SHIATSU ANMA THERAPY
DoAnn's Short & Long Forms

Dr. DoAnn T Kaneko
1ST Editor Ani Cole
2ND Editor Lisa Arnquist
3RD Editor Noel Norwick
4TH Editor Liza Foreman

Layout design by Shawn Gill & Yen Dang
Photography by Trevor Pearson

Published by/Copyright © Dr. DoAnn T. Kaneko
620 Haverford Avenue
Pacific Palisades, CA 90272
Tel: +1-310-459-7239
Cell: +1-310-210-8633

AuthorHouse™
1663 Liberty Drive
Bloomington, IN 47403
www.authorhouse.com
Phone: 833-262-8899

Because of the dynamic nature of the Internet, any web addresses or links contained in this book may have changed
since publication and may no longer be valid. The views expressed in this work are solely those of the author and do
not necessarily reflect the views of the publisher, and the publisher hereby disclaims any responsibility for them.

This book is printed on acid-free paper.

ISBN: 978-1-4520-8818-1 (sc)
ISBN: 978-1-4634-6667-1 (e)

Print information available on the last page.

Published by AuthorHouse   10/28/2022

Shiatsu Anma Therapy
DoAnn's Short & Long Forms

Dr. DoAnn T Kaneko

TABLE OF CONTENTS

ACKNOWLEDGEMENT   I
INTRODUCTION   II
PREFACE   III

CHAPTER 1:
THE WORLD IN WHICH WE LIVE   1
Historical Background in China   2
The Origins of Chinese Medicine   2
Theory of Yin and Yang   4
Five Element Theory of Chinese Medicine   5
Foundation for Today   5
History of Shiatsu and Anma Therapy in Japan   6
Definition of Anma Therapy   6
Heritage of Anma Therapy in Japan   6
The Fall and Resurrection of Anma Therapy in Japan   6
The Development of Shiatsu Therapy   7
Philosophical Background of Oriental Healing Practices   8
Cycles of Life   8
Microcosm and Macrocosm of the Universe   12
The Role of Healer   13
The Goal of Healing Arts   14

CHAPTER 2:
THE BENEFITS OF ANMA (LONG FORM) AND SHIATSU
(SHORT FORM) THERAPY   17
Healing Through Love   18
A Look at the Long and Short Forms   18
Healing General Complaints   19

CHAPTER 3:
TECHNIQUES USED IN DOANN'S LONG
AND SHORT FORMS   23
Techniques of Long Form   24
Soothing Technique (Choma No Jyutsu Keisatsu-Ho)   24
Kneading Technique (Kaishaku-No-Jyutsu)   28
Pressing Technique (Appaku-Ho)   34

Exercising Technique (Undo-Ho, Rikan-No Jyutsu)   42
Correcting Technique (Kyosei-Ho)   44
Vibrating Technique (Shinsen-Ho)   50
Shaking Technique (Shindo-Ho)   52
Tapping Technique (Koda)   54
Semi-Tapping Technique (Kyokude)   58
Snapping Technique   60
Other Techniques   61
Techniques of Short Form   62
Pressure Technique (Appaku-Ho)   62
Correction Technique (Kyosei-Ho)   62
Exercising Technique (Undo-Ho)   63

CHAPTER 4:
APPLYING DOANN'S LONG AND SHORT FORMS   65
Principles of the Long and Short Forms   66
Tips for Good Practice on the Long and Short Forms   69

CHAPTER 5:
BASICS FOR PROFESSIONAL PRACTICE   71
Introduction   72
Preparation for Practitioner   72
Doin: Harmonizing Body, Mind and Spirit   72
Practice of Gassho   72
Clothing   73
Washing of Hands   73
Cutting of Nails, Wearing of Jewelry   73
Advice for Clients   73
Professional Screening   74
Taking Client Information and History   74
Initial Evaluation of Client   75
Screening for Specific Injuries and Appropriate Responses   78
Signing Release Forms   78
Preparation of Working Space   78
Sample Agreements   79
Precautions   80

TABLE OF CONTENTS

Business Issues and Professionalism 81
Ethics 82
Malpractice 83

CHAPTER 6:
PROCEDURES AND TIMINGS 85
Procedure of the Long Form 87
Procedure of the Short Form 90
Energetic Systems 93

CHAPTER 7:
VITAL POINTS AND MERIDIANS IN THE LONG
AND SHORT FORMS 97
Definition of Vital Points (Keiketsu) 98
Characteristics 98
Anatomical Structure 100
Number of Vital Points 100
Function 100
Measurement of Vital Points 100
Definitions of Meridians (Keiraku) 103
Classification of Meridians 104
Characteristics of Meridians 107
Back Paravertebral Region 108
Back of Legs and Feet 113
Side of Feet 115
Bottom of Feet 116
Front of Legs (Outside - Yang) 117
Front of Legs (Inside - Yin) 119
Top of Feet 121
Abdomen 123
Outside of Arms 127
Side of Neck 128
Head 129
Back of Neck 131
Shoulders 133
Summary of Six Meridians in the Arms 135

Summary of Six Meridians in the Legs 136
Locating Pressure Points 138
Anatomical Terminology for Locating Vital Points 138
Methods of Locating Vital Points 138
Four Major Points Among 365 Vital Points 138
The Eight Influential Points 138
Meridians and Vessels 139
Twelve Meridians and Two Vessels 139
Yang Meridians 139
Yin Meridians 139
Vessels 139

CHAPTER 8:
DOANN'S LONG FORM - ILLUSTRATED 141
Types of Techniques in Long Form 142
Back - Paravertebral Region 143
Back of Legs and Feet 153
Front of Legs and Feet 165
Abdomen 180
Arms and Hands 186
Neck and Head 196
Back of Head and Shoulders 206
ACKNOWLEDGMENTS

CHAPTER 9:
DOANN'S SHORT FORM - ILLUSTRATED 231

INDEX 248
REFERENCES 252
RECOMMENDATION 253
POINT LOCATIONS 254

ACKNOWLEDGEMENTS

My prayers go to all our Gods, including my divine parents Hideo and Kimie Kaneko and my wife Heloisa Da Paz Kaneko in Heaven. They inspired and supported me in accomplishing this book.

To achieve my dream was a long and hard journey. My appreciation also goes to my mentors Dr. Nobuyasu Ishino, Masako Yanagiya, Nobuaki Mizukami and all who inspired me through their devoted publications, including Master Sorei Yanagiya and Dr. Katsusuke Serizawa. A million thanks to Noel Norwick who completed editing with Liza Foreman and Debra Lamoureux; Lisa Sterling Arnquist and Trevor Pearson who presented wonderful materials, which gained my deep appreciation. Thanks to Shawn Gill for the design, Eli Albek at Printing Palace for his great help. I can never forget our sweet model Kati Thompson. Special thanks to Alexander Braddel, Katherine Adachi, Renee Silvus and HL Ealy. I would like to thank my beloved brother Sadao Kaneko and daughter Lisa Kaneko who supported this project from the very beginning to the end. Without all of your love, this dream would not have come true. Let me pray Gassho from the bottom of my heart to you all.

INTRODUCTION

Healing the body, mind and spirit is a way of life. My parents, who had met in Tokyo while studying at a healing arts clinic, first introduced me to this way of life. They made another giant commitment that same year of their marriage: to dedicate their lives to the healing of others by opening a healing arts clinic of their own. They accomplished this goal and ran their clinic in Tokyo for more than 50 years. My younger brother ran this clinic until 2005. My own training began when my father and mother, who practiced Sugiyama-style Shiatsu taught me Anma therapy, which is traditional Oriental meridian massage. Determined to live a balanced life and to help others find their natural healer within, I enrolled in the Toyo Acupuncture College, where I learned a variation of Anma therapy called Sujimomi (Keiraku Anma massage, which is traditional Anma massage applied along meridians, muscles and tendons by cross-fiber kneading techniques) through Sensei Masako Yanagiya whose husband, Sensei Sorei Yanagiya, was a legendary Master of Japanese acupuncture. Master Sorei Yanagiya was a source of great inspiration to Oriental body workers in the period preceding Dr. Katsusuke Serizawa's[1] academic study of Anma therapy. Toyo Acupuncture College also introduced me to Shiatsu therapy based on Dr. Serizawa's publications.

In the years of clinical practice that followed, I drew from these various sources to offer my clients the most effective application. From my clinical practice in Tokyo in the late 1960s and in New York in the early 1970s, I developed my own particular style of Oriental body work by in essence synthesizing the two most common styles of body work in Japan (Anma and Shiatsu) with my original training and experience which yielded the best response to the situations I encountered in practice.

Since I began instructing students in my school, I formalized my style into a long form and a short form, similar to the format of the Chinese martial art, Tai Chi Chuan. Both short and long form utilize effective acupressure points in conjunction with other techniques in what I consider to be the best orthodox application of Dr. Serizawa's principle.

Having dedicated my life to healing, and after having over 40 years of clinical experience in the healing arts, I can confidently say that my Long and Short forms are relatively simple for beginner students to master and offer remarkably effective results to clients. I have wholeheartedly enjoyed the rewarding process of bringing my own heritage and healing ability to those in need, and I look forward to the continued spread of traditional Oriental bodywork throughout the world.

---

1. Dr. Katsuke Serizawa is a leading authority in Oriental medicine in Japan. His devoted works, research, publications and education are enormous. He has achieved tremendous results in his life's works. He is recognized as one of the important figures in this field.

I came to Los Angeles for the first time at the end of 1971. Like many others, I was enchanted by the "Californian Dream" and the "Flower Children" whose energy and light had pierced traditional convention globally. Exotic and mysterious fragrances were in the Western air. Zen meditation, macrobiotics, Oki - yoga (a yoga style developed by Master Oki based upon the concepts of Zen), tea ceremonies, flower designs, Mahatma Gandhi's non-violence, and the Hare Krishna movement were but a few of the Oriental treasures attracting interest in the U.S.A. My newfound aspiration was to bring to America the healing practices my parents had taught me in Japan.

On a second visit to the United States in 1979, I observed the hippie culture burgeoning into areas of concern such as agriculture and the environment. Western medicine was also experiencing its own special renaissance as chiropractics and other "alternative" healing practices were gaining recognition. Ancient Oriental practices such as Acupuncture, herbal healings, Shiatsu-Anma massage, Tai Chi, Doin and Chi Qong were being well received. I saw that Oriental culture as a whole was steadily receiving acceptance in the United States as sushi restaurants sprang up across the country, and as tofu and soy products became widely available through supermarkets.

The time had come for me to introduce and practice the most natural of healing arts with one of the most unique systems ever taught in America. I opened a small workshop in New York City where I set about training and teaching my students how to prescribe pressure points and Anma massage. Then I founded the Shiatsu Massage School of California in 1982 and continued teaching Oriental bodywork there. I started to call this traditional Anma massage the Long Form. The Long Form is a full body sequence that takes one hour to perform. The Short Form is contemporary Shiatsu therapy that enables the practitioner to perform a full body sequence in half an hour. This was all done in an academic manner, which offered simple forms of practice designed for beginners. The response was beyond all my expectations; something indescribably divine was occurring as many of the graduates discovered profound spiritual values and inner worlds opening up to them as they embarked upon their new careers in the service of bettering human life through the practice of healing arts. Every time I would hear the students say with awe: "This is not just another massage," or "This is not just another form of superficial touch," I would strengthen my commitment to bringing more of what I had learned in the East to this wonderful Western frontier. Many, many students continued on with their studies of the human energetic systems and have gone on to become acupuncturists, chiropractors, healers and therapists who are leading practitioners in the complementary and alternative healing professions in the United States today. It is my prayer that the world will experience a healthier, and therefore more peaceful, energy in the coming century. This can be greatly facilitated with the safest, most natural, spiritual, and cost-effective healing arts of Shiatsu-Anma and the self-healing art of Doin.

DOANN T. KANEKO
L.A.c., Ph.D., O.M.D.

CHAPTER ONE
THE WORLD IN WHICH WE LIVE

"The Valley Spirit never dies... It is there all the while.. Draw upon it as you will; it never runs dry."

Tao te Ching

The Long and Short Forms of therapeutic massage set forth in this text are based upon traditional philosophies that embrace the natural world. Self-realization and respect for nature are fundamental to the understanding of life and to generating balanced relationships with others and ourselves. Let us examine briefly the historical and philosophical background of traditional Oriental healing practices which have paved the way for the healing techniques we use today.

HISTORICAL BACKGROUND IN CHINA

THE ORIGINS OF CHINESE MEDICINE

Legend and tradition place the origins of Chinese civilization over 5,000 years ago. It is natural to suppose some form of medicine was practiced from the very beginning of Chinese civilization, as illness and injury were surely present from the beginning. Indeed, Chinese medical traditions are both ancient and central to the traditions of Chinese civilization. One may identify
a "protohistoric" period before 1600 B.C., when the forms of medicine documented in later historical periods were developing. This period is dominated by semi-legendary figures, including

Emperor Fu Shi, who is credited with the origination of the yin-yang theory; the creation of the I Ching, or Book of Changes; and the creation of the basic Chinese characters or alphabet. Shen Nong, the developer of agriculture and medicinal herbs is also from this period; as well as Huangdi, the Yellow Emperor, who is hailed as the ancestor of the Chinese race and the founder of Chinese medicine

Archaeologists have uncovered actual records from this period carved on animal bones and shells which contain divining phrases relating to disease. Prayer and witchcraft were evidently among the treatments then in use, and indeed "witch" is part of the ancient Chinese character for "medicine." The earliest records of drug treatments come from the Warring States Period (475 - 221 B.C.) and the Early Han Dynasty (206 B.C. - A.D.8). They are preserved on stone, bronze, and wooden slips. They include herbal tea formulas for specific conditions.

Developing medical practices were systematized and extended during this period, and the earliest great texts of Chinese medicine were written. It was during this period that the original "Huangdi Nei Jing," or "Yellow Emperor's Classic of Internal Medicine," was composed. The fact that this great text is attributed to the legendary father of the Chinese race is evidence of the central position which medicine occupied in Chinese culture.

The "Huangdi Nei Jing" contains the first complete description of the theories and methods of Chinese medicine, including physiology, pathology, health enhancement, disease prevention, acupuncture techniques, and theories of anatomy, meridians, and

PROTOHISTORIC PERIOD	1600 B.C.	770 - 403 B.C.	475 - 221 B.C.
	3 Emperors Period Emperor Fu Shi Shen Nong Huandi Nei Jing - Theories of Chinese Medicine	Spring - Fall Dynasty	Warring States Period Qin Yueren - First Acupuncturist

the organs. The central concepts of yin-yang and the Five Element theory[2] are also fully explained. Since the original "Huangdi Nei Jing" was lost, this classic was believed to be a work of fiction written in later generations in the name of Huangdi. This classic consists of two parts, Suwen and Lingshu. Anma massage therapy is first recorded in the "Huangdi Nei Jing" which states, "When you rub, friction brings heat. This takes the pain out." Sometime in the Spring - Fall Dynasty the "Nan Jing" (The Book on Medical Perplexities) appeared and is probably attributed to Qin Yueren (407 - 310 B.C.). Qin Yueren is traditionally regarded as the first acupuncturist and his text sets forth the four diagnostic methods of traditional Chinese medicine and abdominal evaluation which is a foundation for anpuku therapy (abdominal massage including chest and some back).

The Early and Late Han Dynasties (206 B.C. - 264 A.D.) saw the codification of medicine and a resulting systematization and uniformity of medical methods. These processes allowed the development of a complete medical system of traditional Chinese medicine. The first classics of herbal therapy appeared in this period. The "Shang Han Lun" (Treatise on Febrile Diseases) and the "Jin Kui Yao Lue Fang Lun" (Synopsis of Prescriptions in the Golden Chest) were written at this time by Zhang Zhong Jing (142 - 220 A.D.), a theorist whose herbal classics constitute the first specialist applications of Chinese medicine. His texts set forth formulas and theraputic rules which address infectious and contagious fevers, and digestive, respiratory, urological and nervous system disorders. He introduced "Three yang Three yin theory" which explains how the disease takes place in the meridians

according to the time factor.

Hua Tuo (110 - 207 A.D.) is recorded as China's first surgeon. He is credited with developing drug anesthesia which allowed him to perform stomach and other operations without pain to the patient. In addition to surgical operations, Hua Tuo also performed highly specific acupuncture treatments focusing on using only a few selected vital points. He had notable successes with herbal treatments of parasitism and other problems. Hua Tuo

Hua Tuo (110 - 207 A.D.)

expounded the virtues of exercise and emphasized how one can prevent sickness and maintain good health by imitating the movements of animals. He is one of the first doctors who developed and prescribed the therapeutic exercise called "The Five Animal Plays," which advises the patient to imitate the movements of tigers, deer, monkeys, bears and birds regularly. He also introduced Hua Tuo Jiaji as an additional line containing vital points next to the spine, which I now utilize as Sekisaisen (line by the spine) in my Short Form Shiatsu sessions.

206 B.C. - 8 A.D.

'Early Han Dynasty'
Huandi Nei Jing - Medical
Book on Chinese Medicine

25 - 220 A.D.

'Late Han Dynasty'
Hua Tuo, First Chinese
Surgeon

142 - 220 A.D.

Zhang Zhong Jing -
Herbal Theorist

2. See page 10 which sets forth the Five Element Theory.

Yin

Characterized By Cold
The Kidney
Negative Energy
Winter - The North
Acupuncture
Pressure

B A L A N C E

Yang

Characterized By Heat
The Heart
Positive Energy
Summer - The South
Moxibustion
Soothing

YIN AND YANG THEORY

Behind the development of Acupuncture and Moxibustion,[3] and at the core of all traditional Chinese life (and Chinese healing practices such as Anma), is the concept of yin and yang. Yin is negative and yang is positive energy. Winter and the north are yin in nature (cold), while summer and the south are yang in nature (hot). The heating therapy of Moxibustion is essentially yang in nature and is used to address diseases of a yin nature. Those symptoms can be caused by eating too much yin food (such as raw fruits and vegetables), exposure to cold environments (snow or rain), lack of exercise (causing poor circulation, giving rise to a yang deficiency), overwork or chronic degenerative diseases. The "ma" (soothing or friction) of Anma is the alternative to Moxibustion.

Acupuncture, with its cold metal needles, is yin in nature, and is thus appropriate for treating yang conditions. Diseases of a yang nature can be developed by eating too much yang food (animal products, for example), hyperactivity, over-excitement, and exposure to a hot environment or acute inflammatory conditions. The "An" (pressure) of Anma is the alternative to Acupuncture.

YIN IMBALANCE

YANG IMBALANCE

3. Moxibustion is a heating therapy using combustion of dry and spongy herbs (mugwort or Artemesia Vulgaris). A cone of mugwort or a cigar-like stick of it is applied directly or indirectly (through the burning of the herb) to the vital points to stimulate the energetic system of the patient.

FIVE ELEMENT THEORY OF CHINESE MEDICINE

The Five Element theory was developed to explain more specific correlations between conditions of the body and the natural environment. For example, in the east region of China, Bian (a surgical knife made out of stones) was administered to remove skin diseases due to over-consumption of salty seafood. Herbal remedies were developed in the west where rich food injured internal organs. Anma massage became popular when people in central China suffered with joint pain due to lack of exercise and the flood season. As mentioned above, Acupuncture became an excellent therapy for febrile (fever) conditions in the warm and hot south, as Moxibustion was developed to balance the cold condition in the north of China.

These five classifications (Five Element Theory) are relative and are not fixed. Thus, it is impossible to be 100% certain that one type of treatment will consistently heal every sign of disease. The therapist must choose the appropriate modality of treatment (Acupuncture, Anma, Doin, Herbs, Moxibustion, etc.) according to each person's individual constitution and condition. Thus, just as no one disease ever takes the same form in two different people, no single form of therapy, be it Anma, Acupuncture, Herbs or Moxibustion, can possibly treat all conditions effectively at all times. Nothing in the physical world is absolute in itself. All things in the world of form (anything with yin and yang) are relative. Combinations of the above mentioned modalities are commonly practiced.

FOUNDATION FOR TODAY

Practitioners continue, to this day, to build upon the great and complex structure of Chinese medicine. Since the coming of modern Western medicine to China (and the coming of Chinese medicine to the West), therapists and theorists have enjoyed a new perspective on the workings of Chinese medicine. The values of its empirical traditions have been further validated and today, in the People's Republic of China, government policy has established a "Uniting of Chinese and Western Medicine." Physicians and therapists from the two traditions work together to offer their people what they consider to be the best possible health care on Earth.

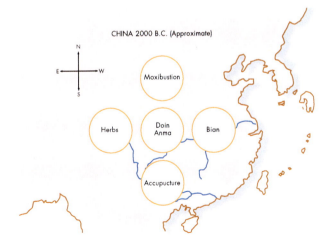

CHINA 2000 B.C. (Approximate)

HISTORY OF SHIATSU AND ANMA THERAPY N JAPAN

DEFINITION OF ANMA THERAPY

Anma (Ankyo Doin) massage therapy as described in ancient Chinese medical history translates in Japanese as "Press" (An) and "Friction or Rubbing" (Ma). Anma is the traditional massage therapy based on the energetic system of Traditional Chinese Medicine, and is in fact one of the five foundations of ancient Chinese medicine[4]. In addition to friction and rubbing, Anma includes other techniques such as kneading, vibrating, shaking, exercising, correcting and tapping. All of these techniques are performed on the meridians and vital points, called TSUBO points, which when stimulated through Anma improve the normal circulation of ki or chi (vital force) by balancing the excess[5] and shortage of ki. Consequently, Anma therapy can promote health in one's body, mind and spirit. Anma can prevent and heal diseases, and it is a powerful tool and technique for the maintenance of good health. Anma massage is an essentially neutral therapy which can be applied when the patient's condition is neither overwhelmingly yin nor yang in nature. For example, if the patient has no severe complaint save general stress, Anma, which does not deplete the system of energy (as may Acupuncture), nor over-stimulate the body (as may Moxibustion), is held to be very safe and effective.

HERITAGE OF ANMA THERAPY IN JAPAN

During the Nara Period (710 - 793 A.D.), the Japanese government set up the first hospital and medical college based on the Chinese medical system. The established three-year course of study included a degree in Anma and a degree in Acupuncture. The Kappo[6] resuscitation technique of Judo martial arts was mastered in the Kamakura Period (1192-1326 A.D.). Chinese medicine gradually established its own style in Japan and during the Edo Period (1603 - 1867 A.D.), many books were published on Anma. The famous blind master of Acupuncture, Waichi Sugiyama (1601-1694 A.D.), made Japanese style Acupuncture unique. Since his success was honored by Shogun Tsunayoshi Tokugawa, many blind Acupuncturists and Anma therapists were trained in his School. Shuan Kagawa introduced Anpuku (Abdominal Anma Therapy) in his book, "Medical Advice of Ippondo," and also during this time Ryohaku Fujibayashi wrote "Anma Tebiki" (Manual of Anma). The "Illustration of Anpuku" by Shinsai Ota was another remarkable publication from this period. Genetsu and Genteki Kagawa were also applying Anpuku in gynecological protocols.

In China pulse and tongue diagnosis were highly developed, whereas in Japan different cultural perspectives led abdominal diagnosis to reach a greater level of sophistication. Shinsai Ota's textbook for abdominal Anma later served to inspire the development of Shiatsu during the Showa Period (1925 - 1989 A.D.). Todo Yoshimasu concluded that 10,000 diseases originate in the abdomen. This led to the practice of self-Anpuku being highly recommended for the preservation of good health.

FALL & RESURRECTION OF ANMA THERAPY IN JAPAN

During the Meiji Period (1868 - 1911), Western medicine and massage came to the East and soon established dominance over traditional Chinese-Japanese medicine. The mass of Japanese people, however, went on trusting and relying on traditional medicine.

710 - 793 A.D. — Nara Period - Anma Therapy was imported along with Acupuncture, Moxibustion, Herbs.

1192 1326 A.D. — Kamakura Period Kappo Art

1603 - 1867 A.D. — Edo Period Books were published On Anma

1601 - 1694 A.D. — Master Waichi Sugiyama

4. The five types of ancient Chinese medicine include Anma, Acupuncture, Herbs, Biane and Moxibustion.
5. "Warming up" by a soothing technique and 'cooling off' by a pressure technique based on tonification for the shortage and sedation for the excess.
6. A Master of Judo applies Katsu (forceful thrust) to activate the cardio-vascular system through the back when the student faints due to choking of the carotid artery.

More recently, there has been a dilution of Anma's therapeutic potential.

Commercialization led to a focus on relaxation rather than thera-peutic treatment. Despite these developments, serious effort and attention has been paid to restoring and recognizing the merits of tradi-tional Anma therapy. The late Sorei Yanagiya, a leading Acupuncturist and translator of many Chinese classics into modern Japanese, organized a scientific theory of Anma therapy early in the Showa Period. He compiled a book for students at his acupuncture school and made great efforts to reintroduce traditional Anma therapy as a significant and scientific healing art. Sorei Yanagiya was immensely influential, and many of his disciples have become likewise well known. Following the death of Sorei Yanagiya, Dr. Katsusuke Serizawa has become the leading scientific authority in the field of Oriental medicine. Dr. Serizawa and his group at the Tokyo Kyoiku University and Hospital continued to research Anma massage therapy.

THE DEVELOPMENT OF SHIATSU THERAPY

Popular attention has shifted to Shiatsu therapy, which first appeared in Japan a few years prior to the end of the Taisho Period (1925). Its origin, however, is rooted in ancient Chinese civilization in the practice of Anma. Traditional Anma massage was modified during the early part of the 20th Century as a result of Western scientific studies of human anatomy and physiology. This lead to the devel-opment of contemporary Shiatsu therapy that subsequently received great support both in Asia and the West. People have found that it is natural, without side effects, cost-effective, holistic, safe, effective and comfortable. Dr. Serizawa defines Shiatsu as associated with Chiropractics, Osteopathy, and the Spondylotherapy of Western science and Anma traditional massage therapy.

Shiatsu gained respectability and official recognition with many authors and medical doctors. Dr. Tadahisa Fujii published "Outline of Shiatsu Therapy and Technique," Master Tokujiro Namikoshi popularized Shiatsu with his very successful "Three Minute Shiatsu," a three-volume best seller. His scientific approach to Shiatsu met with approval by the Japanese medical establishment. He introduced his own non-meridian pressure points. Other authors who contributed to the foundation of Shiatsu are Uchikurayoshi Hirata, Tenpeki Tamai, Rokubai Takagi and Fusajiro Kato. Shizuto Masunage, a disciple of Tokujiro Namikoshi, developed a further style of Shiatsu therapy, Keiraku Shiatsu (Meridian Shiatsu), or Zen Shiatsu. Master Masunage has had considerable success. Unlike his master, Masunage applied traditional Ampuku therapy, based on yin and yang theory, and Five Element theory for evaluation and treatment. Toru Namikoshi also published several books on Shiatsu in English.

Through application of "SHI" meaning finger, "ATSU" meaning pressure, and other techniques such as correction and exercises on the neuro-muscular skeletal system, one can improve structural distortion such as spinal misalignment and pinching of the nervous system. Finger pressure can initiate a nerve reflex that positively affects internal organs, tissues and their various activities. According to Dr. Serizawa, Shiatsu therapy promotes health in two ways. First, Shiatsu directly corrects alignment (in the spine) and second, it also balances the nervous system by initiating reflexive responses in the somatic (cerebrospinal) and autonomic nerve systems in a manner similar to chiropractics, osteopathy and spondyrotherapy.

		1868 - 1911	1912 - 1926	1926 - 1989
Manual of Anma by Ryohaku Fujibayashi	Illustration of Anpuku by Shinsai Ota	Meiji Period Western Medicine was introduced and established	Taisho Period Master Yanagiya	Showa Period Shiatsu Therapy was legalized (1955) Dr. Serizawa Master Namikoshi and Masunaga
1799 A.D.	1827			

PHILOSOPHICAL BACKGROUND OF ORIENTAL HEALING PRACTICES

CYCLES OF LIFE

For all of us, the cycles of our life relate to birth and death, sickness and health, pain and well-being, growth and decay. Lao Tzu, the founder of Taoism, looked for answers about the mystery of creation within the relationship between Father Heaven and Mother Earth; in other words, in the real world or within the very essence of nature itself. Lao Tzu knew that we are physical as well as spiritual creatures that exist ideally in harmony with nature. Taoism teaches us that we live between the two great "poles" of Heaven, our atmosphere, and Earth, the ground we stand upon. Heaven is the domain of the Sun and the Moon; Earth is the domain of ocean water and soil.

The Chinese positioned two aspects of energy, or essential life forces, at work between Heaven and Earth: one positive and one negative. According to this traditional view, the flow of positive energy causes life-creating and enhancing processes, while the flow of negative energy causes life-destroying and restricting processes. These processes interact amidst the five elements: water, wood, fire, earth and metal.

It must be emphasized that the yin and the yang, the negative and positive, are two aspects of a single force which are ideally complimentary with each other and not combative. In fact, when a yin or yang activity has reached its zenith in quantity, it transforms into its opposite, yang or yin, respectively.

Heaven is considered yang and Earth is considered yin.

All of life's processes and experiences depend upon the interaction of energy between yang and yin (heaven and earth). Children are born between the yang (male/heaven) and yin (female/earth). When we die, our mind returns to yang/heaven, our body to yin/earth. As such, the two forces work in a balanced order and in harmony with all of nature.

The ancient Chinese believed that as our human form was created of this world, so we should return to it upon death. Whether buried or burned, our matter returns to the universe.

Our spirit, on the other hand, is believed to join the eternal cosmic energy after departing from the temporary home of form. The yin and yang ki that interacted to shape into flesh go on to create further life from the dissolution of our bodies. This process is at work in nature wherever we look. The cycle of life and death is much the same everywhere: birth, growth, propagation, and decay. The natural cycles are exemplified within the context of seasons throughout a year and of time throughout a day in Figures 1-1 and 1-2.

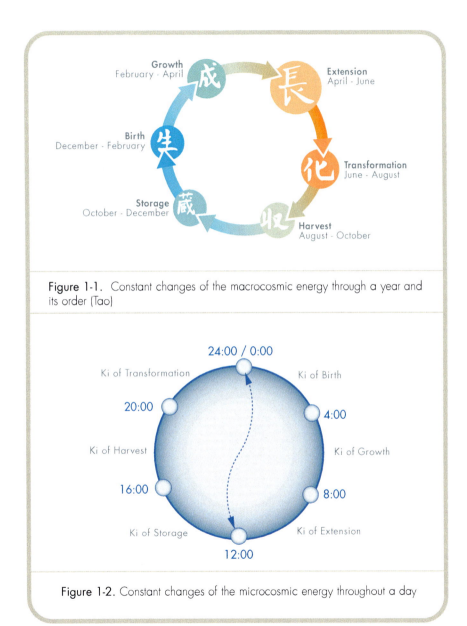

Figure 1-1. Constant changes of the macrocosmic energy through a year and its order (Tao)

Figure 1-2. Constant changes of the microcosmic energy throughout a day

Throughout the cycle of a year, we experience all variations of the cosmic interaction of energy between positive-yang energy and negative-yin energy. Our own lives and human bodies, just like the four seasons of Earth, experience a range of energy influxes varying between hot (summer) and cold (winter). There are seasons for wind (spring), humidity (Indian summer) and dry (fall). Those energies in the heavens are manifested on earth, represented by the five elements of water, wood, fire, earth and metal.

The great universe remains beautiful and perfect because of the harmony created by balancing the two basic cycles, namely positive-creative (yang) cycle and negative-restrictive (yin) cycle during their transitions through the five elements. Sickness is the result of imbalanced relations among the five elements (water, wood, fire, earth, and metal) due to either excess (jitsu) energy, which is too much yin or yang energy, or deficient (kyo) energy, which is not enough yin or yang energy (See Figure 1-3).

As seen in Table 1-2, many phenomena in the universe are also classified according to the Five Element theory. As the Tao, the divine order of the universe, completes its changes, we see repeated phenomena constantly in change every single second of the day. These constant changes are between the yin and yang energy, and this pattern is repeated again and again. It is a never changing pattern. Those who are able to follow these changes of cosmic energy enjoy the harmonious rhythm of ki[7] energy and thus enjoy good health.

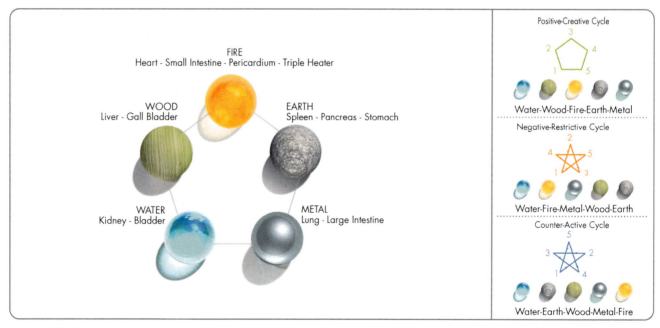

Figure 1-3. Five Elements Chart

7. Ki (Japanese) or Chi (Chinese) represents the vital force or infinite electromagnetic field.

TABLE 1-1	WOOD	FIRE	EARTH	METAL	WATER
Zang or Yin Organ	Liver	Heart Pericardium	Spleen	Lung	Kidney
Fu or Yang Organ	Gall Bladder	Small Intestine Triple Heater	Stomach	Large Intestine	Bladder
Tissues	Tendons, Nails	Blood, Blood Vessels	Flesh, Connective Tissue, Muscles	Skin Body Hair	Bone, Head Hair Bone Marrow
Liquid Emitted	Tear	Sweat	Saliva	Phlegm	Urine
Sense Commanded	Sight, Eyes	Speech Tongue	Taste Lips	Smell Nose	Hearing
Body Smell	Oily, Rancid	Roasted Scorched	Fragrant Baking	Rotten Raw Fish	Putrid Decaying
Motion	Clenched Fists	Suffering	Hiccup, Stuttering	Cough	Tremble Stress
Sound of Voice	Shouting	Laughing	Singing	Sighing	Groaning

TABLE 1-2	WOOD	FIRE	EARTH	METAL	WATER
Time of Day	Morning	Noon	Late Afternoon	Evening	Night
Direction	East	South	Center	West	North
Activity	Birth	Extension	Transformation	Reaping	Storing
Season	Spring	Summer	Late Indian Summe	Autumn	Winter
Color	Green	Red	Yellow	White	Black
Weather	Wind	Heat	Humidity	Dryness	Cold
Flavor	Sour	Bitter	Sweet	Spicy, Pungent	Salty
Domestic Animal	Fowl	Sheep	Ox	Horse	Pig
Beneficial Grains	Wheat, Rye Barley	Corn	Millet	Rice	Beans Buckwheat
Beneficial Foods	Leafy Greens Leeks, Spinach Scallions	Red Berries Watermelon	Pumpkin Yellow Squash Orange Squash	Daikon Radish Onion	Fish, Burdock Coarse Greens

Table 1-1. Five Element Theory in the Organism Table 1-2. Five Element Theory in the Universe

MICROCOSM AND MACROCOSM OF THE UNIVERSE

Ancient Chinese theory held that the original state of the universe was a void-like chaos of gaseous energy. This energy existed without form, and there was neither time nor space, life nor death, heaven nor earth. There was no beginning or ending, no time, no darkness or brightness in space. Prior to the polarization into complementary opposites, this state is likened to the infinite electromagnetic field of ki or chi called Mukyoku in Japanese. (See Figure 1-4).

As the ancient Chinese perceived it, the universe reflects the integration of invisible yang energy (the heavens) with visible yin energy (the planets). When the inexplicable energy of ki took form, the universe separated into an enormous series of complementary opposites. Heaven, the accumulation of light or "pure energy," characterized as hot and bright, became the home of the electromagnetic current of yang energy and is the dominant force of the daytime, as the sun is imbued with yang ki. Oxygen and light are understood as manifestations of yang ki, as is the concept of time. In fact, the ancient Chinese ascribed to yang ki all things without an obvious basis in gross matter or form.

Complementing the formless yang energy is the world of dense matter or yin energy. Earth, as an example, resulted from an accumulation of coarse or "impure" energies, characterized as cold and dark, the home of the electromagnetic yin energy. An example of yin energy is the form and substance of the planets and their relationship to each other. The dominant force of night, the moon is also imbued with yin ki.

The forces of yin and yang are interactive as they compliment and regulate each other. The equilibrium of nature depends upon them working equally together in harmony (See Figure 1-5).

Figure 1-4. Mukyoku: the empty abyss, infinite electromagnetic current and field

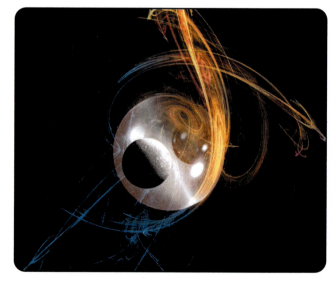

Figure 1-5. Macrocosm: the two polarities of heaven and earth

THE ROLE OF THE HEALER

As with every other part of nature, human beings result from the interaction of the two kis. Thus, humans inevitably embody both yin and yang energies. The ancient Chinese were astutely observant of this process within themselves. In Chinese physiology, this yang ki (chi) is centered on the acupuncture point Conception Vessel 17, "Center of the Church." They identified the heart with heaven, associating it with spirit (shin), emotions and feelings not rooted in gross matter. A similar understanding of the heart energy is found in the Hindu philosophy which believes that the heart is associated with the fourth chakra, or anahata chakra[8]. Our ability to transcend time through memory, imagination and thought is also associated with yang ki. The Chinese identified yin ki with the kidney, which they held to generate and regulate life span, stamina and vitality (sei). They centered this yin ki on the acupuncture points Conception Vessel 7, 6, 5, and 4. In India, the first chakra, muladhara chakra, is also identified with the kidney. Humans flourish only when their yang ki and yin ki are properly balanced[9]. By achieving this balance, we unify the world within, and this unity allows for the growth of the spirit (seishin) (See Figure 1-6).

Good health depends upon our following the natural and divine order (Tao). By doing so, we maintain a harmonious balance of the yin and yang ki within us and our environment. According to the ancient Chinese medical classic Su Wen, each of us has an allotted life span of 100 years. Failure to attain this age was attributed to an imbalance of yin and yang energies, a condition resulting from living life in an unnatural way. The entire basis of Oriental medicine was founded upon the purpose of restoring the balance of energies upon which our well-being depends. The role of the healer is to facilitate the body's own natural healing capabilities to restore balance.

Most forms of healing were first developed as forms of self-healing. "Physician heal thyself" rings true for all of those who seek to help others. One must first restore and maintain the balance of ki in oneself as a necessary precondition to healing others. This restoration may take an endless number of forms, some of which include self-massage, breathing techniques, meditation, exercise, herbal treatments, prayers and/or environmental precautions.

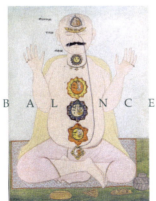

Yin		*Yang*
Space		Time
The Body		The Mind
Kidney		Heart
Water (Cold)	B A L A N C E	Fire (Heat)
Structure		Function
Physical Vitality		God (Essence of Spirit)

Figure 1-6. Microcosm: the composition of the human being

8. Chakras in sanskrit is a number of psychic centers which receive prana (vital energy). There are 7 Chakras through the body.
9. The mind is seen as yang, the body as yin, and any imbalance between the two is an acknowledged component of sickness.

THE GOAL OF HEALING ARTS

When we live harmoniously within our environment, we regulate minor imbalances naturally. However, when our patterns of behavior disrupt that harmony, or when, often for reasons beyond our control, the natural environment itself is disturbed, serious imbalances result.
If these imbalances overwhelm our ability to cope, illness results.

The goal of the healing arts is to encourage the natural healing powers of individuals to act in accordance with the great order of the universe, or Tao. The concept of self-healing is based upon the practitioner's ability to utilize this universal energy in a balanced manner.   The practitioner works with the recipient, rather than against the disease. The implications of this approach are infinite. In restoring the proper balance of universal energy between human being and nature, we are provided with unlimited opportunities to expand our knowledge and awareness of our proper place in the universe. Proper and harmonious interaction frees us to develop an ever-deepening understanding and expression of our love within a universal context. Balance is one of the greatest truths and beauties of the universe[10]. When anyone asks, "Why do we live?" we may well answer, "We live to experience and express universal love." There is no difference between Christianity and Taoism in this very fundamental concern in life. According to Taoism, those who practice unconditional love deserve good karma in this life or in future generations (See Figure 1-7).

Numerous ancient Asian proverbs regard balance as a way of utilizing Oriental medicine into our everyday lives. One of the most popular sayings, yamai wa kikara, "sickness often comes from the imbalanced mind," is a basic principle of Oriental medicine. Most simply it means that discomfort or pain such as stiffness and tensions, as well as more serious diseases such as

tumors or cancer, are the consequences of mental, emotional and spiritual troubles. Ryusui fubu, "the flowing water never gets stale," is another proverb which attributes the cause of disease to a stagnant lifestyle. Those who do not exercise properly develop toxicity and decay. The joints need to move regularly, and Asian culture has developed exercises such as Tai Chi as prevention from stagnation and disease.

Wise healers also practice "i shoku dogen," which translates to "healing and eating have the same root," meaning those who eat well heal themselves. In the diverse and sometimes confusing world in which we live, it is very essential to realize that we are what we eat. Consequently, if we wish to prevent disease, we need to establish harmony between ourselves and the divine order of the universe, or Tao. According to the tenets of Oriental philosophy, a healthy lifestyle should include exercise to prevent toxic buildup, plenty of natural foods to maintain a healthy body, and a good dose of laughter to maintain a healthy mental state. The concept of laughter as healing is found in the saying "warau kado niwa fuku kitaru," meaning "good fortune seeks out laughter." It has been scientifically proven that laughing provides positive mental and physical effects. For example, laughter activates cardio-pulmonary function and increases production of endorphins, natural pain killing substances, in the brain, that change negative moods into healthy ones.

Another proverb tells us "Jyoko wa mibyo o iyasu," which translates to "the best healer cures future disease," which emphasizes the preventive nature of healing arts. Through exercise, eating properly and maintaining positive mental attitudes, we can live in harmony with "The All That Is" and prevent imbalance which leads to unhealthy behavior. Ultimately, the gift of the healing arts is summarized in the saying "I wa jinjutsu," meaning "the healing art is the manner of love and compassion."

10. The exchange of energies between the healer and the client is itself part of the natural and wholesome flow of energy in life and the universe.

Figure 1-7. The healing environment and healing ourselves.

CHAPTER TWO
THE BENEFITS OF ANMA (LONG FORM)
AND SHIATSU (SHORT FORM) THERAPY

HEALING THROUGH LOVE

All healing takes place through the power of God - the divine power of the universe, or ki. All healing methods and healers seek to enhance the flow of this healing power within the recipient's own energetic system, and so repair ailments, maintain a harmonious metabolism and prevent disease.

The supreme goal of the healing arts is spiritual healing. Jesus Christ, and other spiritual masters and saints from all religions who practiced healing, healed without a medical degree or application of painstakingly-studied technical skills. They appear to have simply laid their hands upon the ailing person's body, and by utilizing the spiritual energy of the Godhead, instantaneously produced healing. Their reward lay not in any material payment, but in knowing the unconditional love of God and its application in the service of humanity. Having given themselves over wholly to God's will, they were at one with that will and hence able to actualize it for the good of all. These saints and sages were most likely oblivious to the concepts of pressure points and meridians of traditional Chinese medicine, knowing only the all-important power of universal love through which they achieved their miraculous cures. When we follow in the footsteps of the saints and sages and practice the highest form of healing – healing through the power of faith - we too can fulfill the highest goal of those involved in therapeutic healing.

A LOOK AT THE LONG AND SHORT FORMS

The Long and Short forms presented here are simple and safe enough to perform at home, on the athletic field, at work and at professional therapeutic facilities. There is no special equipment, clothing, massage table, or oil necessary. A Shiatsu table in the professional facility or a futon mat at home is comfortable. Needing none of the accouterments of Acupuncture, Moxibustion, or herbal therapy, it is the most simple and comfortable of the traditional Oriental healing arts. It is extremely cost-effective, generally requiring no instruments or machinery.

Its focus is on preventive healthcare, which when effective minimizes the need for costly Western medical treatment.

Therapeutic healing arts have in some cases been reduced to an instrumental form of massage for relaxation, where it becomes automated and loses its therapeutic value. It can further be debased in the case of so-called "adult entertainment," where massage is associated with sexuality. While sensuous or sexual massage has its place in private life, practitioners and others intent on effecting a holistic healing can only feel sorrow for its commercial debasement. Of course massage for the purpose of relaxation and stress management certainly does have its therapeutic value; however, our concern here goes far beyond the intention of temporary comfort for the recipient. The focus at hand is upon creating lasting effects in the recipient's (and our own) total health.

It is a practitioner's role to guide people (and themselves) to a positive, healthy and peaceful world. Such a state is the natural result of a proper understanding of the universe and a proper realization of the harmony within oneself. "Stress" is often the diagnosis with the prescription being to "relax more." One agrees that this remedy would be a fine thing, but those unable to step outside of a busy schedule and take a vacation every time they feel run down will find Shiatsu-Anma a welcome alternative. Both the Long form and Short forms restore harmony between Body and Mind to enhance spiritual well-being.

Even those inexperienced in any of the healing arts will find that the Long and Short forms presented here, with their focus on stimulating the body's most powerful and commonly used vital points to tap into the recipient's own natural healing energy, will take care of many stress related complaints. The more experienced practitioner, through the use of these forms, will grow in confidence with his or her mastery of healing techniques and will be able to help or heal pain such as four of the most common complaints today: lumbago (lower back pain), neck and shoulder dysfunction, headaches and indigestion.

HEALING GENERAL COMPLAINTS

Let us briefly examine some of the healing styles classified in Traditional Chinese Medicine.

1. HONJI-HO

In Japanese, "Hon" means root source, "Ji" means heal and "Ho" means method. Therefore, Honji-Ho roughly translates as "root source healing method." These healing techniques are fundamental and deal with the source or cause of the complaint or problem.

A. **For general condition** - Long Form or Short Form (whole body).

B. **For specific condition** - yu points[11], bo points[12], tonification[13] and sedation points[14] and other important points according to the syndrome (the pattern of the imbalance).

2. HYOJI-HO

Hyoji-Ho translates as "local or symptom healing method," as "Hyo" means local or symptom, "Ji" is healing and "Ho" is method. These are techniques which focus on the symptoms of the complaint.

A. **Attsuten Method** - treating painful points locally according to perceived tenderness and sensitivity with pressure techniques. (For example, many of them are found on the Additional Hip Line between UB54 and GB30 for sciatica.)

B. **Tai So Method** - treating pressure points distal (far) from the location of the problem. (For example, LI4 for frontal headache TH5 for side headache SI3 for potential headache, etc.)

C. **Tai Sho Method** - selecting pressure points according to the symptoms of the problem. (SP6 for PMS, PC6 for motion sickness, GB21 for frozen shoulder, etc.)

---

11. Points strongly associated with internal organs that directly regulate the associated organ. They are located in the back of the body along the spine on the urinary bladder meridians.
12. Bo, or alarm, points are places associated with internal organs on the front abdomen and chest. They are sensitive to the touch, and when achy indicate that something is wrong with a corresponding organ
13. This is a basic rule to balance the energetic system when its activity is too little. It is used in a healing session to increase the patient's weak ki in that area.
14. Sedation is used to balance the energetic system when the activity from a particular area is excessive. The technique is used to drain off one's excessive ki.

Each style is the result of a carefully considered and practiced therapeutic approach, and each style uses the vital points to stimulate the body's energetic system in its own distinctive way. Thus each style has its characteristic formulas for selecting vital points according to the pattern of the illness or disease in question

Of the two basic styles, Honji-Ho addresses the root cause of the problem (which may be general or specific), while Hyoji-Ho addresses local symptoms. Honji-Ho is the more essential of the two methods. But Hyoji-Ho has its place also, and the most effective therapy will combine the two methods appropriately. For example, when a client complains of allergic sneezing, a practitioner would tonify or sedate the lung meridian[15] and perhaps the kidney or spleen-pancreas meridian, depending on the symptoms associated with the allergy (Honji-Ho). In other words a practitioner doesn't just treat the nose, but treats the lung/kidney or spleen energetic system. But if a client has whiplash due to auto injury, the correct treatment would be to work on the neck. In such a case, the injury has little immediate relation to the internal organs. Therefore, pressure and kneading techniques on and around the injury are appropriate.

A chronic back problem, on the other hand, would have a relationship with internal organs and may be evaluated as, for instance, a weak kidney (energetic system). This would be treated with stimulation of vital points along the kidney and urinary bladder meridians in the leg, abdomen and para-vertebral region (Honji-Ho), as well as by the local healing points directed at the symptomatic lower back pain (Hyoji-Ho).

The Long and Short Forms set forth in this text, called DoAnn's Long form and Short form, are a combination of Honji-Ho and Hyoji-Ho with an emphasis on Honji-Ho, knowing that it is better to treat the body as a whole and the root of a problem, as one effects the other. In applying DoAnn's Long and Short forms, the parts of the body which are most important include:

1. PARA-VERTEBRAL REGION

Due to this region's healing and evaluating functions, Traditional Chinese Medicine deems it one of the most important parts of the body. It is associated with the major Zo Fu organs (five yin organs and six yang organs). The points relating to these organs are called yu (associated) points. Here lies the source of most neuro-muscular problems, problems that also give rise to diverse symptoms of aches, pains and other discomforts throughout the body. This is the region where the autonomic nervous system and the spinal nerves join, and where nerve roots are situated alongside the spine. This region is the root source for numerous problems. For example, numerous complaints in the lower extremities can be treated with techniques applied in the para-vertebral region in the lumbar-sacral levels.

2. ABDOMEN

This region is of primary interest because it is where toxicity generally builds up. The Tanden, or root of the body's energy (kidney energy), is situated in the lower abdomen, one to four fingers below the navel. This area is where most vitality is held[16].

As Todo Yoshimasu, a famous Japanese herbalist of the Edo period said, "man byo ichi doku ron" (One toxicity can cause

---

15.   Meridians are energy channels of the energetic system and are pathways for the circulating ki.
16.   In traditional Chinese physiology, there are three tanden: upper tanden for the spirit, middle tanden for the mind, and lower tanden for the body. Lower tanden is the one under the navel for everyday stamina.

10,000 diseases). Most importantly, bo (alarm) points are located in the abdomen and chest. Healthy individuals should have no pain or aches when being pressed. If something is wrong, then the body will develop pain as an alarm (whether or not points are pressed); this is a warning sign that trouble is inside. For example, if something is wrong with the heart energetic system, pains in the inside of the left arm and middle of the chest often develop, which is where the heart meridian is located. This phenomenon has been well documented in both Oriental and Western medicine.

3. LIMBS AND EXTREMITIES

There are many vital points located on the limbs and extremities. In DoAnn's Long and Short forms, for men, the stomach meridian, which runs the length of the leg, contains the vital point Stomach 36, important for general well-being. For women, Spleen 6, also located in the leg, is an important vital point for gynecological concerns. The Large Intestine meridian offers important points (Large Intestine 4 and 10, located in the hand and forearm, respectively) for both men and women. DoAnn's Long and Short forms also include vital points of the Small Intestine and Triple Heater, which are both located on the neck; Governing Vessel; Urinary Bladder and Gall Bladder, which are located on the head and back of the neck; and finally, vital points for the Gall Bladder and Small Intestine, which are on the shoulder.

Through comprehensive awareness of the ancient healing arts combined with generations of practical therapeutic application, DoAnn's Long and Short forms were developed to best utilize pressure points to stimulate the whole body's natural healing

powers, rather than focusing on local symptoms. This approach of enhancing the body's own power to help prevent disease through detoxifying and strengthening the body's immune system has consistently proven to achieve the greatest long-term health benefits.

CHAPTER THREE
TECHNIQUES USED IN DOANN'S LONG AND SHORT FORMS

TECHNIQUES OF LONG FORM

DoAnn's Long Form method draws from ancient Anma techniques in combination with the more modern Shiatsu style. A thorough understanding of the Anma basics of soothing, pressing and kneading are elemental to application of the form. The soothing technique works at the skin level and is used to warm up poor circu-lation and to tonify; pressing works on a deeper bone or nerve level and is used to sedate. Kneading is used as a general, neutral application and works at a medium level, as a muscle regulator. Additional techniques include therapeutic exercises, correction techniques, vibration, shaking, snapping and tapping

SOOTHING TECHNIQUE

(CHOMA NO JYUTSU/KEISATSU-HO)

Why apply: The skin is the largest organ of the body. The meridians pass through the internal organs, and enter and exit the body through the skin. Imbalances of ki in the meridians and organs will produce symptoms on the skin surface. For example, retention of toxic blood in the lower abdomen can cause consti-pation and dermatological complaints.

Soothing works with the skin's protective energy, or eiki[17], to regulate the pore openings that defend the body against exogenous (outside of the body) environmental elements, to release stagnant energy and heat and to expel toxins from the body. Soothing also creates heat through friction, which like movement, generally results in better circulation. Soothing is administered toward the heart like effleurage in Western massage to aid better circulation of the cardio-vascular system. Light soothing stimulates sensory nerve receptors. This generally induces a spinal nervous system response that stimulates the body. Strong soothing stimulates both ki and blood circulation,

removes the stagnation and may resolve pain[18].

How to apply: Throughout the healing session, it is important that the hands remain relaxed and the wrists flexible (See Figure 3-1). The soothing technique is applied by following the contours of the recipient's body with the hands remaining in contact, pulling down, while maintaining a consistent pressure. Keep the elbows loosely bent with the joints relaxed throughout the application. The application is generally performed from top to bottom, except at the extremities (feet, hands and neck) where one works from bottom to top, or from foot to ankle, hand to wrist. For broader areas of the body (back, abdomen, limbs), use the whole hand, keeping fingers close together. For narrower areas like the neck, use four fingers (Figure 3-2). For narrow areas, such as the client's face, hands and fingers, use two fingers or the thumb only (Figures 3-3 through 3-6).

When to apply: In both the Long form and the short form, always start with a general soothing technique. The soothing

17. Eiki is a Japanese word referring to an aspect of the quality of one's vital force. Eiki dwells on the surface of the skin as a protection and defense energy, which is part of one's electro-magnetic field.
18. Pain is the result of blocked energy; therefore any improvement in energy circulation will reduce the quality and quantity of the pain.

technique is used as a warm up to increase the movement of ki in the area to be worked upon. Soothing also helps put the client at ease. Keep in mind that the first touch of the practitioner can set the tone for the entire session. Therefore the goal in this moment should be to convey reliability, kindness and capability. It is also good to end a session with the soothing technique, which will leave the recipient with a warm, healing effect.

Practitioners commonly encounter yin or yang excess conditions and yin or yang empty conditions. Yang excess is an area where too much yang energy has accumulated. Its symptoms may be hot, as in a fever. Yin excess will produce a cold sensation. Yin and Yang empty conditions are where there is not enough yin or yang energy in the affected area. Not enough yin produces a warm sensation, such as a low grade fever or night sweats. Yang empty would be a cold spot on a normally warm area or a cold body temperature. Specific friction techniques have a specific goal, to bring about heat-warming effects. Gentle soothing on the surface of the body is excellent for yang empty symptoms (cold areas on the surface of the skin), as gentle friction along the surface of the meridian promotes heat. Strong friction against the direction of energy flow in the meridians also promotes heat but is excellent for yin excess syndrome, and acts to drain off the excess cold energy.

Where to apply: Soothing techniques may be applied to most of the body. In DoAnn's Long and Short forms soothing is applied along the meridians on the surface of the body or above the digestive tract. Soothing often covers a couple of meridians together except on the hands and feet where the therapist's fingers soothe specific lines.

When to be cautious: Poor energy circulation, due to weak vital force in that area, is termed "yang-empty" and can be observed when the recipient's skin shows subtle dents, feels hollow to the touch, is cold and has a pale color. In this situation, apply gentle friction to the areas, without powder[19], being careful to avoid irritating the skin. Gentle friction along the energy flow will tonify, or supply energy for yang empty conditions. However, in the case of yin-excess, drain the excess yin (cold) by strong, deep soothing against the energy flow. Some recipients respond quickly to this technique, with an immediate flush or reddening of the skin. A quick response is often indicative of healing power from good ki. Be aware, however, that if this reddening remains for any length of time with accompanied sensitivity of the skin, it may indicate retention of toxicity.

People may benefit from soothing and other therapeutic techniques throughout their lives, literally from the cradle to the grave. Soothing or friction is a wonderful technique for babies, and is recommended in place of kneading or pressing techniques. Be careful, however, not to over-stimulate. Five or ten minutes of light soothing will provide optimum stimulation in pediatric care.

---

19. To aid the soothing technique by reducing friction, one may use powder on areas such as the abdomen or the feet. Unlike Swedish and other massage techniques, oil generally is not applied.

SOOTHING TECHNIQUE

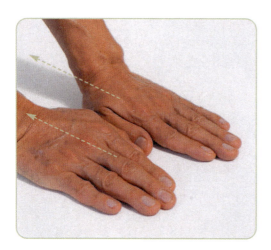

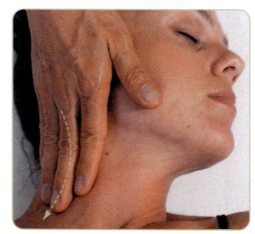

(Fig. 3-1) Soothing with fingers.

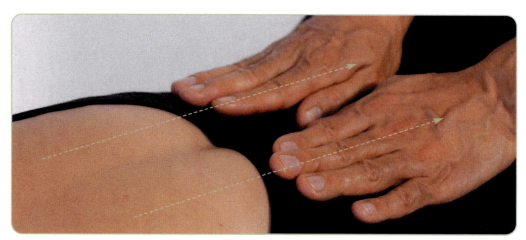

(Fig. 3-2) Soothing with both hands.

SOOTHING TECHNIQUE

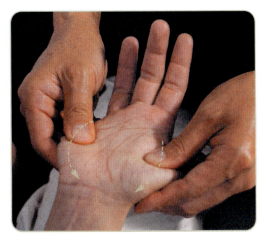

(Fig. 3-3.) Soothing with both thumbs.

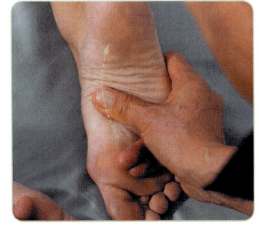

(Fig. 3-4.) Soothing with thumb.

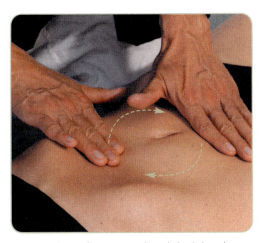

(Fig. 3-5.) Soothing stomach with both hands.

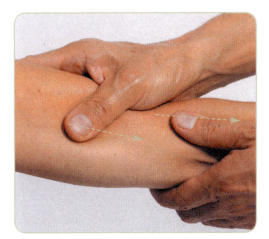

(Fig. 3-6.) Soothing both sides with hands.

CHAPTER THREE

KNEADING TECHNIQUE

(KAISHAKU-NO-JYUTSU/JYUNETSU-HO)

Why to apply: Kneading is an excellent technique to regulate the energy flow by stimulating and thus relaxing stiff muscles. Kneading applied with a good rhythm is profoundly relaxing for the recipient. The same principle as in traditional acupuncture may hold true for kneading, in that clockwise rotation is excellent for tonification and counter-clockwise rotation is optimum for sedation. Kneading, as does petrissage in Western massage, helps break down waste materials and disperse toxins in the muscle tissue, This improves both blood and ki circulation and allows for better absorption of nutrients. Kneading also enhances the metabolism of the muscle tissue, promoting better muscle function. Clinical experience shows that six or seven out of ten cases of pain are usually caused by muscle spasm as in lumbago or lower back complaints and that kneading techniques are much more effective than pressure technique.

How to apply: The appropriate amount of pressure for the area being worked upon is key to proper application of kneading techniques. Although the thumb is used most often for kneading, elbows, wrists and the heels of the hands are also utilized for certain areas. Practitioners may increase the pressure of the application by shifting their balance forward. This will increase the weight brought to bear on the recipient so as to penetrate thick and heavily developed layers of muscle, particularly in the trunk, upper back and shoulders. Elbows can be used to work such areas of dense muscle as the back, along the spine, and where ever thick muscle layers are found, as well as for any large area that is stiff. The heels of the hands are best for strong kneading in sensitive areas. Like a count to five in music, a good, consistent and disciplined rhythm is most effective and encourages the correct accenting of pressure. It is desirable to

create constant changes between slow (yin) forceful pressure (yang) at the beginning and quick (yang) gentle pressure (yin) at the end of the kneading action.

There are two basic kneading techniques introduced in the Long form (the Short Form has no kneading). The first, Senjyo Jyunetsu ("cutting kneading"), uses the thumbs to cut, or cross fiber the tissue across meridians and muscles. In most cases this would be performed horizontally on a standing body since muscle tissue usually runs vertically. For this kind of kneading (See Figure 3-7), the thumbs are placed at right angles to the vertical axis of the practitioner's thumbs. Cutting may be performed in any direction, except when working along the spine. If you are cutting along both sides of the spine at once, cross away from the spine; but when using both hands overlapped to cross on one side of the spine, work either towards or away from the spine.

Cutting kneading is a demanding technique, taking more effort and more pressure than rotation kneading. Keeping the elbow bent helps the wrist and creates softness of movement. Keeping the wrists flexible allows for full movement of the hands. It is important to exert consistent and sufficient pressure throughout the session; otherwise the application is a variation of the soothing technique. However, too much pressure while crossing muscle fibers will cause the recipient soreness later. A sufficient amount of pressure is necessary at the beginning of the cutting motion, with a reduction of pressure applied while cutting across the muscle (See Figure 3-8). The thumbs and wrists do all the actual work. The fingers are used to steady the wrists and to guide the hands. Keeping enough space between the thumb and the fingers avoids pinching the area being worked on. In the case of a recipient with sensitive muscle tissue, cut with the fingers or the palm of the hand rather than the thumb (See Figures 3-9 through 3-13).

The second major kneading technique is Rinjo Junetsu ("rotating kneading"). This technique is faster and requires less pressure than cutting. Like cutting, rotating is done with the thumb and wrist. The hand is held in much the same way, but instead of the lateral motion in cutting, rotating requires the thumb to move in a half circle measuring about a half inch in diameter. The thumb is pressed "under" the meridian and then released "over" it in a half circle or spiral motion as the practitioner moves along the meridian. The direction of the rotation itself is usually clockwise, except when working simultaneously on both sides of the spine whereby it is necessary to rotate symmetrically away from the spine (See Figures 3-14 and 3-18).

When to apply: In the Long form, the kneading technique comes after the initial soothing. Kneading is applied more specifically than soothing along the meridians, according to the recipient's condition. For example, when the muscles surrounding the meridians are stiff and tight, this is an indication of blocked energy. Kneading is the appropriate application to release this blocked energy. In this instance the energy channels to be worked upon are called muscle meridians and are in actuality the muscles themselves.

Where to apply: Muscles, tendons, ligaments and connective tissue all respond well to kneading. Kneading should be focused along the meridians, on subcutaneous (under the skin) tissue above the bone. The major energy flow is located somewhere between the skin and the bone, between the muscles. This is why kneading and stimulating the muscles is so effective in releasing stagnant energy. It is the muscles themselves which provide pathways for the energy to flow. A practitioner must always be on the lookout for "noisy" or "messy" conditions that indicate separated muscle fibers; this may manifest as crunchy sounds like gori-gori , kori-kori and gyoro-gyoro in the muscles. This demonstrates a loss of muscle fiber unity and an energy block in need of release.

When to be cautious: Although kneading generally provides sore and stiff muscles a relief from pain, by much the same token, poor application can aggravate and even cause these very complaints. If the muscles are inflamed, kneading should not be applied. Wisdom must be used to determine if there is an energy flow blockage along the muscle meridian, or whether the muscle is actually inflamed.

The Japanese term Momidako translates as stiffness (or negative reaction) due to strong kneading. See the Figures 3-8 and 3-14 to understand how to modify the amount of the pressure on the muscles along the spine.

KNEADING TECHNIQUE

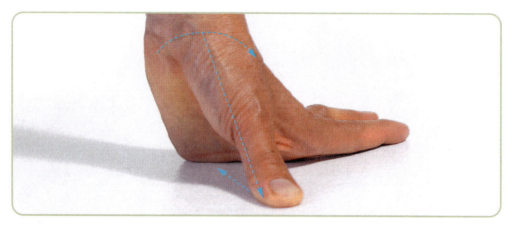

(Fig. 3-7.) Angle of thumb for the kneading technique. Snap wrist, not thumb, as you knead the muscle layer with pressure

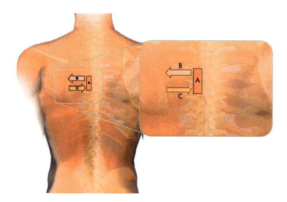

A = Full pressure at the medial edge of erector spinae muscle

B = 1/2 pressure at the lateral edge of erector spinae muscle

C = 1/4 pressure from the lateral to the medial edge of erector spinae muscle

(Fig. 3-8.) Changing of amount of pressure in cutting kneading along the spine.

KNEADING TECHNIQUE

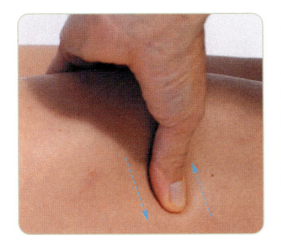

(Fig. 3-9.) Cutting with thumb.

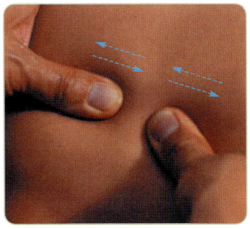

(Fig. 3-10.) Cutting with both thumbs.

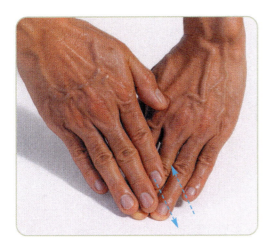

(Fig. 3-11.) Cutting with fingers overlapped.

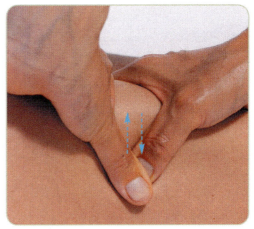

(Fig. 3-12.) Cutting with thumbs overlapped.

KNEADING TECHNIQUE

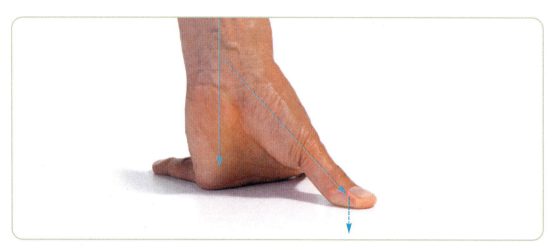

(Fig. 3-13.) Proper alignment of thumb in relation to palm

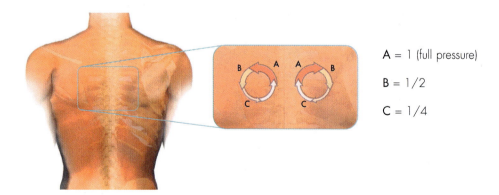

A = 1 (full pressure)

B = 1/2

C = 1/4

(Fig 3-14.) Changing of amount of pressure in rotating kneading technique

KNEADING TECHNIQUE

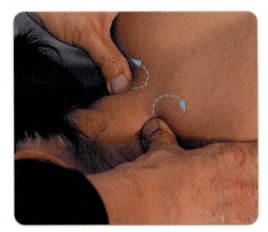

(Fig. 3-15.) Rotating with both thumbs.

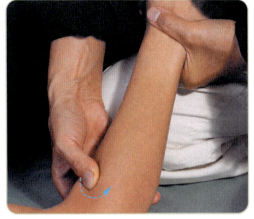

(Fig. 3-16.) Rotating with thumb.

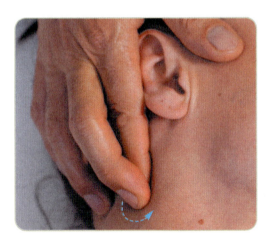

(Fig. 3-17.) Rotating with fingers.

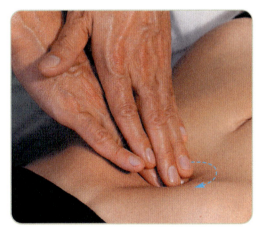

(Fig. 3-18.) Rotating with fingers overlapped.

33

CHAPTER THREE
PRESSING TECHNIQUE
(APPAKU-HO)

Why to apply: Application of ordinary pressure (see below) causes neither discomfort nor a sense of relief unless an energetic imbalance exists. One of the most powerful techniques used in the Long form is the application of pressure to restrict an excess flow of energy that causes stiffness, cramps, discomfort and pain. This commonly occurs when inflammation has not fully subsided, but major symptomatic expression has ceased. When people feel better when a normal amount of pressure is applied, it is a sign that there is an energy imbalance (kyo), or blockage, that has resulted in a deficiency of yin or yang ki (weakness) in the area being treated. In this case, the recipient may experience stiffness and cramping without any inflammation. This can be observed in people with chronic bad posture. However, if the recipient is uncomfortable with ordinary pressure, it is symptomatic of a jitsu condition, an imbalance producing an excess of yin or yang ki. If the recipient is unusually sensitive even to light pressure, it is often symptomatic of a toxic condition. If the area is inflamed, cold should be applied. The pressure technique was not developed in traditional Western massage since there was no concept of pressure points influencing an energetic system. While soothing brings heat to an area, pressing tends to minimize excessive energetic activity, thus controlling excess heat. Therefore, it is an excellent technique for yang-excess or yin-empty syndrome as it will drain the heat of the excess yang or empty false heat. Pressing won't actually cool off the treated area but will create a more stable and stationary condition by calming over-activity.

In terms of Western theory, pressure offers relief to the nervous system and to the muscles. Sustained pressure restricts the over-activity of nerves that causes neuralgia, inflammation of the nerve, and over-activity of the muscles leading to cramping. Intermittent pressure stimulates blood circulation and lymphatic drainage, and aids gastro-intestinal activity.

Two basic applications of pressure (normal/ordinary and inter-mittent) are used in the Long form. Tsujyo Appo (ordinary pressure) is the more simple and basic of the two, thus more widely used. The application of ordinary pressure requires a gradual exertion of pressure, a brief pause followed by a gradual release of pressure. This process should take five to seven seconds per application (five seconds of pressure and two seconds of release) for pressure points along the meridians of the spine, and three to five seconds for meridians of the limbs. The hands should not leave the recipient during the application, as it is important to promote the connection between recipient and practitioner. Kanketsu Appo (intermittent pressure) is a brief (2 to 3 seconds) use of pressure applied to areas with less underlying muscle, such as the head, hands and feet. Although less pressure is needed, the concentration of vital points in these areas will often lead the practitioner to spend quite some time working in these localities, particularly in situations where specific ailments are present.

When to be cautious: Pressure should not be applied to varicose veins, burns, scalds, open wounds, acute and active infections, and inflammations. In such cases, pressure usually aggravates the condition. In general, the amount of appropriate pressure depends on the sensitivity of the individual recipient at the time of treatment. When pressure treatment is first begun, it is important to ask the recipient if the amount of pressure being used is comfortable. Recipients should be asked to let the practitioner know immediately if the amount of pressure being applied is excessive or if, though uncomfortable, it is also relieving pain and blockages. The practitioner should allow himself or herself to be guided by the recipient on this matter; this is especially true for the beginning practitioner. The standard for the optimum amount of pressure is best expressed by the Japanese word "tsukai", which translates as, "it hurts good."

How to apply: In traditional Anma therapy as well as in the modern therapeutic application of Shiatsu, pressing techniques have always been regarded as the most potent form of Oriental bodywork. With this distinction comes a heightened responsibility for absolutely correct application. In both the Long and Short forms, Tsujyo Appo (ordinary pressure) and Kanketsu Appo (intermittent pressure) are the most common forms of pressure used. Specific applications vary: yang excess cases require sharp surface pressure against the energy flow, while yin empty cases require gentle but deep pressure along the energy flow. Follow the six rules listed below to ensure smooth, safe and effective application. Ordinary pressure should be applied when performing according to these six rules:

1. Concentrated Pressure (Shuchu Atsu): To achieve the purpose of concentrated pressure, one must be truly present in mind and body. When this oneness extends to the recipient to be healed, the ability to heal is made manifest. Awareness should be placed on the fact that the practitioner and the recipient both have the same goal. Nothing should be forced or manipulated; rather, one relaxes and becomes a channel through which the cosmic healing energy of the universe may flow. Remember that one's hands will express what is in the heart. Let one's hands (and particularly the thumbs) be sensitive, and let the heart be open to love. Put one's warm heart into the hands, and let one's hands become the eyes. Keep the eyes open and focused for problems or healing opportunities. If greater concentration can be achieved with the eyes closed, this is also acceptable.

2. Vertical Pressure (Sui Choku Atsu): Pressure should always be applied at a 90° angle to the surface of the recipient's body to be most effective. Pressure directed towards the center of

the body will always ensure firm, stable application. Be particularly mindful when following the contour of the spine to ensure that pressure is directed towards the center of the body, for the vertebrae may crack if pressure is purposely directed upwards or downwards along the spine (See Figure 3-19).

3. Sustained Pressure (Sasae Atsu): Once the appropriate amount of pressure is found, it must be sustained, especially along the recipient's spine. To give sustained pressure, the practitioner's elbows must be straight. When working on someone's back, the practitioner's arms and chest should form three sides of a rectangle with the recipient's back completing the fourth side. A knee pressed against an elbow can give additional support and stabilization to the practitioner's working arm (See Figure 3-20 and 3-22). For maximum efficiency, apply pressure by channeling the body's weight through the arms. Those who seek to apply pressure with muscular strength will find the exertion unnecessarily taxing. However, you will need to bend your elbows and use muscular strength when pressure is applied to the recipient's sides.

4. Stable Pressure (Antei Atsu): It is very important to secure and stabilize pressure. If the practitioner's thumbs shake or vibrate in an uncontrolled manner, the recipient will often understandably be unable to relax. Pressure should be secured and stable, particularly when it has reached its maximum exertion level. For this reason, it is the ball of the thumb, rather than the very tip, that is the most effectively utilized and the most comfortable application for the practitioner. Utilization of the four fingers is also a way of providing strong support and stabilization for the thumbs (See Figure 3-21). Again, it is important to keep the elbows and the arms straight, and when necessary to use the inside of a knee to support the outside of the elbow (See Figure 3-22). The thumbs need not be kept parallel; a 30 to 60 degree angle is acceptable (See Figure 3-23). Double-jointed thumbs, whose flexibility makes them unusually vulnerable to injury, will present more problems than do stiff thumbs, which will become more flexible with use. When the thumb is weak, the knuckles may be used, and/or you may support a weak thumb with three fingers (See Figures 3-24 and 3-25).

5. **Gradual Pressure (Kanjo Kangen Atsu):** Exert pressure gradually. Spend more time increasing the pressure than when decreasing the pressure. This technique is basic to the Long and Short forms. At the application of maximum pressure, usually after a three to five count, pause briefly before gradually decreasing pressure. The brief pause is called "Ma". It is believed that this is the therapeutic moment when universal life energy enters the point (See Figures 3-26 and 3-27).

6. **Coordinated Pressure (Chowa Atsu):** This is an important technique that coordinates the application of pressure with the recipient's breathing. As the recipient exhales, pressure is exerted. When the recipient inhales, pressure is released. This is done to increase energy in the recipient or to support energetic activity[20]. This coordination of rhythm is natural and supportive of the therapeutic process. If the recipient's breathing is too shallow to distinguish exhalation from inhalation, the practitioner may direct the recipient to exhale as pressure is applied. However, too many reminders to exhale may bother the recipient. It is therefore a good practice for the practitioner to coordinate his or her breathing with the recipient's. Then the practitioner will automatically know when the recipient is exhaling. Synchronized breathing also promotes the oneness of body and mind that inspires significant healing, but as with all technical applications, this should be done unobtrusively so the recipient will neither be distracted nor disturbed by the practitioner's breathing. Proper

abdominal breathing saves therapist's energy based on the sense of divine consciousness from the universe. Our faith in God prevails and he manifests his love through healing.

Exhaling from the tanden (lower abdomen) sends a strong energy through your hands to the recipient. This technique lends a quality of focus to the treatment independent of the amount of pressure exerted and promotes a healing interaction between practitioner and recipient. Thoughtful breathing from the tanden is essential to becoming conscious of one's connection with the universal energy of life. Working with closed eyes often makes it easier to visualize this vital connection.

When to apply: Pressing techniques are performed most effectively, and with the least risk of causing soreness, after tissues have been kneaded. Those advanced practitioners, who have mastered the Long form and have thorough control over the pressure they exert, can use pressing techniques safely without soothing and kneading techniques.

Where to apply: Pressure is applied on the numerous vital points to help balance the flow of ki along the meridians. Especially when the stiffness has deep roots such as in a chronic or more accumulated condition, pressure should be applied through specific vital points. In circumstances where pain is chronic, this rigid energetic blockage reflects a long-standing buildup (accumulation). The energy blocks responsible for such conditions can be released with pressure applied to the major vital points of the twelve primary meridians and to those of the muscle meridians. Oriental and Western massage theory both agree that pressure along these meridians positively affects the nerve roots and deep muscle tissue. Pressure applied with the thumb is more specific and concentrated than that applied with

20. To decrease energy (such as in a yin or yang excess condition) pressure would be exerted on the inhalation.

the knee, elbow, or foot; thus it is the generally preferred method of application. The others are used for stiffer, more heavily muscled areas. The amount of pressure applied varies according to the needs of the individual recipient. For example, a large man who performs heavy labor or lifts weights may benefit from pressure being applied from an elbow, foot or knee. Indeed you can use all different parts of the body for applying pressure in the Long form and short form, including the fists, palms and feet (See Figures 3-28, 3-29 and 3-30).

Additional cautions: If the pressure applied causes discomfort or aggravates the recipient, such pressure should be stopped immediately. Only in certain chronic conditions such as a long-standing physical complaint may the practitioner consider continuing treatment despite the pain. Even in these circumstances practitioners should be conservative, especially beginning practitioners. "No pain, no gain" is a most dangerous concept; it's just too risky. Always consider the recipient's age, sex, occupation, nature and stage of complaint (acute injury, inflammation, etc.), as well as her or his previous experience with Shiatsu-Anma therapy. Some recipients may be sensitive or very fragile and must be treated very gently or not worked at all. Other recipients may have chronic conditions that require the use of an elbow or knee. Through experience, one learns how much pressure is best for each case. A Japanese concept that translates as, "Only disciplined practice enables one to perfect the art of Shiatsu-Anma," provides the necessary frame of mind to properly master the Long and Short forms.

PRESSING TECHNIQUE

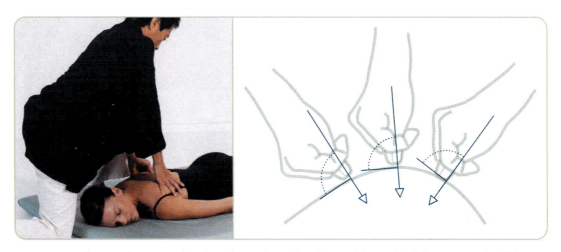

(Fig. 3-19.) Elbow and wrist must be aligned one above the other and the angle of the pressure should be 90 degrees against the surface.

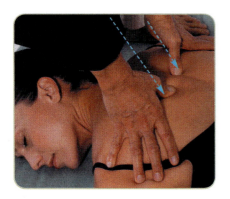

(Fig. 3-21.) Stable pressure.

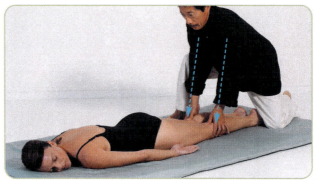

(Fig. 3-22.) Support the elbow against the inside of the knee.

PRESSING TECHNIQUE

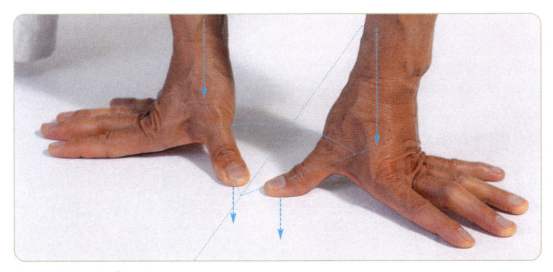

(Fig. 3-23.) Angle of thumbs.

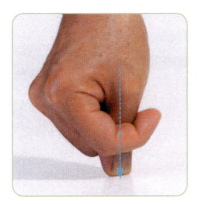

(Fig. 3-24.) Pressure with supported thumb for double-jointed practitioners.

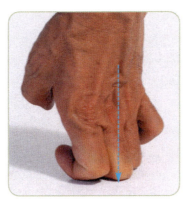

(Fig. 3-25.) Pressure with knuckles to substitute for weak thumbs.

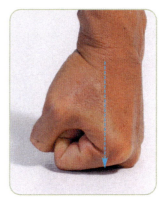

(Fig. 3-28.) Pressure with fists.

PRESSING TECHNIQUE

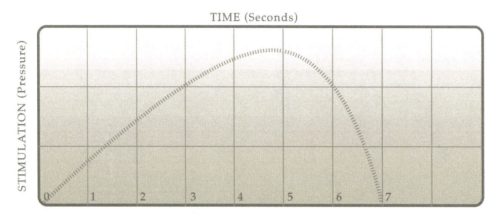

(Fig. 3-26.) Gradual increase and gradual decrease in ordinary pressure.

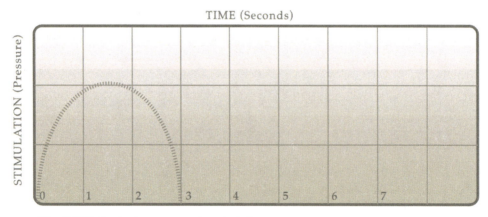

(Fig. 3-27.) Gradual increase and gradual decrease in intermittent pressure.

PRESSING TECHNIQUE

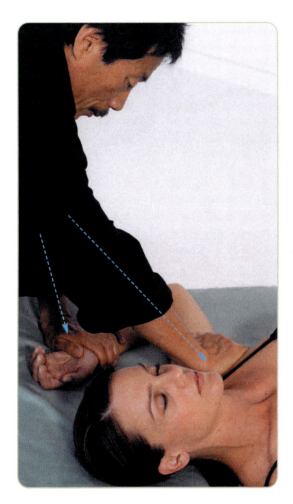

(Fig. 3-29.) Pressure with palm.

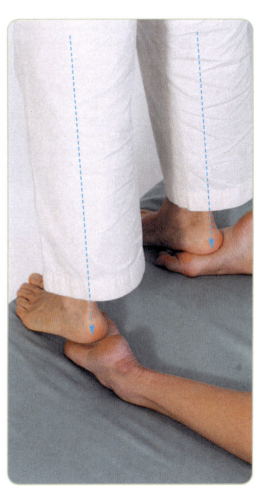

(Fig. 3-30.) Pressure with feet.

CHAPTER THREE

EXERCISING TECHNIQUE

(UNDO-HO/RIKAN-NO JYUTSU)

Why to apply: Exercises are administered to promote the circulation of ki energy through the internal organs and the joints. Exercises also stretch the meridians and promote flexibility of joints, muscles and tendons. In terms of Western theory, exercises will improve blood circulation and stimulate the secretion of articular fluid, enhancing smooth functioning of joints and preventing rigidity and calcification of joints. Modern physical therapy divides exercises into three general categories: active exercise, passive exercise and exercise against resistance. The exercises administered in Anma massage therapy fall into the category of passive exercise. The passive exercises included in the Long form have a unique concept of "Yoga with a therapist" not found in classical oil massage due to its draping condition.

How to apply: It is initially necessary to ask the recipient if they have prior joint dislocations. Then one can evaluate range of movement: checking for stiffness in limbs and joints, for flexibility, and for any pain or irregular limitations. Within the safe range of motion established, exercise the person by working joints, extending and flexing the muscles and limbs, and by stretching the meridians. With great care, it is sometimes appropriate to extend the recipient's range of motion beyond that initially established as safe. Such extension of the recipient's range may be done by simple repetition of an exercise.

The practitioner must remember to perform each exercise in the reverse direction as well. It is also important to keep one's grip relaxed and gentle while performing passive exercise techniques.

When to apply: Exercises are safest and most effective after the muscles have been warmed up and relaxed; therefore they are administered after the application of the soothing, kneading and pressing techniques. These exercises techniques are also included in the Short form.

Where to apply: Exercises are applied throughout the body, basically on the joints and muscles.

When to be cautious: Always be cautious when administering exercises to elderly recipients because their bones and connective tissues are more fragile and they are generally more easily injured. When treating recipients who complain of stiffness, let the recipient guide you regarding pacing and range of motion[21]. Ask about previous traumas such as broken bones, whiplash, and damaged ligaments and tendons. Be careful of injured ligaments and tendons as inappropriate treatment can occasionally cause internal bleeding. Recipients with osteoporosis, whiplash, and those undergoing cortisone therapy should be carefully treated due to the fragile condition of their bones. Numerous exercises are presented in the Long form in Chapter 8 and the short form in Chapter 9.

---

21. As mentioned earlier, a useful technique to help alleviate stiffness in a patient is to synchronize breathing with the application of therapeutic passive exercise. By having the recipient exhale as the practitioner applies the exercise, resistance to passive movement will be greatly reduced.

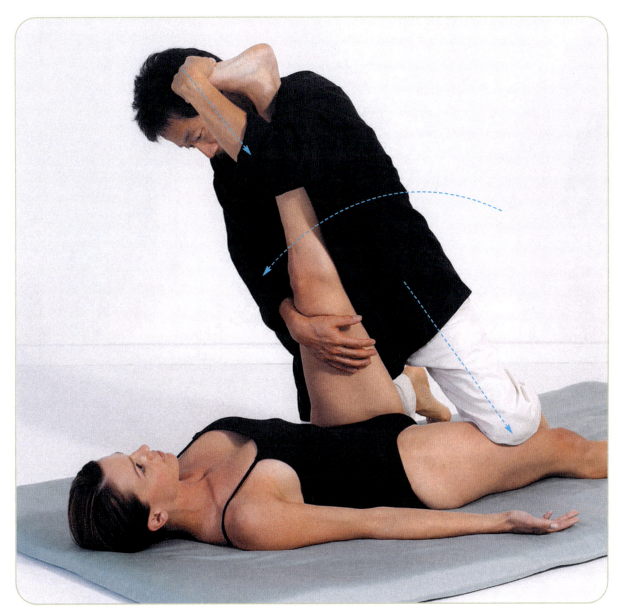

(Fig. 3-31.) Leg Exercising Method II: Bladder Meridian

CHAPTER THREE

CORRECTING TECHNIQUE

(KYOSEI-HO - STRETCH)

Why to apply: Both the exercise and correcting techniques improve R.O.M. (range of motion). In the exercise technique, the therapist rotates a joint 90 to 360 degrees, depending on the limb. The correcting techniques involve pressing, pulling or twisting on the skeletal system such as the joints, spine, pelvis, neck and/or scapula (on the back of the shoulder or "shell bone") to extend the range of movement in these areas. When there is an energy blockage, a corresponding accumulation of toxicity, stiffness and even bone deformation may result. Aging, poor diet, lack of exercise, excessive imbalanced exercise or repetitive movement may all contribute to a condition of ill health. Correcting the skeletal system and aligning the spine, pelvis and thorax will help to keep the proper energy pathways clear and secure. In Western terms, it also stretches out ligaments, tendons and the articular or joint capsule surrounding tissues of the joints, which keep the limbs and joints flexible and pliant. Application of the correcting technique frees pinched nerves and improves blood circulation. This works to enhance the function of internal organs. It also helps ensure correct spinal and skeletal alignment,

a prerequisite for healthy functioning of the body.

The similarity of Shiatsu therapy with Western chiropractic science is seen most clearly in the corrective technique. There has always been a great concern for proper posture in both Oriental and Western culture. In Asia, this is reflected in a method called Seitai ho, which is used to improve bad posture. Chiropractic, Osteopathy, Cranio-Sacral therapy, Rolfing and the Alexander Technique are some of the Western therapies that address posture.[22] Of course, Shiatsu-Anma approaches structural alignment in the context of soothing, kneading, pressing and other techniques, whereas classical chiropractic and some of the other techniques work primarily by manipulation of the skeletal system through abrupt forceful thrusts called adjustments.

How to apply: The correcting technique is applied by pressing or pulling on the joints, spine, pelvis, neck and/or scapula, to release rigidity from these areas. While applying pressure to the area being treated, the practitioner's hands are often pulled or stretched in two opposite directions (See Figures 3-31 through 3-40).

---

22. Chiropractics:
    Dr Daniel David Plamer (1845-1913) started Chiropractic diagnosis and treatment for patients who suffer disorders of the spinal and other joints by adjusting the spinal column or through other corrective manipulation.
    Osteopathy:
    Dr Andrew T. Still(1828-1917) founded osteopathy and he developed the complete system of health care based on correcting mechanical imbalance and bone pathology and alignment issues within the neuro-musculoskeltal system.
    www.academyofosteopathy.org
    Cranial Sacral Therapy:
    CST was pioneered and developed by Osteopathic physician John E Upledger following extensive scientific studies from 1975 to 1983 dealing with of the membrances and cerebrospinal fluid that surround and protect the brain and spinal cord.
    www.upledger.com
    Rolfing:
    Rolfing technique was invented & developed by Dr. Ida Rolf (1896-1979), a biochemist. Rolf uses connective tissue manipulation to put your body into better vertical alignment.
    www.rolf.org copywrite2000the Rolf Institute
    Alexander Technique:
    Alexander Technique was invented by F. M Alexander (1869-1955) an actor, Alexander Technique is a way of learning how you can get rid of harmful tension in your body by changing movement habits during every day activities.
    Spondylotherapy:
    Dr. Albert Abram (1863-1924) originated Spondylotherapy which is the treatment of disorder of the spinal column by percussion traction, vibro traction or concussion only. Royal Raymond Rife (1888-1971) was one of many Abram's imitators and created a generator of radio-waves to shatter bacteria that he believed to cause cancer.

23. Unforced snapping of stiff joints sometimes occurs and is not considered harmful.
24. This is a technique which has become important to Shiatsu therapy. It helps align the body properly, one of the primary goals of Shiatsu therapy.

CORRECTING TECHNIQUE

Shiatsu-Anma correcting does not have as its purpose the snapping or popping of joints[23]. The effectiveness of its slow and gentle techniques depends on the considered timing and soothing rhythm that practitioners will develop with experience. Correcting technique is introduced in the Long form as an additional technique of Anma massage.

When to apply: This technique is applied after pressure techniques, and may be used to re-align the skeletal system. This Kyosei technique is included in the Short form.

Where to apply: The correcting technique is applied to the joints, spine, pelvis, neck, and scapula. Spinal alignment, correcting joint articulation, and improving smooth functioning of the joints are all objectives of this technique.

When to be cautious: Improperly applied, the correcting technique may cause troubles in soft tissues. Very stiff and elderly recipients pose the greatest risk of misapplication of this technique. Great caution must be exercised with such recipients as well as with people undergoing cortisone therapy or those recipients suffering from osteoporosis. Never practice the corrective technique in an abrupt, uncontrolled or forceful manner. Before application, muscle and other soft tissues must be warmed and relaxed, either through soothing, kneading, pressing, or by using a heating pad.

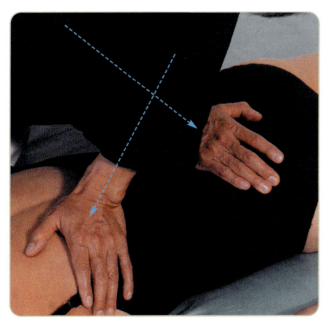

(Fig. 3-32.) Back correcting technique I.

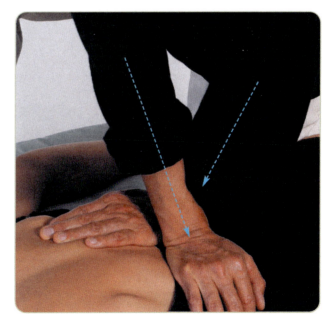

(Fig. 3-33.) Back correcting technique II.

CORRECTING TECHNIQUE

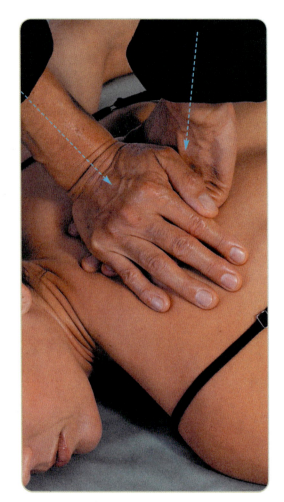

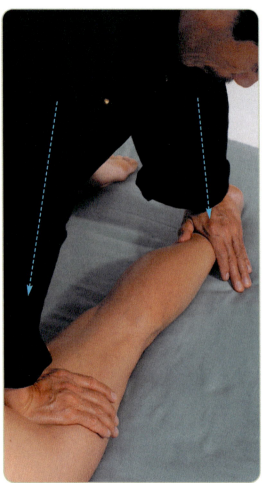

(Fig. 3-34.) Back correcting technique III.

(Fig. 3-35.) Leg correcting technique.

CORRECTING TECHNIQUE

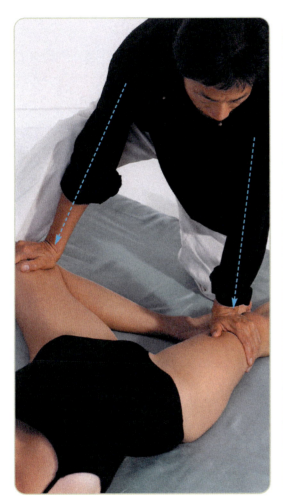

(Fig. 3-36.) Pelvis correcting technique.

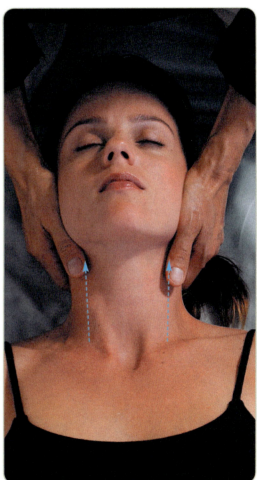

(Fig. 3-37.) Neck correcting technique.

CORRECTING TECHNIQUE

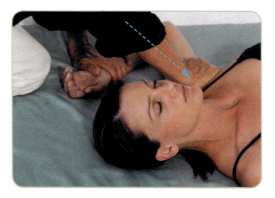

(Fig. 3-39.) Scapula correcting technique.

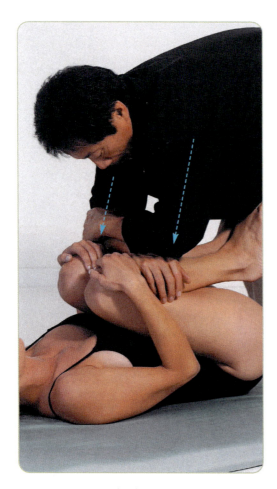

(Fig. 3-38.) Lower back correcting technique.

CORRECTING TECHNIQUE

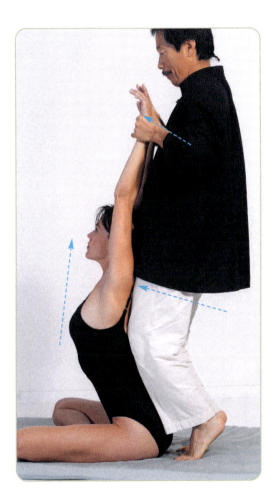

(Fig. 3-40.) Spine and shoulder joint correcting technique.

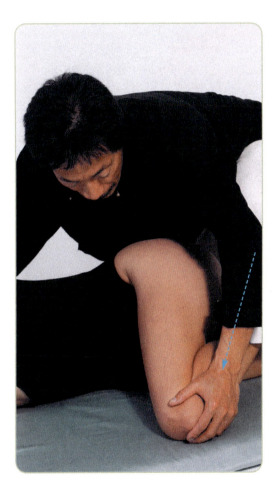

(Fig. 3-41.) Lower back and hip joint correcting technique.

CHAPTER THREE

VIBRATING TECHNIQUE
(SHINSEN-HO)

Why to apply: Vibrating disperses blockages of the meridians, helping to restore the correct flow of ki. Light vibration tends to excite the nerves, muscles, internal organs and energy flow, while deep vibration restricts them and releases energy blockages. Strong vibration also releases stiffness and disperses or drains excess energy.

Vibrating the abdominal area should always be done gently. Vibration helps to release congestion, which if allowed to accumulate, may give rise to various conditions such as toxicity of blood, fluid, gas, feces and so forth. Abdominal vibrating stimulates the digestive, reproductive and excretory functions. Vibrating on the head, which may be applied more forcefully, releases stagnant or excessive ki. Vibrating is generally very relaxing for a recipient. When it is applied extensively on the forehead, he or she may fall asleep toward the end of the session.

How to apply: Vibrating is performed with both hands in a vibrating movement. Pressure in this technique is applied by the palms, which are often overlapped but sometimes separate, the tips of the fingers and the sides of the hands. When applying the vibrating technique to the abdomen or to the upper forehead with the heel of the palms, place the palms together with the dominant hand in the lower position (See Figures 3-42 through 3-44). The upper hand should be placed with a light touch above the lower hand for the purpose of focusing the vibration. The lower hand will be the hand that provides the pressure and the vibration.

After placing the heel of the hand on the area to be vibrated, exert pressure with both hands. Vibrate the lower hand from the elbow, moving the heel of this hand rapidly from side to side. Be sure to hold the hands with the fingers lifted out of the way on the face (to avoid the nose). To vibrate the side of the head, place one hand around each ear and vibrate while pressing the hands together.

There are two kinds of vibration technique, one slow and gentle, and the other rapid and deep. As the recipient inhales, apply the gentle technique, and when the recipient exhales, apply the deep technique. Sustain each application for 3-5 seconds. Be careful not to change pressure from one to the other abruptly, as this will cause discomfort to the recipient, especially when treating the abdominal area. With practice, forceful isometric contraction will produce a good vibration.

The fingertips may also be utilized during the vibration technique and this style may be employed throughout the body, including application to the head, face, and extremities, as well as to the abdomen and to the back. The sides of the hands are used on the abdomen, the base of the skull, the shoulders, and the extremities.

When to apply: Vibration is applied after the pressure technique as an additional Anma technique.

Where to apply: Vibration is applied primarily to the abdomen and to the head.

When to be cautious: It is necessary to apply a softer and more sensitive vibration to the abdominal area due to the delicate nature of this area.

VIBRATING TECHNIQUE

(Fig. 3-42.) Vibrating the head.

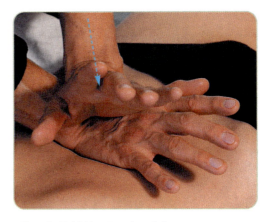

(Fig. 3-43.) Vibrating the abdomen.

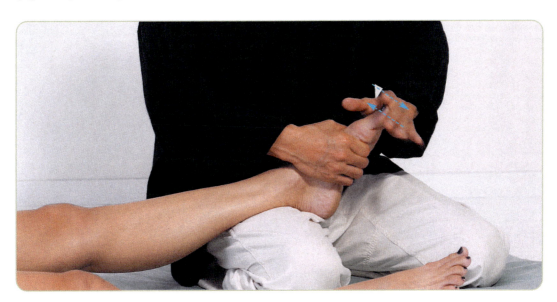

(Fig. 3-44.) Vibrating the toes.

SHAKING TECHNIQUE

SHAKING TECHNIQUE (SHINDO-HO)

Why to apply: Shaking breaks up stagnant energy and improves the flow of ki. It also stimulates muscles and break up the stiffness of the joints as well as improving the blood and lymphatic circulation. It has also been shown that muscles recover faster from fatigue and/or are revitalized through shaking.

How to apply: The shaking technique is applied to the limbs and extremities. The practitioner first takes hold of the recipient's wrist and hand, or ankle and foot, and begins stretching the arms or the legs and then shakes the limb rhythmically (See Figures 3-45 through 3-46). Holding the extremities, the practitioner shakes them up and down, left and right (vertical and horizontal). The practitioner starts slowly and then increases the frequency of the shaking. Although this technique may tire the practitioner, it is generally very pleasant for the recipient and will promote excellent circulation.

When to apply: This is an additional technique used most appropriately once muscles and joints have become limber after soothing, kneading and pressure technique.

Where to apply: In addition to the limbs, the toes and fingers themselves may be shaken.

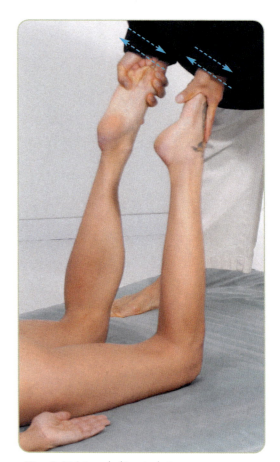

(Fig. 3-45.) Leg shaking technique.

SHAKING TECHNIQUE

(Fig. 3-46.) Arm shaking technique I.

(Fig. 3-47.) Arm shaking technique II.

TAPPING TECHNIQUE
(KODA)

Why to apply: Light to moderate tapping stimulates the flow of ki and heavy tapping can restrict the ki flow. Heavy tapping may be applied if there is a major stiffness or an energy blockage that is causing muscle tension. Tapping helps break down stiffness and stimulates the muscles by stimulating electrical activity in the nerves. The tapping technique called tapotement in Western massage is designed to stimulate blood circulation. In the Orient, numerous tapping techniques have been developed to achieve a greater range of effects. Ten tapping techniques are included in the Long form.

How to apply: Fast, light, and rhythmic impacts should be applied to the area being treated. For correct application the elbows should be bent, the shoulders dropped, and the hands and wrists relaxed and coordinated. Tapping can be performed with the side of the fists, backs of the fists, sides of the fingers, backs of the fingers, or with chopping or cupping hands. The hands and fingers tap out a synchronized rhythm to treat the designated area with alternation of the left and right hands.

When to apply: Tapping is an additional optional Anma technique usually applied after soothing, kneading, and pressing to further enhance treatment. In the Long form it is applied at the end of the session, along with kyokude, or a semi-tapping technique.

Where to apply: Tapping may be applied to any part of the body, including the abdomen. In the Long form it is applied on the recipient's neck and shoulders while they are sitting up.

When to be cautious: Unless the practitioner's wrists, hands, and fingers are fully relaxed and both hands are well coordinated, tapping techniques can cause the recipient unnecessary discomfort. Special caution need be displayed when treating recipients who have suffered whiplash. If treatment is being sought right after an injury, movement of the neck must be avoided and the practitioner is advised to use a collar or neck brace if one has been prescribed by a D.C. or M.D. Do not perform tapping treatment of the neck area for a few days, or possibly not even for several weeks, after any injury to this area. Applications of soothing techniques are better suited for the neck in these circumstances. Caution also needs to be used when tapping a recipient's back in the kidney region. Practitioners should only apply light tapping to the kidney area (See Figures 3-48 through 3-53).

TAPPING TECHNIQUE

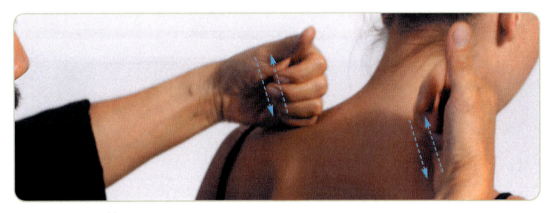

(Fig. 3-48.) Side of fists.

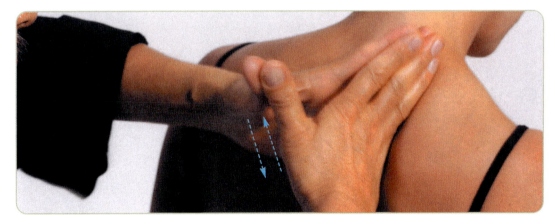

(Fig. 3-49.) Side of fingers.

TAPPING TECHNIQUE

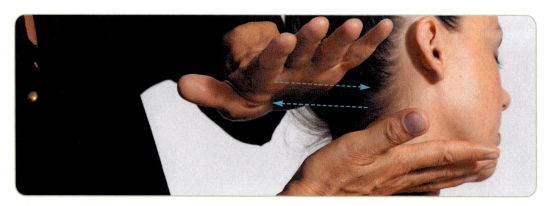

(Fig. 3-50.) Chopping.

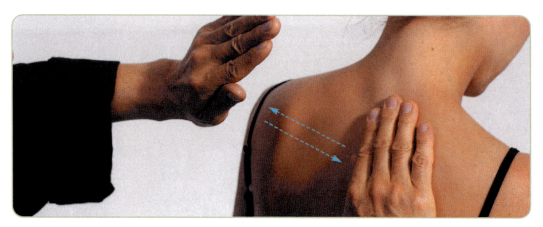

(Fig. 3-51.) Cupping.

TAPPING TECHNIQUE

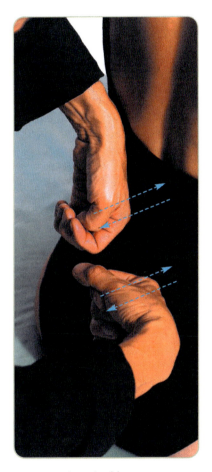

(Fig. 3-52.) Back of fists.

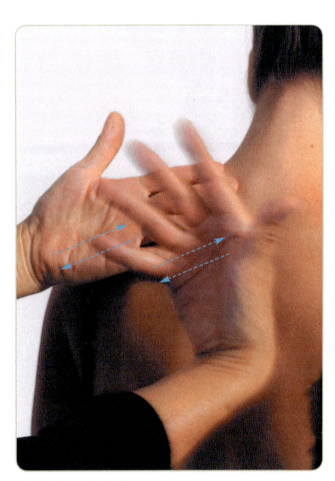

(Fig. 3-53.) Back of fingers.

SEMI-TAPPING TECHNIQUE

(KYOKUDE)

"Kyokude" translates as "bend" which also has reference to musical sounds in Japan. Semi-tapping techniques make musical sounds and are very traditional variations of tapping. The same advice given previously for traditional tapping techniques largely holds true for the methods set forth in this section on semi-tapping techniques. Each of the forms below has its own speed and rhythm, and is made up of various unique elements combined with movements from tapping, shaking, vibrating and soothing techniques.

Tsukide (horse hands): In Japanese, this technique is likened to a horse trotting. Application of the technique begins by stretch one's fingers straight and then making gentle impacts on the recipient's body with the tips of the fingers. As soon as the practitioner makes contact with the recipient, the practitioner collapses his or her fingers and forms a fist. The fingers next go once again into a straight position and the motion is repeated. Both hands should be used to establish a fast rhythm. The practitioner should make impact first with one hand and then with the other. This technique requires much practice to achieve good coordination and a pleasing rhythmic sound (See Figure 3-54).

Kurumade (wheel hand): The wheel hand technique is applied by first extending the fingers flat on the recipient's body, and then rolling the hand into a fist, while letting the finger joints make light contact. When the knuckles make contact, the hands open and then the procedure is repeated. Both hands are to be used, alternating contact from hand to hand, while moving up the body (See Figure 3-55). For variety, you may roll up both fists at the same time.

Kujikide (butterfly hand): This technique is usually applied alongside the spine. While the thumbs apply pressure, the fingers flap like butterfly wings over the surface of the recipient's body to support the movement of the thumbs. The thumbs should be placed about one to two inches apart on either side of the spine, with the fingers extended above the recipient's body. As pressure is applied, the thumbs bend and flex, in and out, in and out, with the knuckles knocking together and striking the area being treated. This bending and flexing motion of the thumbs causes the fingers to "flap." With each application, the hands are "flapped up" (moved up) right next to the recipient's spine (See Figure 3-56).

Yokode (fish-tail hand): To apply this technique, place the side of the little finger flat on the area to be treated. While rotating the wrist, with the palm moving rapidly from side to side, the little finger presses down and the hand slides upward. The other four fingers flapping give the impression of a "fish-tail." This technique is used primarily on the neck. This application may be given to the arms, legs, and even along the spine as well as Tsukide and Kurumade (See Figure 3-57).

SEMI-TAPPING TECHNIQUE

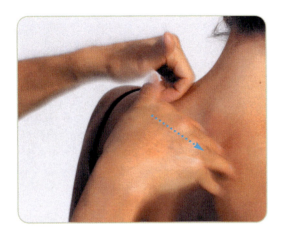

(Fig. 3-54.) Horse hands (striking).

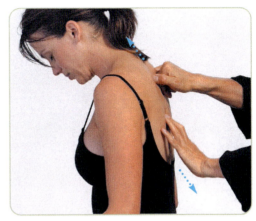

(Fig. 3-55.) Wheel hands (rolling).

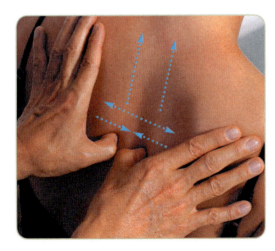

(Fig. 3-56.) Butterfly hands.

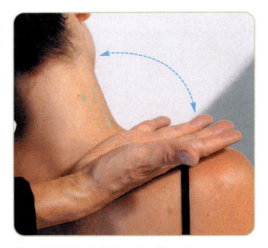

(Fig. 3-57.) Tail of fish (side of hand).

SNAPPING TECHNIQUES

Why to apply: Snapping is applied to stimulate the flow of ki in the particularly important area of fingers and toes. Since meridians generally begin and end at the base of the toenails and fingernails, where energy flows begin or end, this technique is very valuable since it impacts the entire channel flow.

How to apply: Gently pull out and shake each finger and each toe. While tractioning fingers and toes, snap your fingers together with a quick pull when arriving at the tip. A nice snapping sound comes after much practice.

When to apply: Snapping technique is applied immediately before the exercise technique in the Long form. Snapping is not applied in the Short form.

Where to apply: Snapping technique is applied to the fingers and toes.

When to be cautious: Be careful not to strongly pinch the fingers and the toes while snapping. Be aware that some of the joints in the fingers and toes may pop during this technique, but if the practitioner does not pull too strongly, then popping may be avoided. Some people like the sensation of popping, while others do not. Popping is not the purpose of this technique and is not the usual result, but if it does occur, it is generally not harmful. Practitioners should always be cautious not to pull too strongly as this may cause the recipient unnecessary pain (See Figures 3-58 and 3-59).

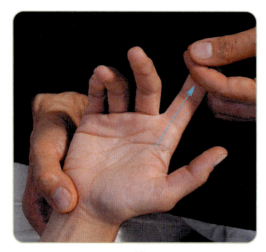

(Fig. 3-58.) Snapping of fingers.

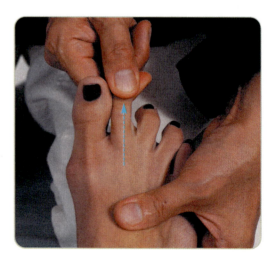

(Fig. 3-59.) Snapping of toes.

OTHER TECHNIQUES

Various other techniques applied in the Long form include tossing and squeezing. Tossing is applied by "tossing" the recipient's relaxed limbs into the air. This technique has no specific therapeutic value but is very pleasant for the recipient. Squeezing of shoulders and hands releases tension and gets the ki flowing properly (See Figures 3-60 through 3-62).

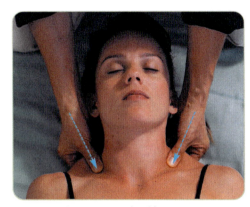

(Fig. 3-61.) Squeezing shoulders.

(Fig. 3-60.) Tossing arm.

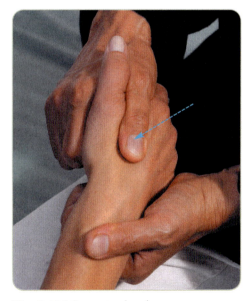

(Fig. 3-62.) Squeezing hand.

CHAPTER THREE
TECHNIQUES OF SHORT FORM

The short form is based upon the principles of Shiatsu. A primary focus of Shiatsu is on the application of pressure to vital points and meridians, proper alignment of the spinal column and skeletal system. The various correcting techniques in Shiatsu are also designed for this purpose. By combining pressure techniques with correction techniques, one may achieve the alignment essential to good health. Both the Long and Short forms use a hand application technique similar to Western chiropractic, but without the chiropractor's characteristic abrupt forceful thrusting motion.

PRESSURE TECHNIQUE (APPAKU-HO)

Pressure technique helps correct spinal and skeletal misalignment, without "cracking" or "snapping," by relaxing muscles, ligaments, tendons, and articular capsules. For example, application of pressure on the sekisaisen (lines by the spines) can correct a spinal misalignment. Every part of the skeletal system is attached to muscles; these muscles tighten up under stress, pulling the body's structure into misalignment. Pressure technique may address spinal alignment directly through the sekisaisen and indirectly through paravertebral muscle groups. Please review all the descriptions of Pressure techniques in the prior section on DoAnn's Long Form

Shiatsu, unlike Anma, emphasizes pressure techniques. Pressure may be exerted with fingers, palms, knuckles, fists, feet, elbows and knees, in addition to the thumbs. These advanced forms of pressure should be utilized after the basic pressing techniques have been thoroughly assimilated. By then, the practitioner should have achieved a level of strength and dexterity sufficient for the application of advanced techniques.

The various pressure techniques of Shiatsu can produce definite effects without the application of the Anma techniques of soothing, tapping and kneading. Those advanced techniques are Nidan Oshi (two step slow pressure), Sandan Oshi (three step slow pressure), Jizoku Appo (continual pressure), Soku Appo (rapid pressure), Sho Appo (quick pressure) and Kyu Appo (negative pressure).

Many Western therapists associate Trigger Points[24] with a release of pain and aches. When you include those un-numbered numerous tender points called Attsuten, many Trigger Points are within the practice of Shiatsu Anma therapy. However, the concept and application of Trigger Point therapy is completely based on Western science.

CORRECTION TECHNIQUE (KYOSEI-HO)

"Don't slouch! Sit up straight." Our childhoods are full of such admonitions from parents and teachers alike, concerned for our posture. In the West, actors, dancers and athletes, among others, carry this concern into their adult and professional lives. In Japan, all those who practice Zen meditation, martial arts, the tea ceremony and No performance (classical masked ritualistic dance) must also focus on their posture. Likewise, posture is in many ways the main concern of this technique.

In Asia, it is further believed that only those with excellent posture are truly healthy. Modern anatomy and physiology also emphasizes the importance of posture in the protection and proper functioning of our internal organs; however, proper spinal alignment is also essential to the nervous system and the thorax, as well as to the pelvis, the limbs and to the body as a whole.

---

24. The theory of Trigger Point was recently introduced by Janet Travell, M.D. for pain control and as a method utilizing Attsuten (painful on compression) which is characterized as referred pain, referred tenderness and autonomic phenomena.

Traditional Chinese physiology identifies the body, the mind and spirit as the three vital centers. In order for the ki to flow optimally, these centers must be kept open. The tanden, or center of the body, should be kept strong and in proper alignment by the strength of the pelvis. The center of the mind, represented by Conception Vessel 17, should be secured by the thorax. The center of the spirit, the "third eye" which blossoms in the forehead, should be protected by the neck. Correct posture, and by extension, correct skeletal and spinal alignment, is vital to all three of these centers.

As mentioned earlier, a number of therapies such as Chiropractic care, Osteopathy, Alexander Technique and Rolfing have been developed in the West to deal with posture and its related health issues. In Japan, there are several kinds of posture correcting methods, called Seitai, which "crack" the body as effectively as chiropractic adjustments. As mentioned earlier, Shiatsu never has such adjustment as its aim, and Shiatsu therapists must not practice abrupt forceful thrusting techniques in the United States as this is outside of their legal scope of practice. Shiatsu correction techniques focus on passive exercising, muscle stretching, soft tissue stretching and relaxing the joints[25]. When joints pop during Shiatsu, it denotes stiffness, fatigue in the tissues and a stagnation of ki energy. For a more detailed description of the technique of manipulative correction, please refer to the previous explanation of long form techniques.

EXERCISING TECHNIQUE (UNDO-HO)

The exercising technique is also applied in the short form in order to enhance the flexibility of joints and circulation of ki. Correction techniques (Kyosei-ho) and exercising techniques (Undo-ho) have complementary effects in practice. Correction stretches and pulls the joints between the left and right, top and bottom. This technique, however, does not rotate the joints. Exercising also works on the soft tissues and the joints, but in a different way. Exercise works more to improve the general range of motion. By performing exercise and manipulative correction, both joints and soft tissue can be positively influenced. Please refer to the description of exercise techniques previously set forth in the Long form. Shiatsu is referred to in this book as a "Short form," yet Shiatsu can easily be developed into a longer treatment simply by extending the number of vital points and meridians treated, including a side posture form and by methodically repeating sections of the treatment.

25. In Japan, a license to practice Shiatsu-Anma allows the practitioner to specialize in chiropractic care (spinal adjustment), for which there is no separate license. In the U.S., chiropractic care requires its own specialized license.

CHAPTER FOUR
APPLYING DOANN'S LONG AND SHORT FORMS

A product of the modern lifestyle we have created for ourselves is what can be called being half-sick, half-healthy. The characteristic of this condition are symptoms that often defy medical diagnosis but are manifested as general aches and pains, discomfort, irritability, fatigue, poor concentration, insomnia, heaviness, depression, low energy, and other such symptoms that may be termed "subjective." Application of the Long and Short forms can often effectively improve what poor living conditions, a stressful life style, incorrect diet, lack of exercise and pollution have helped to create.

During a one-hour long form session, one may entirely rejuvenate the whole body by improving the flow of vital energy. This speeds elimination of stagnant toxins by enhancing circulation that has been compromised by long-standing conditions resulting from hereditary conditions or illness. The Long form is best at relieving congested energy or toxic conditions affecting the muscles and organ energetic systems. More specifically, the techniques of Anma therapy, applied as local or systemic therapies, are very helpful in treating sports and occupational injuries. They are particularly useful for addressing problems related to muscle groups and soft tissues (where ki is stagnant) such as the ligaments and tendons because they employ soothing, kneading, shaking, vibrating and tapping techniques which are excellent for improving the circulation of ki.

Therefore, Anma therapy improves the circulation of ki that naturally results in overall detoxification and strengthening of the immune system. The body's natural healing power is increased. This, in turn, helps the body prevent disease—one of the most valuable aspects of Anma therapy.

On the other hand, Shiatsu therapy is excellent for balancing the autonomic nervous system (which regulates organs, glands and biochemistry), the spinal nervous system (which regulates motor and sensory conditions), and the skeletal system. Pressure techniques often help re-establish a healthy balance to resolve autonomic nervous system imbalance (dizziness, tinnitus, stiff shoulders, headaches, insomnia, night sweats, irregular rhythm of bowel movements, menstrual cycle problems, irregular heart beat and other symptoms whose etiology may be difficult to diagnose). These techniques of pressure, exercise and kyosei (correcting) are best at enhancing nerve reflexes and establishing harmony between the sympathetic and parasympathetic nervous systems (the two components of the autonomic nervous system). This occurs as each nerve receives information from the technique (pressure) and sends a message to the brain, which then sends a corresponding reflex down to the appropriate organ. Shiatsu therapy may lessen or resolve pain caused by unhealthy posture and stress by application of pressure, passive exercise and correcting techniques. Shiatsu therapy excels in promoting relaxation and healing throughout the nervous and skeletal systems. The techniques applied in the Short form (Shiatsu) are most applicable for localized or limited symptoms and may be used as a complement to Chiropractic and Acupuncture treatments.

PRINCIPLES OF THE LONG AND SHORT FORMS

The following underlying principles of the Long and Short forms will help to prevent rote memorization and performance of a sequence of techniques that can result in an uncaring approach to therapy.

1. In the Long form, the practitioner should spend about an hour, using nine different techniques[26]. The practitioner should always begin with the recipient face down (prone). After approximately

---

26. Soothing, kneading, pressure, correcting, exercise, vibration, shaking, tapping, and semi-tapping.

twenty minutes of application, the recipient changes to the face up (supine) position. After another twenty minutes, the recipient is moved to the sitting position.

2. In the Short form, the practitioner spends about half an hour basically using three different techniques[27]. A fourth technique, soothing is only applied exceptionally at the beginning and ending of the form. The recipient should be moved from the prone, to supine, to sitting positions in about ten minute intervals.

3. The Long and Short forms both follow the same sequence, except for the addition of sekisaisen (a line alongside of the spine) in the Short form. The sequence starts along the spine from the top of the shoulder and follows along the pressure points (next to the cavity of each spinal segment) down to the sacrum. During this time the practitioner has an opportunity to evaluate the recipient's condition and decide on a specific treatment that will provide the best possible therapy.

4. Stomach (yang) and Spleen (yin) are paired organs in Traditional Chinese Medicine. The meridians are likewise paired. The Stomach meridian, which runs down the outside front of the leg, is important both for men and women. However, since man is yang, this earth element meridian is particularly effective for men. In the same way, the yin earth element, Spleen meridian, that runs up the inside front of the leg, is particularly effective for women, as it addresses gynecological and menstrual issues. Vital points Spleen 6, 9, and 10 are also important points for specific female problems. In the arms, the Large Intestine meridian (running up the arm) is beneficial for men and women equally for face, sinus, eyes, neck and shoulder issues. This meridian is also helpful for toothaches and headaches.

Other essential meridians significant for both men and women include: Conception Vessel (in the abdomen), Small Intestine and Triple Heater meridians (in the side of the neck), and Governing Vessel, Urinary Bladder and Gall Bladder meridians in the top of the head and the shoulders.

5. From the shoulders, it is normal to proceed down the spine from top to bottom. Then the limbs are worked from the larger to the smaller joints (from the body to the extremities). However, when working the extremities (feet, hands and neck), the direction to work is reversed (from the tips of the toes and fingers to the ankles and wrists).

6. In the Long form, the practitioner soothes, then kneads, and finally presses. Thus he or she moves from the more general applications to the more specific. This is always the sequence, except when treating the head[28]. These three techniques applied in this combination constitute the basic methods of traditional Anma massage.

7. Yu points in the paravertebral region (along the Urinary Bladder meridian) and Bo points in the abdominal region (along the Conception Vessel) need both cutting-kneading and rotating-kneading techniques followed by pressing techniques for about 7 seconds (5 seconds pressing, 2 seconds releasing).

More time may be spent on the abdomen, chest and along the spine (paravertebral region) because these areas are closer to the major vital organs. Less time may be spent on vital points in the limbs (3 seconds pressing, 2 seconds releasing) and the extremities (head, hands, and feet) where only 2 to 3 seconds of intermittent pressure technique need be applied. Pressure applied for 2 to 3 seconds in these areas provides for a basic minimum of stimulation. Individual circumstances may demand more, such as severe conditions where tightness and pain exist.

---

27.   Pressing, kyosei, and exercise.
28.   In the head there are fewer muscles and basically skin and bone. Kneading and soothing that could pull the hair are generally not appropriate. For the head, pressure is the most practical application; soothing can be performed on the forehead as well.

8. The practitioner should choose either cutting or rotating-kneading for the limbs and extremities, except for the head where pressure techniques are preferable to soothing and kneading.

9. Pressure techniques are generally applied once on each vital point through the whole series. However, pressure may be repeated on important vital points in the limbs and extremities, such as Stomach 36, Spleen 6, Large Intestine 4, Large Intestine 10, Kidney 2, and Gall Bladder 21 and 22.

10. Kneading techniques (including both cutting and rotating) are repeated 5 times along the spine and abdomen. On other parts of the body, either cutting kneading or rotating kneading is applied 3 times, except for the top of the feet, where the practitioner should employ a spiral rotation technique[29] The aforementioned provides a therapeutic minimum of basic stimulation. Individual circumstances may demand more.

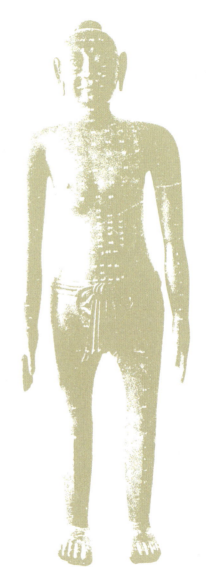

29. This technique is applied as a continual, full circle motion. It is applied to areas where there is not much muscle and where the practitioner doesn't wish to spend much time such as the top of the feet where it is mostly bone and tendon.

TIPS FOR GOOD PRACTICE OF THE LONG AND SHORT FORMS

In both the Long and Short forms, practitioners should strive to avoid becoming mechanical and formulaic in their application and sequencing of techniques.

Practitioners are advised to vary:

- Speed
- Amount of pressure
- Number of repetitions

Variations in speed, pressure and the number of repetitions are necessary to accommodate the individual requirements of recipients.

Practitioners should also seek to establish:

- Good rhythm
- Spiritual focus using breathing techniques to channel the universal life force
- Harmony

It is also important for practitioners to be responsive to changes in the recipient's:

- Skin, muscles and nervous system
- Limitations to range of movement (R.O.M.)
- Emotional state

This sensitivity should be located in and expressed through the practitioner's hands, which, as stated throughout this text, become his or her heart and eyes. By the same token, the practitioner should beware of relying on his or her physical strength. Successful therapy is not a matter of beating or forcing energetic blockages and tissue disturbances out of recipients.

Practitioners are advised to:

- Make themselves an open channel for heaven's divine energy
- Calmly let the divine energy flow into the recipient
- Remember that the practitioner is merely an instrument of divine power – only God heals

CHAPTER FIVE
BASICS FOR PROFESSIONAL PRACTICE

CHAPTER FIVE

INTRODUCTION

Whether performing the Long form or Short form, at home, in an office, or in a clinic, certain issues must be addressed to ensure safe and effective practice. Practitioners must understand and know well both the Long and Short forms before attending to recipients. Practitioners must first screen clients for limitations, contra-indications and risks prior to devising a treatment plan best suited for each recipient's specific needs. Follow-up sessions must be charted and planned for optimum care and treatment of each and every client. This chapter covers the fundamental considerations for setting up a professional practice and for the maintenance and growth of a safe and effective healing arts enterprise.

PREPARATION FOR PRACTITIONER

Doin: Harmonizing Body, Mind and Spirit

It is important for the practitioner to be in the best possible condition (physical, mental and spiritual) when attending to clients. Errors and mistakes can best be avoided through disciplined practice. A practitioner must be disciplined physically, mentally and spiritually and must strive for balance, integrity, harmony and peace in all of these areas. Yang ki is the manifestation of God's healing power. Those who have wonderful yang ki emanate its healing vibrations through their smiling and cheerful attitude. Clients instinctively welcome and take succor from such smiles and cheerfulness. A positive attitude is always significant but may play an even more important role when clients, friends or family members are suffering from terminal diseases. Projection of negative energy may accelerate disease. When dealing with clients and with those closest to our hearts, it is particularly important to accept the cycles of life with peace and equanimity. It helps to be secure in the knowledge that life is a continual process of transformation, and that the spirit never dies. In this way one can offer real support to those with incurable disease. Even if one is able to do little for another on the physical level, there is much that can be accomplished on the mental and spiritual levels. Moreover, when we open ourselves to God and his divine unlimited power, that power is capable of lifting any and all limitation

When a practitioner prays and meditates for peace and contentment to prevail in the world, especially through the use of Doin practice[30], he or she harmonizes the body, mind and spirit, becoming one with nature. This truly prepares one for a healing session. The peace and serenity that meditation confers is essential for concentration on the Long and Short forms. From a position of peace and serenity, practice of the forms actually becomes a peaceful moving meditation.

Doin exercises make it easier to perform the forms by helping to develop the overall flexibility and strength essential for comfortable practice. If the practitioner's back is tight and inflexible, he or she is susceptible to lower backache. Doin exercises should be practiced constantly, as part of a daily exercise regime along with yoga stretches.

PRACTICE OF GASSHO

As one centers one's mind, concentration grows stronger and communication becomes clear and respectful. It is in this context that we greet clients with Gassho. Gassho means to put palms together, signifying respect, trust, thanks, apology, blessing, sympathy, forgiveness, humility and love. Practicing Gassho in front of people and in nature is a wonderful way to discipline oneself and to nourish one's mind through the heart. By practicing Gassho toward the morning sun, we commission the yang healing energy, and by practicing Gassho toward the moon, we may properly reflect upon the day's clients.

The greeting of Gassho opens the practitioner to better communication with his or her clients and to the flow of the divine healing

30. Doin is the self-healing art comprised of meditation, breathing exercises, self-massage and prayers. For further reading on this subject, see "DoAnn's Doin for Self Healing."

power itself. The practitioner opens and closes a session with Gassho to let his or her sincere concern and God's divine healing power flow over the imbalanced body and mind of the client. Daily practice of Gassho will establish and expand a constant sense of balance, love and care toward all.

Clothing

It is important for a practitioner to wear loose-fitting and comfortable clothes, and that such clothing is clean and fresh. In addition to presenting the image of a professional health-care provider, cleanliness is a basic part of establishing a hygienic clinical environment. Spots, stains and residual body odor in one's clothing should be avoided. Cotton is highly recommended, as it is a natural fiber that is comfortable and good at absorbing perspiration.

Washing of Hands

It is essential to wash one's hands before and after a session. Hygienically, one may wish to wash their hands during a session (before moving from any other part of the body to the face). Instead of breaking off to do this, an alcohol napkin might be kept close at hand for this purpose especially in practicing on the face. This way, the continuity of the form will not be interrupted.

Cutting of Nails, Wearing of Jewelry

Hygiene and comfort dictate that the practitioner keep his or her nails moderately short. Likewise, rings and bracelets can be both distracting and uncomfortable, both for the practitioner and for the client.

ADVICE FOR CLIENTS

There are a number of things one may wish to communicate to clients before performing the Long or Short form:

1. The client should not to eat for a minimum of 30 minutes before the session, and preferably not a large meal for two to three hours after the session.

2. The client should empty the bladder before beginning the session.

3. The client may dress in a robe provided (if one is so provided), leaving their underclothes on beneath the robe. Nudity is prohibited in massage establishments in most cities in California. Light, comfortable clothes (such as sweat pants, shorts, T-shirts, or bed clothes) which can be separated into two pieces (a top and a bottom) are an alternative. One should always apply draping with sheets or towels for undressed clients.

4. A client should not hesitate to inform the practitioner of any special symptoms. This is particularly important in the case of infectious or contagious diseases, so that we can take appropriate precautions to protect ourselves and other clients. Please note that we must respect the client's privacy and maintain confidentiality as required by law.

5. A client should be advised that there is a distinction to be made between the pain of contracted tissues being mobilized and "unproductive pain." Clients must trust themselves to draw this distinction and should not hesitate to immediately tell the practitioner if they feel "unproductive pain." To reduce the likelihood of experiencing such pain, clients need to warn the practitioner before sessions begin of any surgery they have undergone, any significant injuries suffered, and any vein problems, bruises or areas of unusual sensitivity.

6. The client should hope and expect to feel great after the session. Frequently, clients express feelings of enjoyment and relaxation, of getting back into harmony and re-energizing themselves. Both the Long form and the Short form are excellent methods of stress-reduction that release considerable amounts of healing energy within the client's body. To enjoy the full benefits of the session, it is recommended that clients rest an additional ten minutes after treatment has been completed.

Sometimes, particularly after the first session, clients may experience soreness. This may be symptomatic of a toxic constitution. It may also occur after strong, deep application of pressure in the case of large, stiff or old clients. Should a client feel tired or worse after the session, he or she may be experiencing what is called Meigen, or Menken, which translates as a healing crisis in which the client's condition deteriorates before it improves. The client should be assured, however, that he or she may look forward to a strong recovery.

Sometimes, a case of bruising results from application of normal/ordinary pressure. This is generally due to Oketsu, a Japanese term meaning "old blood." Some women bruise easily due to gynecological problems such as P.M.S., reflecting periodically stagnant blood.`

7. Encourage the client to feel comfortable and to enjoy DoAnn's Long and Short forms. Shiatsu-Anma naturally rejuvenates the body, mind and soul. It stimulates the healing powers and strengthens the immune and metabolic systems. It is also recommended to practice various programs for continued health and vitality, such as Yoga, Tai Chi Chuan, Doin, Kiko and nutritional counseling to enhance the effects of Shiatsu Anma.

PROFESSIONAL SCREENING

TAKING CLIENT INFORMATION AND HISTORY

It is customary to open a case history for a new client before administering the long or short forms. Such a case history should include the following information: name, address (including zip code), telephone (work and home), age, date of birth, marital status, number of children, occupation, employer, and who referred them. The case history should also record medical details such as the client's chief complaint, date of first symptom, current medication(s), personal history, habits (including exercise and meditation), family history, and so forth.

Such information is essential to the practitioner gaining a whole picture of the client to initially categorize the client's condition. The practitioner should always ask the client for any diagnosis from physicians who may have been consulted previously. The practitioner must establish whether a complaint is: chronic or acute; psychosomatic or traumatic; contagious, infectious, or not; constitutional; environmental; stress-related; deemed medically curable or incurable; and so on. Understanding the root of a client's complaint is the key to effective healing.

Time spent at the beginning of a session establishing such an understanding is clearly time well spent. The format on page 76 is the first page of the client evaluation form used in our Santa Monica clinic.

INITIAL EVALUATION OF CLIENT

Having gathered the essential information on the client's condition, the practitioner should be in a position to decide whether it is appropriate to apply DoAnn's forms. According to official Japanese manuals on Oriental bodywork, orthodox Western medicine is more effective than Oriental body work for treating severe, infectious diseases with symptoms such as excessive fatigue, high fever, swollen glands, and severe aching body (including headache); thus application of DoAnn's Long and Short forms may be unsuitable. In such cases, medical treatment to prevent the progress or spread of the disease may be necessary to avoid an epidemic. However, medically diagnosed chronic conditions where massage has not been deemed contraindicated can often be greatly relived by application of the Long and Short forms. The following conditions should be avoided unless working under the direct super-vision of qualified medical personnel:

A. Contagious illnesses (typhoid, dysentery, cholera, gonorrhea, Weil's Disease, tuberculosis, whooping cough, measles, cerebro-spinal meningitis, polio, leprosy, scarlet fever, small pox, syphilis, trachoma) and infectious skin ailments (gonorrhea, syphilis, leprosy, trachoma). These diseases are highly contagious. Risk of death is high in many of them. If such illness is suspected and the client has not already received a medical diagnosis, directed him or her to seek appropriate emergency care. In the chronic degenerative stages of some of these conditions, following emergency treatment, Shiatsu-Anma, acupuncture and herbal treatments may become appropriate (such as in the case of polio).

B. Blood diseases (thrombosis, embolism, pyemia, varicose veins). Blood diseases are contra-indicated due to the risk of moving blood clots into the brain, heart and lung, with possibly fatal results.

C. Any life-threatening condition (peritonitis, pleurisy, appendicitis, acute or chronic ailments of the internal organs such as ulceration, heart failure or heart attack, pneumonia, heavy bleeding, spitting up blood, febrile disease, liver cirrhosis, hepatitis, cancer). You should refer clients to a physician upon any indication of such conditions. Be aware that in various combinations, fever, pain, headaches, fatigue, and swollen glands can all presage severe conditions.

D. Any local conditions characterized by fractures and severe inflammations which need paramedical assistance. When confronted with an inflammation (symptoms include local heat, swelling, aching and redness), always approach it cautiously since working on it may well aggravate the condition. In such instances, avoid the inflamed area. You may work inches away from the inflamed area and focus on the rest of the body. Appropriate restraint and recognition of one's limitations usually raises one's standing with clients. When you are confronted with a condition that calls for some other form of therapy, do not hesitate to suggest it. Many sports injuries, for example, respond well to "ICERS" (I for ice, C for compression, E for elevation, R for rest, S for support).

E. Conditions that call for limited application of DoAnn's Long and Short form include high fever, extreme debility (such as in the case of immediate post-surgery), pregnancy, and states of altered consciousness from alcohol or drugs.

In the case of high fever, try to establish what is causing the fever, as it may be symptomatic of a severe condition. Fever itself is not the problem causing pain; it is only a signal of our natural defense mechanisms at work. The body defends itself by increasing its temperature so that some bacteria may not be able to survive. The healing process generally causes some pain or discomfort; this is only healing energy at work. Thus we need to deal with the cause of a fever, not only the fever itself.

It is not wise to constantly depend upon anti-biotics to control fever and pain. It is preferable to prevent most infections by strengthening one's immune power with suitable alternative, complimentary and integrated methods. However, practitioners should be aware that if fever nears 104 degrees, risks of fatal dehydration and other damage are present.

For pregnant clients, DoAnn's forms are very effective for lower backache, constipation, poor circulation in the legs, breathing difficulties, and stiffness in the shoulders. However, the practitioner must be extremely careful around the lower abdomen and the sacrum, applying only gentle soothing. According to classical acupuncture, the vital points Large Intestine 4, Spleen 6, and Urinary Bladder 60 are contra-indicated. Urinary Bladder 67 and Gall Bladder 21 are effective for difficult labor. The pregnant client should adopt the side posture during the application of DoAnn's forms. For a newborn baby, only 5-10 minutes of soothing technique and exercises are appropriate. No pressure is recommended for newborns.

In cases of extreme disability, apply DoAnn's forms gently and with appropriate modifications. The same is true for clients recovering from surgery. If for example, a client is disabled following surgery, the practitioner needs to be particularly cautious with the affected tissue, making sure not to cause any more problems. This may be done by limiting the pressure to that area or by skipping the area entirely for an appropriate time period (about two weeks). It is also appropriate to ask for the attending physician's recommendation.

Clients suffering the intoxicating effects of drugs or alcohol need careful attention. Their reactions to DoAnn's forms are unusual and it may be difficult to follow the normal sequence of the form. With such highly intoxicated clients, they should be referred for medical attention. However, if bodywork is still considered suitable and the client may be helped, focus on certain limited areas such as feet, hands, neck, head and ears. The client may calm down as a result of work on these distal areas.

When working on clients with cancer or AIDS, precautions should be taken not to aggravate the condition by stimulating so much that the disease spreads more rapidly to the rest of the body. The practitioner's objective is to increase the client's natural self-healing powers by the laying of warm healing palms on the affected area or on the root of the healing source (tanden) along with the practitioner's prayers for the client's well-being. Distal vital points in the ears, head, hands, feet and area next to the spine are safe and effective points to apply pressure techniques for AIDS and cancer patients unless the areas of distal points are infected.

For more information please contact a local AIDS support group in your area. In Southern California, special training is provided for massage therapists by The Heart Touch Project. They can be reached at (310) 391-2558 or visit their website at: www.hearttouch.org.

Date: _____

How did you find us?_____
Advertisement (specify):_____
Friend's referral (specify):_____

Name:
Address:_____
Email:_____
Phone: (H)_____
             (W)_____
Age:_____
Birth date:_____
Body weight:_____
Height:_____
Marital Status:_____
Children:_____
Occupation:_____
Employer:_____
California Driver's License Number:_____
(in case of payment by check)

Major Complaints_____
Date of first symptom:_____
Your doctor's diagnosis (if any):_____

Personal History_____
Injuries:_____
Surgeries:_____
Abortions:_____

Condition_____
Blood pressure: _____Blood sugar: _____Height:_____

Other Treatment

1. Medication by physician: 6. Chiropractics:
2. Orthopedics: 7. Colonics:
3. Diets: 8. Psychological counseling:
4. Homeopathy: 9. Nutritional counseling:
5. Acupuncture and/or herbs   10. Other:

Habits_____
Smoke: Y / N   Drink: Y / N

Preferred food taste: Sour / Bitter / Sweet / Pungent / Salty

Condition
Blood pressure:_____Blood sugar:_____Height:_____

Exercise
What kind: Daily / Weekly / Occasionally

Meditation
What kind: Daily / Weekly / Occasionally

Have you ever had Hepatitis? Y / N AIDS? Y / N
Are you happy with your lifestyle? Y / N

Family Health History

Mother:_____
_____

Father:_____
_____

Note: This information is confidential and not accessible without
your permission.

SCREENING FOR SPECIFIC INJURIES AND APPROPRIATE RESPONSES

The following procedure is helpful when screening for specific injuries:

A. After taking a client's personal details, medical history and any physician's diagnosis, encourage the client to locate and describe the root of his or her complaint. If the client is unable to pinpoint the complaint, then the practitioner must uncover the root of the complaint. It is useful to begin this process by first evaluating the client's range of motion by moving joints around to assess any limitation in range of motion. Then by palpating[31], one can establish with the client exactly those areas, and more specifically those meridians and vital points, which are sensitive and tender. It is also effective to stimulate tender spots not coinciding with vital points. In other words, if the area between the vital points is sore, treat these areas. In Japanese, these spots are known as Attsuten ("ouch spots").

B. Another way of determining the root of the complaint is to look for visible conditions such as inflammation, varicose veins, deformations, scars and so on which may be visible externally, indicating a problem in that area. Having screened the client for such indications, it becomes possible to evaluate whether DoAnn's forms may be safely and appropriately applied.

SIGNING RELEASE FORMS

In some circumstances, a practitioner may feel it wise to have clients sign a release form. This is particularly advisable if you advertise your services or have clients who were not referred by regular clients. Your release form should establish the following salient points:

A. That services provided complement, and in no way are in opposition to, that of a medical doctor. Thus a clause such as, "I understand that all services, practice, sessions and applications given here are in no way intended to replace any medical care by a licensed medical doctor, Signed Signature:_____ Date:_____, should be included.

B. That any dispute that arises shall be settled through binding arbitration rather than in the courts.

C. That clients are responsible for all fees properly accrued.

PREPARATION OF WORKING SPACE

Your working space should be a clean, hygienic and peaceful place. Any materials to be utilized by the practitioner should be prearranged and the telephone answering machine turned on, with beepers and cell phones turned off. Outside noise should be reduced as much as possible. Try to ensure good, natural ventilation, and monitor the lighting. Subdued lighting is always the most relaxing. Be careful not to let incense or background music become intrusive. DoAnn's forms are most effective in an atmosphere of tranquil simplicity.

Have a blanket or cover of some sort available should the client feel cold. A heating pad can be most effective for poor circulation or pain and may be applied to a cold back or feet. Remember that comfortable warmth is an important part of your efforts to improve the client's circulation of ki and blood.

FEES, INSURANCE, AND PAYMENT AGREEMENT (SAMPLE)

The fees charged in this office are comparable to those charged by other specialists with similar qualifications in this geographic area.

---

31. Palpating is therapeutic touch for purpose of evaluation. It is similar to soothing and pressing but is done at a slower pace and with more pressure.

The fees for office services are payable at the time of the visit, except in cases enumerated below. For your convenience, we accept cash, personal checks, MasterCard and Visa.

If you carry health insurance covering any service that we offer, it is your responsibility to provide us with the proper insurance claim forms and a proper identification card showing proof of coverage on your first visit. Please remember, responsibility for the fee for an application is your obligation.

If you are the victim of an industrial accident, you must provide us, on your first visit, with an authorization from your employer or supervisor authorizing the clinic to provide medical services to you. It is also your responsibility to provide us with the name and address of the worker's compensation carrier.

If you carry private health insurance, please bring your portion of the insurance form completed and signed on your first visit. You will be expected to assign payments to the clinic. We urge you to review your insurance coverage carefully prior to your office visit. Policies are often confusing, misleading, and rarely pay everything. Please understand we have no payment agreements with insurance companies. Insurance benefits are a matter between the client (i.e., the insured) and his or her insurance company. Should you enter into a dispute with your insurance company, and should the insurance company refuse to make payments to us, you will become directly liable for payment of the medical bill. In those cases, we reserve the right to charge interest at the rate of 1.5% per month, for every month the account remains overdue after thirty days.

If you agree to the above terms, please sign in the space provided adjacent.

Signature:_____ Date: _____

Group Insurance, Personal Injury, and Worker's Compensation Client:

Assignment and Release: I hereby authorize my insurance benefits to be paid directly to the practitioner and I accept financial responsibility for non-covered services. I also authorize the practitioner to release any information necessary to process this claim.

Signature:_____ Date: _____

PAYMENT AGREEMENT (SAMPLE)

The fees charged in this office are comparable to those charged by other specialists with similar qualifications in this geographic area. The fees for office services are payable at the time of the visit, except in cases enumerated below. For your convenience, we accept cash, personal checks, MasterCard and Visa.

OUR CANCELLATION POLICY IS AS FOLLOWS:

If you need to cancel your appointment, please call at least 12 hours in advance of your scheduled time. When we receive no call prior to a broken appointment, you will be charged the full fee. There is no charge for cancellation when you reschedule.

There will be a charge of $15.00 on any checks returned unpaid by the bank. I have read the above agreement and agree to be completely responsible for my bill.

Signature:_____ Date:_____

PRECAUTIONS

Gentle, comfortable, gradual stimulation is always safe. Adjust the "dosage" according to the age, gender, experience with Shiatsu-Anma, and the physical condition of the client. Dosage is defined by: (1) type of stimulation, (2) amount of stimulation, and (3) duration of stimulation. The gentler and slower the stimulation, the lighter the dosage.

The practitioner should closely observe changes in the client's skin color, body temperature, range of movement and so on (as they relate to the client's condition). A nice, pinkish tinge to the skin and a comfortably warm body temperature are indicative of a good response to therapy.

Proceed from the general to the specific. Having first identified the area of client concern, investigate the relevant meridians and muscles to better understand the client's energy. Lastly, work on the specific vital points indicated by signs of the client's condition. Try to balance the application of DoAnn's forms to respond both to local symptoms and to the root causes of the client's condition. Do not hesitate to concentrate the application on a specific ailment if it is deemed appropriate. Repeat soothing, kneading and pressure techniques as necessary. Thirty-six repetitions might not be excessive, but prepare the client for the possibility that soreness may occur the day after the session.

Unless it results from inflammation, sensitivity in vital points is an indication of their relevance to the client's condition. In other words, when the pressure causes severe discomfort and provokes a surprised or angry reaction from the client, such as, "Oh my goodness, it is too painful," or "What are you doing to my body?" Stop immediately. When a client's condition has rendered certain areas painful, it may be advisable to begin the application of DoAnn's forms away from these areas: perhaps on the opposite side, around the edge of the injured tissue, or at a distant point. For example, if the client has a sensitive back, the practitioner might begin with the lower extremity of the leg or a healthy area of the back.

Let a natural rhythm, melody and harmony infuse the application. Don't be over-eager to see results from the work. Healing is a process of change. Conditions developed over months and sometimes years are unlikely to disappear overnight.

Prepare the client (when appropriate) for the process known as menken or meigen, a healing crisis during which the client's condition worsens before improving. When clients experience such a healing crisis, a warm Epsom salt bath may be a good recommendation to make.

Lonely clients often wish to talk to practitioners about their happiness or unhappiness in life, and it is sometimes important for clients to express themselves in this way. Practitioners should therefore cultivate good listening habits. However, unless the topic relates to the application of DoAnn's form or some other aspect of the healing process, there is no need for the practitioner to talk at any length with the client. If the practitioner feels that a talkative client is hindering the application through lack of focus, it is useful to instruct him or her to stop talking and to concentrate on effortless breathing.

A variety of clients may benefit from receiving Shiatsu-Anma in a side posture. Pregnant clients, clients suffering lower back pain, elderly clients whose bodies are stiff, and obese clients may particularly benefit from this position.

Immediately following the session, if at all possible, allow a period of about ten minutes for the client to rest, relax and become fully energized. Jumping out into a busy street and engaging in the busy activities of the day can render a wonderful treatment worthless. The energy of the session can be preserved and fully integrated by this precious time of rest after a treatment.

BUSINESS ISSUES AND PROFESSIONALISM

To ensure that a practice complies with existing legal ordinances and regulations, the local Chamber of Commerce or clerk's desk at City Hall should be consulted to obtain local licensing requirements. When constructing a professional identity and persona (business cards, advertising, and all aspects of presentation), it is well worth the effort to create a unique presentation that reflects the practitioner's unique self-image. It is also important to remember that the services provided aren't just another massage, but a very special healing opportunity.

Be as flexible and accommodating with clients as possible. Before establishing professional offices, a practitioner may wish to establish and generate income first by making their services available to clients in the clients' homes or workplaces when it is legal. It is a sensible precaution to carry malpractice insurance. When dealing with the public at large, a practitioner has little control over whom they encounter. Should a dispute arise between client and practitioner, it is better to be prepared. In addition, general liability insurance is essential to protect against accidents that may occur on the business premises.

Clear communication with clients is essential at all times, but most particularly address the following issues with new clients:

A. PRICING. Fees should be set in accordance with what is customary in the area of practice for a practitioner of comparable experience. A practitioner may wish to discount his or her fee for a number of reasons such as promotional value, financial situation of the client, seasonal fluctuations in the volume of business, or advance purchase of a block of sessions.

B. TIME. Be clear about the length of your sessions so that clients know what to expect in advance. Be punctual for appointments. Research has shown that fear of being kept waiting for their appointment is one reason people are often reluctant to visit doctors. Moreover, clients will follow your lead. If clients see that the practitioner does not respect punctuality, they are unlikely to either. Such an attitude will soon play havoc with the practitioner's attempts to schedule clients, and since the practitioner's income is directly related to his or her efficiency, it is certainly in the practitioner's best interest to keep on schedule.

C. CANCELLATION OR NO SHOW. Though frustrating, cancellations and no-shows are an inevitable part of doing business. It is sensible to formulate a policy and establish clear ground-rules with clients (see our own policy above). A practitioner may wish to be flexible with these rules when the situation seems to warrant it.

D. CLIENT FEEDBACK. Be open to client reactions to the services provided. The customer may not always be right, but it is a foolish practitioner who ignores the customer! In our clinic we have a suggestion box (useful for clients who wish to comment anonymously), and from time to time we find that clients complain about such things as, "The room was too cold," "The therapist talks too much," or "There was too much pressure." Honor the clients' constructive input wherever possible. It will benefit your business.

E. CLIENT EDUCATION. If open to the general public, a practice will occasionally attract clients seeking "adult entertainment." These clients need to be educated about therapeutic Shiatsu-Anma and the goals of the Long and Short forms. Be sure that clients understand what services are being offered so there is no misunderstanding. Any misleading behavior, such as touching inappropriate spots on clients or letting the client touch a practitioner, need to be avoided, even if done unintentionally.

F. SEXUAL HARASSMENT. Unfortunately, this is an issue constantly confronted in the healing arts. Honor and trust are essential between practitioners and their clients and this is why tact and rectitude is of the utmost importance; some degree of reserve may be appropriate, particularly when dealing with the opposite sex. Any sexual motivation needs to be eliminated with control and self-discipline. Always be content with God as you practice Doin meditation and prayers to deal with any inappropriate feelings.

G. PROFESSIONAL ASSOCIATIONS. Practitioners may wish to join one of the associations in our field (such as the American Oriental Bodywork Therapy Association: www.aobta.org), to keep abreast of interesting developments. Such organizations provide opportunities for continuing education and nationwide networking with other practitioners to achieve optimum professionalism. Other associations are ABMP (Associated Bodywork of Massage Professionals) and IMA (International Massage Association). Their websites are: www.abmp.com and www.imagroup.com.

ETHICS

Ethics must always be a prime concern when making efforts to maintain the highest professional standards. A conscience which is intact and in accordance with the Tao, or divine order of the universe, should serve as one's most helpful code of ethics. Another useful guide is the code of ethics drawn up by the American Oriental Bodywork Therapy Association (AOBTA). Important ethical considerations may be summarized as follows:

A. Harmony with the divine order of the universe (through following the Tao). A practitioner's ultimate goal should be to create harmony with nature, people, society and the community. Nature is the greatest master and should be respected and trusted. Practitioners need to act as disciplined and healthy individuals in order to gain respect and trust from our clients as practitioners and educators.

B. Healing is a form of love, companionship, benevolence and virtue. Healing is not just a technical or theoretical skill or knowledge; it is the manner of communicating God's wisdom. We do not heal; God is the one who heals. A practitioner needs to be modest and not too boastful of himself or herself, avoiding such statements as "I cured him."

C. Healing and therapy are based on professional and legal conduct which fall under a specific scope of practice. For example, practitioners do not offer chiropractic adjustment or medical diagnosis.

D. Healing and therapy are administered in an atmosphere of clear communication and understanding. All information about clients remains confidential and may only be disclosed to others with the client's permission. Healing and therapy should be practiced in a therapeutic, academic, honest, safe, effective and comfortable atmosphere. Healing and therapy should be practiced in an ethical and professional way during the session.

E. AOBTA members respect the client's physical/emotional state and do not abuse clients through actions, words or silence; nor do they take advantage of the therapeutic relationship. A practitioner may in no way participate in sexual activity with a client. A practitioner must consider the client's comfort zone for touch and degree of pressure, and honor the client's requests as much as possible within personal, professional and ethical limits. A practitioner must acknowledge the inherent worth and individuality of each person and therefore not unjustly discriminate against clients or colleagues.

F. Practitioners need to keep upgrading their knowledge, skills and experience through continued education. Research and further education are essential for continual progress and greater effectiveness.

MALPRACTICE

We have already touched on the value of malpractice insurance. Malpractice itself is a complicated issue which may involve the following aspects:

A. Bodyworkers should respect their scope of practice and not invade other health professionals' fields (such as physicians, chiropractors, physical therapists and acupuncturists). To better negotiate the inevitable gray areas between the various professions, consult available city or state laws and regulations for their official definition of massage. It is, however, professionally acceptable to know the various concepts or principles of related professions and their methods, which may help make a practitioner's sessions more effective. It must be clear, though, that the practitioner is not practicing those professions. As mentioned previously for example, Shiatsu therapists never administer forceful thrusts along the spine; only chiropractors specialize in this practice.

B. Bodyworkers should not use the terms "patient," and "diagnosis," nor perform any actions based upon these concepts. The following are examples of such misconduct: "You have liver and heart trouble." "You should stop your doctor's medication and take this herb instead." "I'll give an adjustment like chiropractic treatment." "My treatment is very effective. I have many patients who love my treatment."

C. Careless practice leading to aggravation or fracture should be avoided. Although fractures are extremely unlikely, one must be extremely cautious with frail, elderly clients or those undergoing cortisone treatment. It is also important to be careful with the application surface and the amount of pressure being applied. The proper range of movement needs to be assessed, so as not to cause joint problems. If one is at all unsure, it is best to stay safe and conservative and, if applicable, to refer clients to a well-experienced specialist.

D. Careless screening creates a greater possibility of malpractice problems. A practitioner should spend as much time as is necessary to understand the nature of a client's complaint and medical history. This helps to screen out high risks. For example, by screening before a session, a practitioner should be aware of such facts as a client's pregnancy, whether they are taking any medication or whether they have had any surgeries.

CHAPTER SIX
PROCEDURES AND TIMINGS

LONG FORM

"Ishi no ue ni mo san nen"

"Three years on the rock." One should stay sitting on the stone for three years before setting out on one's way. If one can stick to something for three years, success is almost assured.

    It is very important, particularly in the beginning, for practitioners to stick to the kata (the form) and master it, if their practice is to be effective. It is only through client experience and keiko (training) over an extensive period (such as three years) that a practitioner may come to see the fruits of his or her labor.

    Diligent practice should enable the practitioner to develop a fine sense of timing. When a practitioner makes a point of practicing the one-hour Long form sequence timing through the kata, it is amazing how precisely timed one's practice can become. Pages 87 through 92 set forth a standard time schedule for the Long and Short forms for the beginning practitioner.

PROCEDURE OF LONG FORM

MERIDIANS:

UB = Urinary Bladder	CV = Conception Vessel	GB = Gall Bladder
GV = Governing Vessel	HC = Heart Constrictor	LI = Large Intestine
LG = Lung	LV = Liver	SI = Small Intestine
SP = Spleen	ST = Stomach	TH = Triple Heater

TIME (Minutes)	BODY PARTS	VITAL POINTS	TECHNIQUES
Gassho Greeting Prone Position	Shoulder Upper back Between shoulder blade	UB 11-17	1. soothing (3) incl. mid-lower back 2. kneading - cutting (5) - rotating (5) 3. pressing (7 sec.)

:00	Middle back
	Lumbar-sacral
	Buttocks (additional hip lines)
	Whole back
		UB 17-30
		
		UB49 - GB30
			1. kneading - cutting (5)
			    rotating (5)
			2. pressing (7 sec.)
			3. kyosei - stretching (2-3 sec.)
			    a. crossing arms
			    b. crossing hands
			    c. crossing fingers

:10	Thighs Legs Feet	UB 36-40 UB 60-67	1. soothing (3) 2. kneading - cutting or rotating (3) 3. intermittent pressure (2-3 sec.)
	Feet (plantar)	3 lines	1. soothing (3) 2. kneading - rotating (3) 3. intermittent pressure (2-3 sec.) 4. fist pressure (2-3 sec.)
	Thighs and legs		1. kyosei stretching (1-2 sec.) 2. exercising (3 ways) 3. foot pressure (2-3 sec.) 4. pressing back (2-3 sec.) 5. stepping on the feet (30 sec.) 6. stepping on calf & shaking (2-3 sec.)

PROCEDURE OF LONG FORM cont'd.

TIME (Minutes)	BODY PARTS	VITAL POINTS	TECHNIQUES
Supine Position :20	Thighs Legs Ankles	SP 11-6 (For Women) ST 31-41 (For Men)	1. soothing (3) 2. kneading - cutting or rotating (3) 3. pressing (5 seconds)

	Feet (dorsal)
	
	Both feet
	One leg
	
	Other leg
	Lower back
		SP 1-5
		LV 1-4
		ST 45-41
		GB 44-40
			1. soothing (3)
			2. kneading - spiral rotation (1)
			3. intermittent pressure (2-3 seconds)
			4. snapping toes, both sides (1)
			5. vibrating toes while pressing toes (5 sec.)
			6. exercise - rotating ankle (3x & reverse)
			7. kyosei stretching & exercise (4 ways)
			    a. rotating hip joint (3)
			    b. stretch bladder meridian (3)
			    c. stretch gall bladder meridian (3)
			    d. stretch 3 yin meridians of leg (1)
			8. repeat 5, 6 and 7 above
			9. optional lower back kyosei exercise,
			    knee to chest (2 ways)

:32	Abdomen
	Under ribs
	Above pubic bone
	(2/3 of lower abdomen)
		CV 14-4	1. soothing, 2 ways
			    a. diamond shape (9)
			    b. clockwise circle (9)
			2. kneading - cutting (5)
			    rotating (5)
			3. pressing (7 sec.)
			4. roto (canoeing) (9)
			5. vibrating - 2 ways (5 sec.)
			    superficial on inhale, deep on
			    exhale, on 5 spots
			    around the navel (1)
			6. lifting with up and down movement (1)
			7. vibrate lower abdomen, quick release(1)

:37	Arms Hands Fingers	LI 15-1	1. soothing (3) 2. kneading - rotating (3) 3. pressing (5 seconds)

PROCEDURE OF LONG FORM cont'd.

TIME (Minutes)	BODY PARTS	VITAL POINTS	TECHNIQUES
Supine Position :37 (cont'd)	Hands Fingers	LG 11-9 HC 9-7 HT 9-7	1. soothing (3) 2. kneading - rotating (3) 3. intermittent pressure (2-3 sec.) 4. snapping fingers (1) 5. squeezing hand (1) 6. rotating wrists (3) 7. kyosei stretching hand and fingers (1-3) 8. kyosei stretch arm & shake (5 sec.) (1) 9. kyosei shoulder joint and scapula (1) 10. stretching arm and shaking (1) 11. tossing (1)
:47	Neck	SI 16	1. soothing, toward clavicle (3) one side at a time
	Neck	TH 17	1. kneading - rotating - both sides (3) 2. pressing (5 seconds)
Sitting Position	Forehead & top of head Top of head Neck and forehead	GV 24-20 UB 1-7 GB 14-17	1. pressing - intermittent (2-3 sec.) 2. squeezing shoulders (3) 3. arching cervical vertebra & kyosei stretch with vibration (3) 4. vibrating forehead, temples (3) 5. kyosei - stretching trapezius, 3 ways (1)
:50	Back of neck	GV 15-14 UB 10-11 GB 20-21	1. soothing - neck - shoulders -upper arms (3) 2. kneading - rotating, both sides (3) 3. pressing (5 seconds)
	Shoulder	GB 21 - LI 16 SI 13, 12 - LI 16	1. kneading - cutting or rotating (3) 2. pressing (5 seconds)
:60 Gassho	Whole neck & shoulder		1. exercise - neck a. superficial (3), b. deep (3) 2. kyosei stretching, 2 ways a. arms up (3) b. arms down (3), rotating shoulder 3. shake (5 sec.up, down, 5 sec. left , right) 4. kyosei stretching and foot pressure (1) 5. kyosei stretching - chest, 3 ways (3 sec.) 6. tapping (10 techniques - 5 sec. each) 7. soothing (3)

PROCEDURE OF SHORT FORM

MERIDIANS:

( )=Repetitions

UB = Urinary Bladder	CV = Conception Vessel	GB = Gall Bladder
GV = Governing Vessel	HC = Heart Constrictor	LI = Large Intestine
LG = Lung	LV = Liver	SI = Small Intestine
SP = Spleen	ST = Stomach	TH = Triple Heater

TIME (Minutes)	BODY PARTS	VITAL POINTS	TECHNIQUES
Gassho Greeting Prone Position :00	Shoulder Upper back Between shoulder blade	UB 11-17	1. soothing (3), opening exception 2. pressing, sekisaisen 1st urinary bladder meridian (7 sec.)

	Middle back
	
	Lumbar-sacral
	Buttocks (additional hip lines)
	Whole back
		UB 17-30
		
		UB 49- GB 30
			1. pressing, sekisaisen
			    1st urinary bladder meridian (7 sec.)
			2. kyosei - stretching (2-3 sec.)
			    a. crossing arms
			    b. crossing hands
			    c. crossing fingers

	Thighs Legs	UB 36-40	1. pressing (5 sec.)
	Feet	UB 60-67	1. intermittent pressure (2-3 sec.)
	Feet (plantar)	3 lines	1. intermittent pressure (2-3 sec.) 2. fist pressure (1-2 sec.)
	Thighs and legs		1. kyosei stretching (2-3 sec.) 2. exercising (3 ways) 3. foot pressure (2-3 sec.) 4. pressing back (2-3 sec.) 5. stepping on the feet (30 sec.) 6. stepping on calf (2-3 sec.)

PROCEDURE OF SHORT FORM cont'd.

TIME (Minutes)	BODY PARTS	VITAL POINTS	TECHNIQUES
Supine Position :11	Thighs Legs Ankles	SP 11-6 (For Women) ST 31-41 (For Men)	1. pressing (3 sec.)
	Feet (dorsal)	SP 1-5 LV 1-4 ST 45-41 GB 44-40	1. intermittent pressure (2-3 sec.)
	One leg Same leg Other leg Lower back		1.. exercise - rotating ankle (3) 2. kyosei stretching & exercise (4 ways) a. rotating hip joint (3) b. stretch bladder meridian (3) c. stretch gall bladder meridian (3) d. stretch 3 yin meridians of leg (1) 3. repeat 1 and 2 above 4. optional lower back exercise, (3) knee to chest (2 ways)
:15	Abdomen Under ribs Above pubic bone (1/2 of lower abdomen)	CV 14-4	1. pressing (7 sec.) 2. pressing 5 spots around the navel 3. lifting the back 4. quick release after pressure on tanden
:18	Arms Hands Fingers	LI 15-1	1. pressing (7 sec.)
	Hands Fingers	LG 11-9 HC 8-7 HT 8-7	1. intermittent pressure (2-3 sec.) 2. exercise rotating wrist (3) 3. exercise stretching hand & fingers (3)

91

PROCEDURE OF SHORT FORM cont'd.

TIME (Minutes)	BODY PARTS	VITAL POINTS	TECHNIQUES
Supine Position :18 (cont'd)	Arm	LI 15 - LI 1	1. kyosei stretching arm 2. kyosei shoulder joint and scapula 3. kyosei stretching arm 4. tossing 5. repeat arms, hands and fingers on the other side
:22	Neck	SI 17-16 TH 17-16	1. pressing (5 sec.) front of trap
	Forehead Top of head Neck and forehead	GV 24-20 UB 1-7 GB 14-17	1. pressing - intermittent (1-2 sec.) 2. squeezing shoulders (3) 3. arching cervical vertebra & kyosei stretch without vibration (3) 4. pressing forehead, temples (3) 5. kyosei - stretching trapezius, 3 ways
Sitting Position :25	Back of neck	GV 15-14 UB 10-11 GB 20-21	1. pressing (5 sec.)

	Shoulder
	
	Whole neck & shoulder
		GB 21 - LI 16
		SI 13, 12 - LI 16
			1. pressing (5 sec.)
			2. neck exercise
			    b. superficial (3)
			3. kyosei stretching, 2 ways
			    a. arms up (3)
			    b. arms down (3)
			4. kyosei exercise and foot pressure (1)
			5. kyosei stretching - chest 3 ways (3 sec)

:30 Gassho			

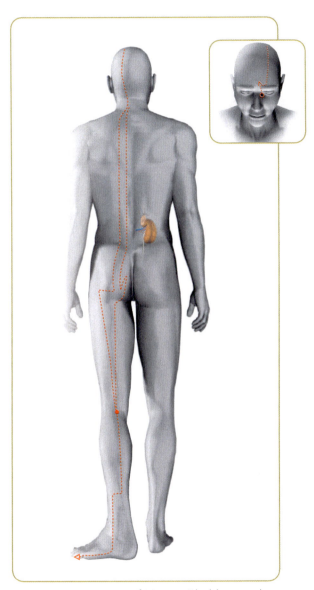

Entire energetic system of Urinary Bladder meridians.

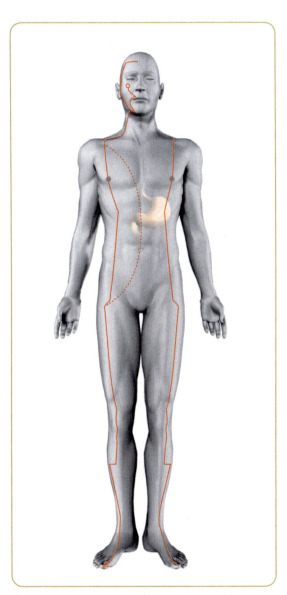

Entire energetic system of Stomach meridians.

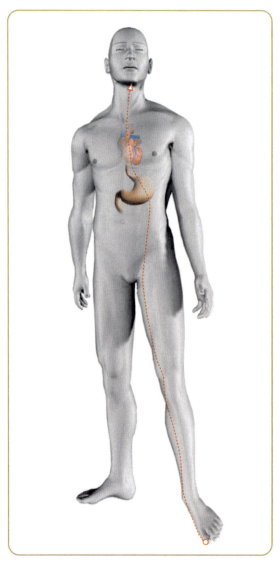

Entire energetic system of Spleen & Pancreas meridians.

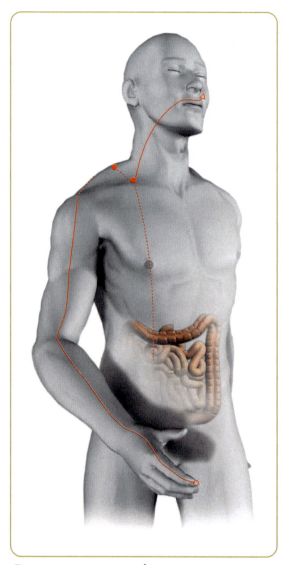

Entire energetic system of Large Intestine.

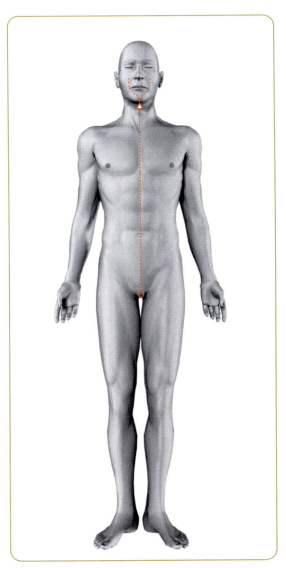

Entire energetic system of Conception Vessel.

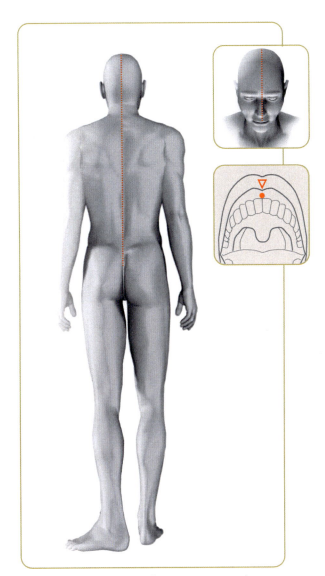

Entire energetic system of Governing Vessel.

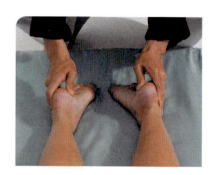

CHAPTER SEVEN

VITAL POINTS AND MERIDIANS IN THE LONG AND SHORT FORMS

DEFINITION OF VITAL POINTS

Vital points are known by a number of names: acupuncture points, pressure points, tender points and sometimes trigger points. A thorough and complete knowledge of vital points is the basis of any understanding of Acupuncture, Moxibustion and Anma therapy. In the healing arts, the student's first task is to study the vital points, and this study is not complete until the student knows the location of each point, its function and use in clinical treatment, and how to select the point according to the client's specific condition.

Vital points are like tuning points for the body's energetic system. The Japanese word for vital point is tsubo, which means a jar or pot. When a person's bio-energy is low, the tsubo feel soft, cavernous, or cold (yang empty). When the person's bio-energy is excessive, the tsubo feel swollen, tight, and feverish (yang excess). Some vital points are familiar to us from everyday life. When in pain, we seek relief, rubbing our bodies in certain places intuitively. Vital points reflect the ever-changing state of human physiology and psychology. Each point, as a vital and active responding unit of the body and mind, may be used to treat those changes as and when desirable (See Figure 7-1).

In health as well as in sickness, we have strong affinities to vital points. Chakras correspond to vital points. For example, the vital point known as Indo is in the same place as the 6th chakra (where Indians put the red mark on their foreheads). When we are sick, our affinity to vital points becomes even more striking. In the case of appendicitis, the vital point Spleen 14 (known to Western medicine as McBurney's Point) located in the right lower abdomen becomes tender. Urinary Bladder 19 (the healing point to the gall bladder), UB 20 (healing point to the spleen), and UB 21 (healing point to the stomach) are all important indicators of stomach ulcers and gallstones.

Clients with lower back pain can show "zoning" (dark skin discoloring sometimes around the waist level) or broken veins behind the knee) at UB 54 or 40. Freckles, discoloring and pimples may appear around UB 23, 24, 25 or exactly along the course of meridians in the arm and face when the case is unusual. Boils and lumps may appear on the sites of other vital points related to the pathological changes.

Vital points are introduced to Westerners through a numbering system, with the lowest number (1) being the starting point and the highest number being the terminating point at the surface level.

CHARACTERISTICS

Most vital points are located on the twelve primary meridians and on the two vessels (conception and governing vessels). Vital points occupy specific places on the meridians, and there are various ways to locate them[32]. There are a number of extra vital points not connected to the major meridians and vessels. In Japanese, these are called Kiketsu (extra, or miscellaneous points), which include Taiyo at the temple, Hachi jyo ketsu at each web of the extremities, and Shitsumin at the bottom of the heel and many more points out of the meridians. Each vital point is named according to anatomical, geographical, symptomatic, physiological, psychological, and three dimensional indications, each point reflecting its unique characteristics.

Vital points are often more sensitive to palpation than other spots[33]. Those "tender points" which are not listed among major meridians and vessels are called Attsuten (painful with pressure), or Azeketsu ("ouch" points). They are significant for clinical treatment in that points often move within a particular line, and although the tender spot may not be a vital point, it may still be significant as an indication of an unhealthy condition.

32.. Location of the vital points is subject to slight alterations, particularly in depth, according to the condition of the body. See also "Measurement Of Vital Points" on Page 100.
33.. The clinical significance of this sensitivity is most pronounced when the vital point becomes suddenly and drastically sensitive.

Vital points are often characterized by different textures in skin, muscles and bones; and by differences in temperature and invisible electromagnetic current. They often occur at bumps, cavities, bone curvatures, junctions of muscle and tendon, hair lines, bases of nails, joints, folds and creases of skin, edges and grooves of muscles, and at the borderline between red and white skin[34].

(Fig. 7-1.) Energetic system of stomach organ and stomach meridian C.V. 12 of Bo–alarm point and U.B.22 of Yu–associated point are linked as electro magnetic activity.

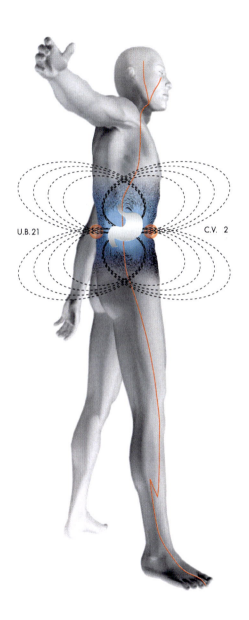

U.B.21   C.V. 2

34.. This borderline may be found along the arms or feet or any topical area where the skin changes color.

ANATOMICAL STRUCTURE

Vital points, much like meridians, currently enjoy an essentially hypothetical existence. Though they have been identified with fibrous nodules in the fatty layer between the skin and the muscle, their physical existence has yet to be scientifically established by Western medicine. It is not our purpose here to question the actual existence of vital points. As with meridians, they serve to describe a real and clinically observable series of complex relationships and interactions within the physical body (See Figure 7-2).

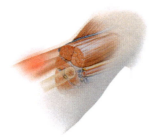

(Fig. 7-2.) Imaginary vital point in the subcutaneous tissue. A tsubo contains stagnated energy that is manifest as thickening tension of muscle and soft tissue.

NUMBER OF VITAL POINTS

It would at first appear that there are 365 vital points as there are 365 days in a year. However, upon closer examination of the classical acupuncture texts, we find some divergences. In earlier times, there were certainly far fewer vital points chronicled. For example, the Nei Jing (Yellow Emperor's Classic) of the second century B.C. lists only 160 vital points. By the end of the 14th century A.D., this number had grown to 354. In the last 30 years, many new vital points have been recognized in China (many of these have been discovered in the ear), with no official number count universally acknowledged.

FUNCTION

Vital points are the gateways, or barriers, through which ki passes as it travels along the meridians. Through vital points, one can regulate both the internal organ and associated meridian tissue as well as the mental and emotional complaints of the client. For therapeutic purposes, vital points are valuable in the evaluation and treatment of disturbed internal organs and their local symptoms, such as muscular stiffness and pain. As stated, vital points shift along the meridians and between the skin and the bones.

MEASUREMENT OF VITAL POINTS

There are several techniques to locate a major vital point, one being to inspect the anatomical "landmarks." One such landmark is the ear lobe with Triple Heater 17 lying below. Likewise, Conception Vessel 17 is situated between a landmark of the two nipples. Landmarks may also be created by manipulating the body, such as bending the elbow and following the crease of the inner arm to its outside to locate Large Intestine 11. Landmarks can also be used when selecting a segment in order to scale two proportional divisions (i.e., horizontal and vertical landmarks such as the nipple line and waist line). Another method uses the sun unit[35] of measurement by means of the client's finger-width to locate vital points. Spleen 6 can be found next to the tibia, four fingers-width above the ankle.

Relating the location of vital points to the various portions of the body is a further device. In this way, Conception Vessel 5 lies two-fifths of the way from the navel to the pubic bone, and LI 10 is located one-sixth of the way from the elbow towards the wrist. A very precise measuring technique, as might be required when inserting a fine needle into an acupuncture point, is to use a rubber band measured to scale and stretched out on the limb or area to be measured. Please refer to Figures 7-3.

35. The sun unit of measurement is based on the width of the patient's own fingers, thus allowing for varying body shapes and sizes (ratio: 1 sun = approx. 1 inch).

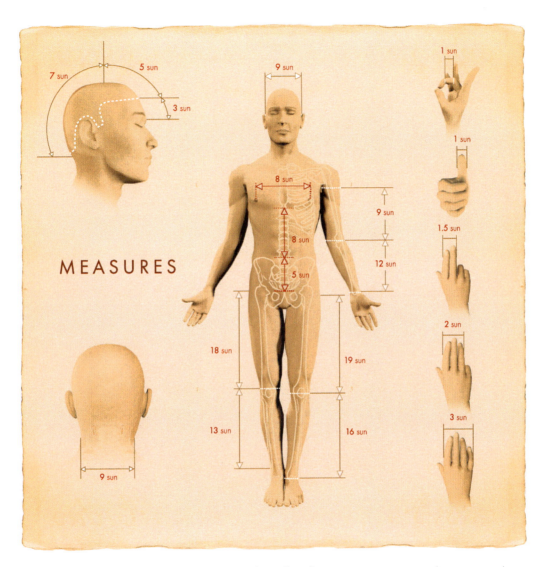

MEASURES

(Fig. 7–3) Methods of locating vital points based on finger measurements and proportional dividing units.

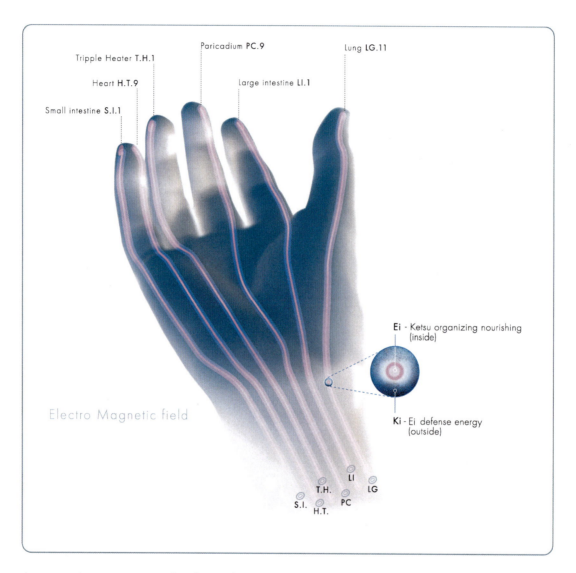

Small intestine S.I.1

Heart H.T.9

Tripple Heater T.H.1

Paricadium PC.9

Large intestine LI.1

Lung LG.11

Electro Magnetic field

Ei - Ketsu organizing nourishing (inside)

Ki - Ei defense energy (outside)

LI

T.H.

LG

S.I.

PC

H.T.

(Fig. 7–4.) Imaginary meridian flows of energetic systems in the hand (electro–magnetic current and its field).

DEFINITION OF MERIDIANS (KEIRAKU)

The Japanese word for meridian is keiraku, which means vertical and horizontal, in reference to the energetic system running through the human body. One might liken this system to the vessels of a plant which supply nutrients and water from root to leaf. The meridian, or channel, is the vessel through which the life force flows, circulating through the whole body and mind. This system of electromagnetic current regulates internal organs, muscles, ligaments, flesh and other tissues, bones, skin, and psychic functions. Each of the primary 12 meridians, except Triple Heater, has a corresponding organ's name since it is associated with that specific internal organ.

There are 12 primary meridians, in addition to collaterals[36] such as the 12 divergent channels, the 8 miscellaneous vessels, the 15 connecting vessels, the 12 muscle meridians, the minute connecting channels, the superficial connecting channels, and the blood connecting channels. The specific and symmetrical directions in which they flow are established by a pattern of energy flow from hands to face, face to foot, foot to body, and body to hands (See the Figure 7-4).

Meridians have proved to be quite an enigma for Western medicine. All efforts to identify their actual physical existence have so far proven fruitless, yet treatments based on their hypothetical existence have proved remarkably effective – even with animals, where one may presumably discount the placebo effect. Although modern science's understanding is far from comprehensive (finding no evidence of an energetic system), it is fair to say that current research focuses more on establishing the neurological and biochemical responses of the organism to effective Acupuncture, Moxibustion and acupressure treatments, rather than searching for evidence of meridians and thus validating practical pain relief through traditional Chinese therapies such as acupuncture and acupressure. Until such time as modern science does achieve a comprehensive understanding, traditional Chinese medical theory remains our best, albeit most subtle guide to understanding the healing arts.

CLASSIFICATION OF MERIDIANS

The meridians and their collaterals are classified according to location, quality of yin or yang, and associated organs. For example, the Lung meridian is formally classified as Arms Greater Yin Lung Meridian; the Stomach meridian is formally classified as Legs Sunlight Stomach Meridian. Table 7-1 sets forth a summary of the 12 meridians and 2 vessels and details the 12 divergent channels, 12 muscle meridians, 8 miscellaneous vessels, the numerous minute connecting vessels, the superficial connecting vessels, and the blood connecting vessels. The primary 12 meridians and 2 vessels are fundamental to the complicated energetic system.

FUNCTION OF MERIDIANS

The meridians provide the pathways and channels for ki and ketsu energy to circulate through the body. The meridians provide a means of bringing ki and ketsu to the internal organs, muscles, bones and all the other body tissues. Ki and ketsu sustain all the organism's activities, both physiological and psychological.

Any dysfunction of the organism, or injury to it, is indicated at some point along the meridians. For instance, a stomach disorder may be indicated by stomatitis (canker sore) in the corner of the mouth where the vital point Stomach 4 is located. The abnormal sensation along Heart meridian in the ulna side[37] of the arm that often accompanies a heart attack is another example of meridian activity. The function of the meridians offers us an opportunity to evaluate the organs, as well as providing considerable prognostic value.

36. Collaterals are branches off the primary meridians.
37. Ulna refers to the bottom side, the medial is the middle and the radial is the top side of the arm.

103

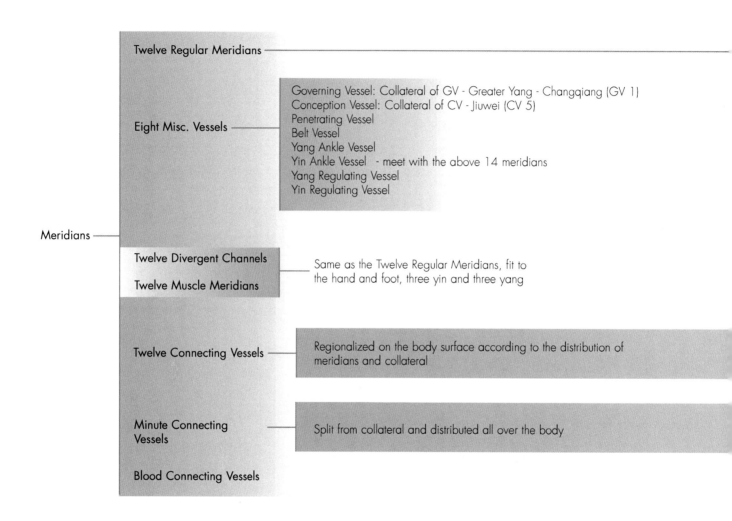

Table 7-1: Classification of meridians and collaterals.

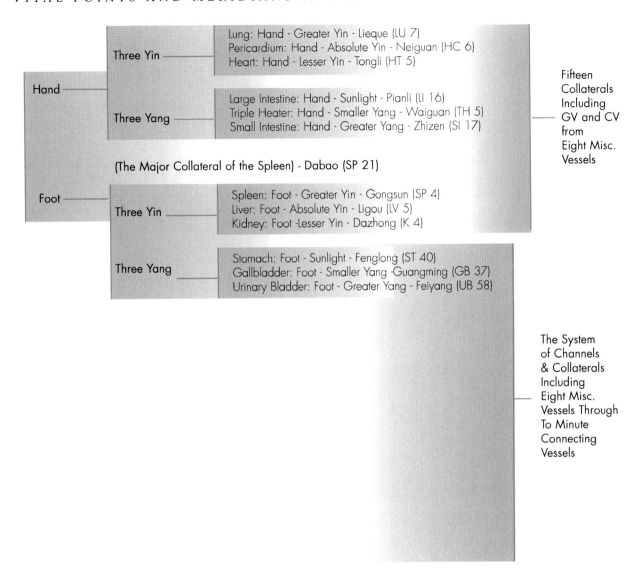

Hand

Three Yin
Lung: Hand - Greater Yin - Lieque (LU 7)
Pericardium: Hand - Absolute Yin - Neiguan (HC 6)
Heart: Hand - Lesser Yin - Tongli (HT 5)

Three Yang
Large Intestine: Hand - Sunlight - Pianli (LI 16)
Triple Heater: Hand - Smaller Yang - Waiguan (TH 5)
Small Intestine: Hand - Greater Yang - Zhizen (SI 17)

(The Major Collateral of the Spleen) - Dabao (SP 21)

Foot

Three Yin
Spleen: Foot - Greater Yin - Gongsun (SP 4)
Liver: Foot - Absolute Yin - Ligou (LV 5)
Kidney: Foot -Lesser Yin - Dazhong (K 4)

Three Yang
Stomach: Foot - Sunlight - Fenglong (ST 40)
Gallbladder: Foot - Smaller Yang -Guangming (GB 37)
Urinary Bladder: Foot - Greater Yang - Feiyang (UB 58)

Fifteen Collaterals Including GV and CV from Eight Misc. Vessels

The System of Channels & Collaterals Including Eight Misc. Vessels Through To Minute Connecting Vessels

105

Classification	Nature	Origin	Function
Life Force Ki	Shin Energy Prenatal Energy Ki	Divine Order Soki Father's Spirit	Organizing Life: Guiding the flow of emotional, mental, spiritual and other psychic forms
Blood Ketsu	Sei- Vital Energy Prenatal Yin Ki	From Mother's Vital Liquid In Her Kidney Primordial Genki	Physical Manifestation: structural, body, tissues,cells,organs
Defense Ei	Postnatal Yang Ki Defense Energy	From Heaven Through Sei - Clear Energy Light	Practicing, defending immunities Inhalation of Air and Nourishment
Yin Ki Nourishing Ki	Homeostasis and Health Ei	From Mother's Milk, Energy	Regulating the metabolism, maintaining Organic Foods (Earth) Grains and Water

(Table 7.1.2.) The four established ingredients of ki flowing within the meridians are summarized above.

CHARACTERISTICS OF MERIDIANS

Meridians are the pathways of vital force, an electromagnetic current and its field, or ki. To better understand the concept of ki in its original context, let us examine some Japanese phrases: Ten ki is translated into English as "weather," but literally means "Energy of Heaven," gen ki is translated as "fine" and means "primordial energy," byo ki is translated as "sick" and means "congested energy," den ki means "electricity."

Ki suggests movement, activity, agency and flow. In human beings this life force flows through the meridians, or channels. Ki consists of four elements: prenatal yang ki, prenatal yin ki, postnatal yang ki and postnatal yin ki. Prenatal yang energy is when a man loves a woman and she conceives a child: the man's spirit is greatly involved in this child's life. It is believed that the essence of the father's spirit that comes from Heaven (called Shin) grows in his child. It is pretty much the same factor as genetic influence. This spirit of heavenly father is named as prenatal yang ki.

Postnatal yang energy is an acquired energy. With delivery, the baby's environment is completely altered and the baby is no longer dependent on the mother alone for its power of life. Postnatal yang energy is produced from the heart's spiritual energy reacting with the oxygen a baby draws through its nose into its lungs after delivery. This process also produces protective resistance power that is distributed in the muscles and the skin. This resistive power, called ei ki, warms, nourishes and smoothes the surface and subcutaneous (just below the skin) tissue. It also controls body temperature through the opening and closing of the pores, and it influences the internal organs. This defensive energy protects the body from outside factors.

There is also prenatal and postnatal yin energy. Yin energy is called ketsu and sui in Japanese. Ketsu means "blood," sui means "fluid." Prenatal yin energy comes from one's parents and dwells in the kidneys. The yin energy flows from the mother through the umbilicus into the fetus, planting sei ("essence") which nourishes the body. Postnatal yin energy, ketsu, is produced from vital energy from the kidney when the spleen first takes in milk and food. Nourishing power is also produced at this time.

Seiki (clean energy) is obtained from the atmosphere and energy of heaven. It is considered very pure. Oxygen, according to the Chinese concept, is regarded as clean energy. Seiki is very important. According to traditional theory, it produces blood when combined with the ki of fluid and the ki of grain from the stomach and the spleen. Soki (ancestral or essential energy) is formed in the chest when the postnatal ki of seiki meets the nourishing postnatal ki of ketsu. Soki nourishes the heart and lungs and promotes circulation, respiration and speech. Travelling as high as the throat and as low as the abdomen, soki is centered in the middle of the chest, at the vital point Conception Vessel 17. Refer to Table 7.1.2.

The remaining pages of this chapter contain charts of vital points introduced in the Long and Short forms in the sequence to be practiced. Also contained are the:

(1) Corresponding numbers of vital points

(2) Japanese names of vital points

(3) Location of vital points

(4) Indications related to vital points

Like sailing, when navigating your healing hands with the compassion of your heart, remember these charts (maps) and have successful sailing. One must master these basic point locations and indications before applying the forms. One must always remember to modify the applications when dealing with fevers and high levels of pain. Serious symptoms should be diagnosed by a proper specialist such as a medical doctor, chiropractor or acupuncturist before application of these forms.

1. BACK PARAVERTEBRAL REGION

1st Urinary Bladder (UB) Meridian (Bilateral[38])
Associated Points: UB13 - UB30

TV: Thoracic Vertebra - Governing Vessel: (1st posterior line)
LV: Lumbar Vertebra - Sekisaisen : Line by the spine
    (2nd posterior line)
CV: Cervical Vertebra - 1st Bladder Meridian (3rd posterior line)
    2nd Bladder Meridian (4th posterior line)

LOCATIONS 12 YU POINTS

UB13: Lung
Between 3rd and 4th TV

UB14: Heart Constrictor
Between 4th and 5th TV

UB15: Heart
Between 5th and 6th T

Diaphragm Line UB17

UB18: Liver
Between 9th and 10th TV

UB19: Gall Bladder
Between 10th and 11th TV

UB20: Spleen/Pancreas
Between 11th and 12th TV

UB21: Stomach
Between 12th and 1st LV

UB22: Triple Heater
Between 1st and 2nd LV

UB23: Kidney
Between 2nd and 3rd LV

Circle Line from UB 48 (49) to GB 30

UB25: Large Intestine
Between 4th and 5th LV

UB27: Small Intestine
At 1st Sacral Crest, 1 sun
Sacral Foramen

UB28: Urinary Bladder

At 2nd Medial Sacral Crest, 1 sun lateral to
2nd Dorsal
Sacral Foramen

On 2nd Bladder Meridian next to UB53

UB28, 2 fingers lateral

GB30: On Superior and Anterior Major Trochanter

(hip area or hip joint).

From side posture, GB30 is on the tip of the
crease created by bending the hip joint. A normal
response is for one to feel a sharp sensation to the
lower extremities. Chinese method places GB30
1/3 way further medial and inferior to the coccyx.

38.   Bilateral refers to having two sides. In this case it is of the existence on both sides of the body of a meridian. Thus, it is symmetrical (left and right).

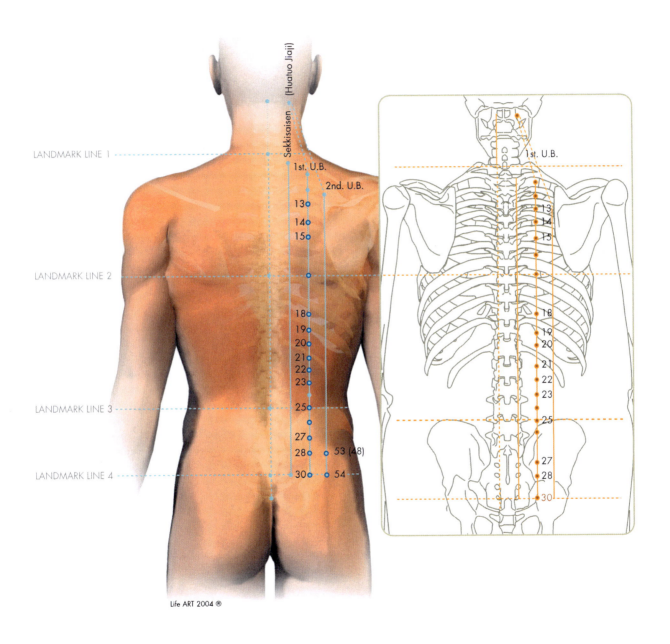

LANDMARK LINE 1

LANDMARK LINE 2

LANDMARK LINE 3

LANDMARK LINE 4

Sekkisaisen (Huatuo Jiaji)

1st. U.B.

2nd. U.B.

13
14
15

18
19
20
21
22
23

25

27
28   53 (48)
30   54

1st. U.B.

13
14
15

18
19
20
21
22
23

25

27
28
30

Life ART 2004 ®

1. BACK PARAVERTEBRAL REGION

1st Urinary Bladder (UB) Meridian (Bilateral)
Associated Points: UB13 - UB30

 INDICATIONS

UB13 Hai Yu: Healing point for (HPF) Lung
- Respiratory ailments
- Common cold
  Coughing, chills, fever and sinus
  Discomfort and pain in the lung
  Difficulty in breathing
  Stiff neck and shoulders
  Itchiness and irritation in skin (allergy)
  Sadness, melancholy
  Controls dryness in body and general mental activity

UB14 Kecchin Yu: HPF Pericardium
- Cardiovascular ailments
  Irregular heart beat
  Palpitation
  Chest pain
  Hypertension
  Circulation problems
  Stiffness and aching between shoulder blades
  Hysteria
  Controls supplemental fire (false heart) in the body

UB15 Shin Yu: HPF Heart
- Cardiovascular ailments
  High blood pressure
  Hypertension
  Post Stroke Syndrome
- Discomfort and pain in the chest
- Epilepsy
- Too much excitement
- Controls heat in the body

UB18 Kan Yu: HPF Liver
- Liver ailments
  Distention below ribs (swelling)
  Abdominal pain and discomfort
  Indigestion
  Nausea
  Chest Pain in side
- Muscle problems
  Cramps
  Degeneration
- Eye problems
  Yellow eyes
  Turned up eyes
  Weak vision
- Anger, impatience, frustration
- Controls wind in the body

UB19 Tan Yu: HPF Gall Bladder
- Same as HPF Liver
- Bitter taste in mouth
- Dry tongue
- Headache
- Controls bile

UB20 Hi Yu: HPF Spleen/Pancreas
- Digestive ailments
  Discomfort in abdomen
  Acidity
  Belching and vomiting
  Diarrhea
  Fatigue

1. BACK PARAVERTEBRAL REGION

1st Urinary Bladder (UB) Meridian (Bilateral)
Associated Points: UB13 - UB30

 INDICATIONS CONT'D.

UB20 - Continued

Prolapse of the stomach
Obesity or losing weight
- Aching joints
- Jaundice, diabetes
- Edema (accumulation/retention of bodily fluids)
- Worry and anxiety
- Controls humidity in the body

UB21 I Yu: HPF Stomach
- Same as HPF Spleen/Pancreas
- Loss of appetite or excess appetite
- Stomach chills
- Gurgling abdomen
- Controls food metabolism

UB22 Sansho Yu: HPF Triple Heater
- Digestive ailments
  Vomiting
  Abdominal pain and gurgling
- Distension (swelling)
- Lumbago (lower backache)
- Headache
- Dizziness
- Febrile (fever) disease with pain
- Controls body warmth and body fluid

UB23 Jin Yu: HPF Kidney
- Excretory ailments
  Painful or irregular urination

Edema (accumulation/retention of bodily fluids)
Draining of body fluid
- Hot flashes to the head
- Reproductive ailments
  Irregular menstruation
  Losing sperm without intercourse, Impotence
- Emaciation (becoming thin and feeble)
- Fatigue
- Ear ailments
  Ringing ears
  Difficulty in hearing
- Fear
- Lumbago, lower backache
- Knee joint problems
- Controls water metabolism

UB25 Daicho Yu: HPF Large Intestine
- Digestive ailments
  Abdominal pain
  Diarrhea
  Constipation
  Gurgling colon
  Hemorrhoids
- Controls food transformation
- Lumbago, sciatica

UB27 Shocho Yu: HPF Small Intestine
- Digestive ailments
  See HPF Large Intestine
  Swollen abdomen
- Lumbago

111

1. BACK PARAVERTEBRAL REGION

1st Urinary Bladder (UB) Meridian (Bilateral[7])
Associated Points: UB13 - UB30

INDICATIONS CONT'D.

UB28 Boko Yu: HPF Urinary Bladder
- Urogenital/excretory ailments
  Irregular urination
  Painful or difficult urination
- Lower digestive problems
- Reproductive ailments
- Controls water metabolism
  Additional Hip Line:

UB53 (48) (Yoko: Principle of Yang) to GB30
(Kancho: Bouncing Ring)
- Hip joint ailments
- Lumbago
- Sciatica

UB31 (Joryo Yu: Healing point at upper hole) to
UB34 (Geryo Yu: Healing point at lower hole)
- Lumbago
- Sciatica
- Reproductive ailments
- Hormonal imbalance
- Gynecological ailments
- Uro-genital ailments

Points in Additional Hip Line (AHL)
- Sciatica
- Muscle cramps around hips
- Hip joint ailments

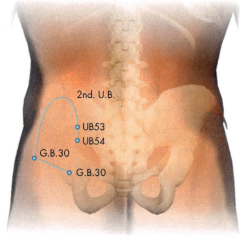

Chart 7.2

Life ART 2004 ®

2. BACK OF LEGS AND FEET

Urinary Bladder (UB) Meridian
Associated Points: UB36 - UB40, UB57 - UB67

LOCATIONS

UB36 (50):
Midpoint of gluteal fold at tip of
ischial tuberosity (sitting bone).

UB37 (51): 6
sun inferior to UB36 (50) About halfway but slightly
superior to midpoint between UB36 (50) and UB40 (54)
(3/7- way). (Deep inside the fleshy part of the leg, you can
feel a hard ball-like tissue).

UB40 (54)
(54):Midpoint of popliteal fossa, (behind the knee in the middle of the crease of bent knee); pulse is perceived and it has
an electrifying sensation.

UB57:
Halfway between UB40 (54) and UB 60 8 sun inferior to
UB40. (Soothe the skin carefully, UB57 is where muscle
texture changes).

UB58:
1 sun (1 finger) lateral to UB57.

UB60:
Halfway between external malleolus (outside ankle bone)
and the Achilles tendon back of ankle. (Use tip of thumb).

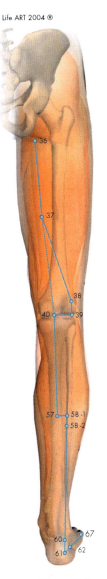

Life ART 2004 ®

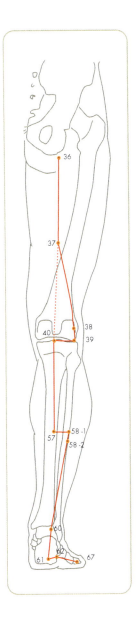

Chart 7.3

113

2. BACK OF LEGS AND FEET

Urinary Bladder (UB) Meridian
Associated Points: UB36 - UB40, UB57 - UB67

 INDICATIONS

UB36 Shofu:Receiving Support
- Constipation
- Sciatica
- Backache
- Weakness or Hemiplegia (paralysis of lower extremities on one side of the body)

UB37 Inmon: Gate of Abundance
- Backache (difficulty in bending the back)
- Spasm of hamstring

UB40 (54) Ichu: Disputing at the Middle
(One of four major points for lower back problems - Masterpoint for lower backache)
- Fever without sweating
- Fever in the limbs
- Pain in the back
- Knee problems
- Sciatica, lumbago
- Weakness (Paralysis of lower extremities)

UB57 Shozan: Receiving the Mountains
- Constipation
- Hemorrhoids
- Sciatica
- Lumbago
- Calf muscle spasm

UB58 Hiyo: Flying Yang
- Hemorrhoids
- Swollen leg
- Dizziness
- Eyeache
- Epileptic condition
- Fatigue in the legs

3. SIDE OF FEET

(Lateral Aspect)
Urinary Bladder (UB) Meridian

LOCATIONS

UB60
Halfway between medial posterior border of external malleolus (ankle bone) and Achilles tendon. At level of tip of ankle.

UB 63
Halfway between UB 64 & UB 62 (0.5 sun inferior to the inferior border of external malleolus.

UB 64
In the depression on the lateral side of the dorsum of foot below the Tuberosity of the 5th Metatarsal bone.

UB67
About 0.1 sun proximal (closer to the center of the body) to the lateral (outside) base of the 5th toenail.

INDICATIONS

UB 63
Kinmon Golden Gate
Pain the ankle, legs, lower back, weakness of lower extremity
epileptic seizure, children's convulsion

UB 64
Keikotsu Capital Bone
Headache, epileptic seizure, neck rigidity

UB67
Shiin: Reaching Yin
Labor pains
Reversing the fetus (improper position of fetus)

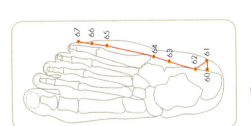

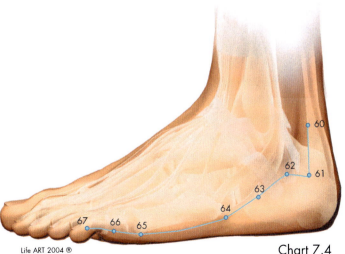

Life ART 2004 ®

Chart 7.4

4. BOTTOM OF FEET

(Plantar Aspect)
Kidney (K) Meridian , Vital Points: K1, K2

LOCATIONS

K1
On the sole between 2nd and 3rd toe, about 1/3 of the way from anterior (front) to posterior (back of foot) plantar line. K1 is on the line between K2 and small toe.

K2
Anterior and inferior to navicular bone. (Bend the toes; K2 is located in the middle of the arch.) Also from the base of 5th toe, K1 and K2 are found in one straight connected line.

Shitsumin
Midpoint of calcaneus bone (bone of the heel).

INDICATIONS

K1 Yusen: Bubbling Spring
- Edema
- Unclear eyes
- Dizziness
- Heart ailments
  Palpitation
  Weakness
- Cold feet
- Kidney ailment
- Uterus ailment

INDICATIONS CONT'D.

K2 Nenkoku: A Light Valley
- Gynecological ailments
  Irregular menstruation
  Infertility
  Prolapse (dropping) of the uterus
- Sore throat
  Bladder ailment

Shitsumin: Lost Sleep
- Insomnia

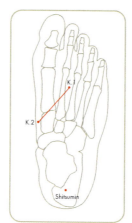

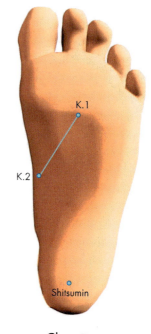

Chart 7.5

5. FRONT OF LEGS (OUTSIDE - YANG)

Stomach (ST) Meridian
Vital Points: ST31 - ST41

LOCATIONS

ST31
Crossing point of pubic symphysis and anterior iliac spine. (Flex knee; ST31 is located in the middle of crease under the iliac spine, approximately at the level of the inferior border of the pubic symphysis).

ST34
2 sun (3 fingers) superior to lateral superior ridge of patella (knee cap).

ST35
Lateral to patellar ligament in middle of cavity just below patella (Flex knee; ST35 is in the middle of cavity).

ST36
3 sun (4 fingers) inferior to lateral interior ridge of patella (Soothe top of tibia bone until the beginning of its prominence. ST36 is located in between this point and head of fibula bone, 1 sun lateral to anterior crest of tibia). Or, grasping patella vertically with thumb and index finger, ST36 is at tip of middle finger.

ST40
2 sun lateral to tibia bone, 8 sun inferior to ST35. (Midpoint between middle of knee and top of ankle).

ST41
At midpoint of transverse (horizontal) malleolus (ankle) crease. (Flex toes toward anterior of ankle; ST41 is in middle of cavity).

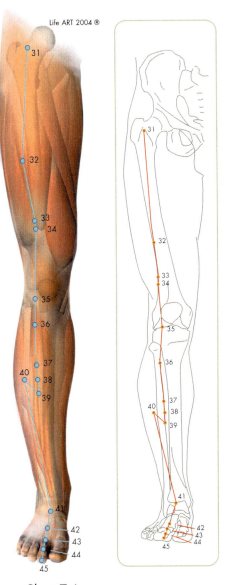

Life ART 2004 ®

Chart 7.6

5. FRONT OF LEGS (OUTSIDE - YANG)

Stomach (ST) Meridian
Vital Points: ST31 - ST41

 INDICATIONS

ST31 Hikan: Barrier at the Buttocks
- Shooting pain due to lower backache
- Weakness such as hemiplegia (paralysis on one side)
- Pain in anterior thigh

ST34 Ryokyu: Hill of Beam
- Special point for acute abdominal pain
- Gall stones
- Diarrhea

ST35 Tokubi: Calf's Nose
- Knee joint ailments
- Neuralgia (inflammation of nerve)
- Arthritis (inflammation of knee joint)
- Spasm of muscles

ST36 Ashi No Sanri: 3 Miles in the Leg (One of four major points for abdominal problems; Master point for well being)
- Digestive ailments
Gastralgia (inflammation of stomach)
Chronic stomach and intestinal problems
Loss of appetite
Nausea and vomiting
- Swollen extremities
- Breast ailments
- Uncontrolled laughing
- Neurasthenia (mental fatigue, listlessness)
- Incoherent speech
- General well being; tonic purpose (energizes)

ST40 Horyu : Copious Abundance
- Swollen lower extremities
- Difficult urination
- Abdominal pain
- Constipation and hard stools

ST41 Kaikei: Loosened Current
- Swollen lower eyelids
- Headache
- Dizziness
- Ankle joint ailment

6. FRONT OF LEGS (INSIDE - YIN)

Spleen/Pancreas (SP) Meridian
Vital Points: SP11 - SP5

LOCATIONS

SP6
3 sun (4 fingers) superior to medial malleolus (ankle) at posterior border of tibia bone, opposite GB39.

SP9
Medial inferior ridge of medial condyle of tibia (bumpy ridge below inside of knee cap), opposite ST36. (Soothe the posterior ridge of tibia; SP9 is where soothing fingers stop).

SP10
2 sun (3 fingers) superior to superior border of patella, opposite ST34.

SP11
Slightly inferior to midpoint between medial superior ridge of patella and superior ridge of pubic symphysis. (6 sun above SP10, or 8/19-way between patella and pubic symphysis).

SP12
3.5 sun (4.5 fingers) lateral to midpoint of superior border of pubic symphysis in the bottom of the abdomen. (CV2)

Life ART 2004 ®

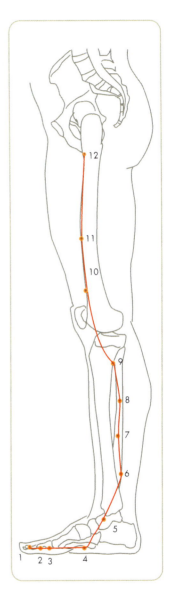

Chart 7.7

119

6. FRONT OF LEGS (INSIDE - YIN)

Spleen/Pancreas (SP) Meridian
Vital Points: SP11 - SP5

INDICATIONS

**SP6 Saninko: Three Yin Channel Crossing
(Masterpoint for female disorders)**
- Special point for yin disease
- Gynecological/reproductive ailments
  Irregular menstruation
  Leukorrhea
  Pain in genitals
  Impotence
  Nocturnal emission (uncontrollable sperm
  discharge during sleep)
- Menopausal symptoms (hot flashes)
- Indigestion
- Urinary retention
- Cold feet and body

SP9 Inryosen: Yin Tomb Spring
- Edema (accumulation/retention of bodily fluids)
- Chill in abdomen
- Urinary retention
- Knee pain and swelling
- Pain in genitals
- Irregular menstruation (Menopause)
- Abdominal pain (P.M.S.) due to stagnant blood

SP10 Kekkai: Ocean of Blood
- Gynecological ailments
  Irregular menstruation
  Menopause
  Leukorrhea (vaginal discharge)
- Abdominal pain due to stagnant blood (toxicity)
- Knee pain or swelling

SP11 Kimon: Gate of Basket
- Lower abdominal pain
- Shooting pain due to lower backache
- Urinary retention

SP12 Shomon: Gate of Pouring
- Lower abdominal pain
- Inguinal (groin; prostate gland; hernia)
- Reproductive ailment

7. TOP OF FEET

(Dorsal Aspect) Spleen/Pancreas (SP), Liver (L), Stomach (ST) & Gall Bladder (GB) Meridians
Vital Points: SP1 - SP5, LV1 - LV4, ST45 - ST41, GB44 - GB40

LOCATIONS

LV1
About 0.1 sun proximal to the lateral base of big toenail, outside corner.

SP1
About 0.1 sun proximal to the medial base of big toenail, inside corner.

LV3
Between 1st and 2nd toe, 2 sun (3 fingers) proximal to margin of web (Pulse is present).

LV4
1 sun anterior to the medial malleolus (Bend toes up; LV4 is in the depression in front of medial malleolus; about halfway between ST41 and SP5).

SP5
In depression of anterior inferior ridge of medial malleolus (ankle bone).

ST45
About 0.1 sun proximal to the lateral base of 2nd toenail.

GB44
About 0.1 sun proximal to the lateral base of 4th toenail.

UB67
About 0.1 sun proximal to the lateral base of 5th toenail.

ST41
At midpoint of transverse malleolus crease (Stretch foot and bend toes; ST41 is in middle of cavity.)

GB40
In the depression of anterior inferior ridge of lateral malleolus (ankle bone).

UB60
Halfway between medial posterior border of external malleolus and Achilles tendon.

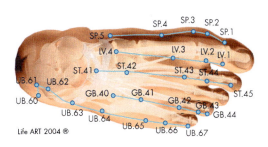

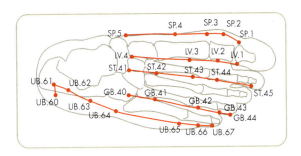

Life ART 2004 ®

Chart 7.8

121

7. TOP OF FEET

(Dorsal Aspect) Spleen/Pancreas (SP), Liver (L), Stomach (ST) & Gall Bladder (GB) Meridians
Vital Points: SP1 - SP5, LV1 - LV4, ST45 - ST41, GB44 - GB40

INDICATIONS

GB44 Kyoin: Shady Hole (Foot)
Coughing with breathing difficulty
- Difficulty in perspiring
- Dryness in mouth
- Eye ache
- Deafness (temporal)
- Distorted mouth (numbness caused by wind)
- Tight tongue (affecting speech)

GB40 Kyukyo: Ruin at the Hill
- Abdominal pain
- Distention (swelling) in chest and abdomen (gas)
- Lumbago (pain in mid-back)
- Pain in side of chest
- Ankle ailments (sprain)

ST45 Reida: A Strict Exchange
- Fever without perspiration
- Nasal Congestion
- Irritable skin at the corner of the mouth
- Swollen face and neck due to sinus
- Epileptic condition
- Dream-disturbed sleep

ST41 Kaikei: Loosened Current
- Swollen lower eyelids
- Headache
- Dizziness
- Ankle joint ailments (sprains)

LV1 Taiton: Big Performance
- Pain in genitals
- Difficulty and pain when urinating

- Gynecological ailments (menstrual)
- Swollen abdomen
- Pain in the chest

LV3 Taisho: Great Rush
- Abdominal spasms and cramps
- Gynecological complaints (uterus)
- Convulsions in children
- Headache
- Pain in genitals

LV4 Chuho: Central Blockade
- Hernia in the abdomen
- Pain in genitals
- Swollen abdomen
- Lumbago (pain in left to right movement)

SP1 Inpaku: Hidden White
- irregular blood condition
  Nose bleed
  Irregular menstruation
- Cold feet
- Indigestion (vomiting)

SP5 Shokyu: Hill of Deliberation
- Digestive ailments
  Swollen abdomen (gas)
  Loss of appetite
  Stomach ache
  Gurgling colon
- Fatigue
- Ankle joint ailments

8. ABDOMEN

Conceptual Vessel (CV)
Vital Points (Bo or "Alarm" Points): CV14 - CV3

LOCATIONS

LG1 Lung
1 sun inferior to the middle of infraclavicular fossa (cavity below the collar bone). LG2 lies in the middle of infraclavicular fossa.

LV14 Liver
On mammary line in the intercostal space (space between ribs) between 6th & 7th ribs.

GB24 Gall Bladder
On mammary line in the intercostal space between 7th and 8th ribs.

LV13 Spleen/Pancreas
At tip of 11th costal bone (rib not attached to rib cage).

GB25 Kidney
At tip of 12th rib (Floating rib).

ST25 Large Intestine
2 sun (3 fingers) lateral to center of navel.

CV17 Heart Constrictor or Pericardium
On sternum between the two nipples, about 1/3-way from inferior tip of sternum to jugular notch (cavity below the throat, at the top of the sternum).

CV14 Heart
1/4-way from inferior tip of sternum to navel.

CV12 Stomach
Halfway between inferior tip of sternum to navel.

CV5 Triple Heater
2 sun inferior to navel or 2/5-way from navel to pubic bone.

CV4 Small Intestine
3 sun inferior to navel or 3/5-way from navel to pubic bone.

CV3 Urinary Bladder
4 sun inferior to navel or 4/5-way from navel to pubic bone.

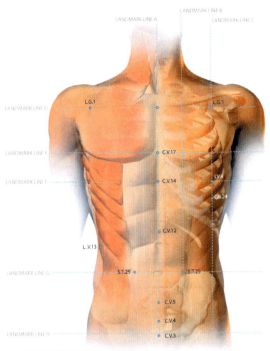

Life ART 2004 ®

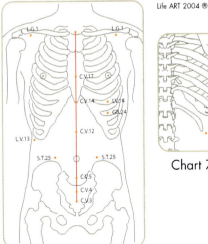

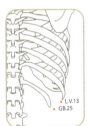

Chart 7.9

123

8. ABDOMEN

Conceptual Vessel (CV)
Vital Points (Bo or "Alarm" Points): CV14 - CV3

 INDICATIONS

LG1 Chufu: Central Residence
- Respiratory ailments
  Common cold
  Coughing
  Panting
  Asthma
  Chest pain
  Excessive sweating
- Pain in shoulders
- Upset (flash)
- Swollen face (sinus)

CV17 Danchu: Middle of the Chest (One of eight influential points for emotional and breathing problems)
- Respiratory ailments
  Congestion and pain in chest
  Coughing
  Panting
- Circulatory ailments
- Hiccups
- Lack of milk for nursing mother
- Panting
- Nausea
- Upset, unstable emotion, moodiness

CV14 Koketsu: Huge Void
- Circulatory ailments
  Palpitation
  Chest ache
  Discomfort and weakness in the heart
- Distention under the ribs
- Vomiting, nausea
- Phlegm
- Madness

**CV12 Chukan: Middle of the Stomach
(One of eight influential points for all yang organs)**
- Digestive ailments
  Stomachache
  Duodenum ache (small intestine)
  Cramps
  Nervous stomach (tight, pulsating)
  Indigestion (vomiting, acidity, diarrhea, distention)

CV5 Sekimon: Gate of Stone
- Digestive
  Blood stagnation (toxic blood)
  Water stagnation (swelling, edema)
- Reproductive ailments (gynecological lower)
  abdominal pain due to stagnant blood)
- Uro-genital ailments
  Residual urine
  red color in urine
  pain in lower abdomen
  feverish due to infection

CV4 Kangen: Barrier of Origin
  Urogenital and reproductive ailments (gynecological)
  Difficulty in urinating
  Irregular menstruation
  Impotence
  Leukorrhea (discharge)
  Male sperm problems such as nocturnal emission,
  or spermatorrhea
- Chill in lower abdomen
- Pain around the navel
- Fatigue

8. ABDOMEN

Conceptual Vessel (CV)
Vital Points (Bo or "Alarm" Points): CV14 - CV3

 INDICATIONS

CV3 Chukyoku: Central Pole
- Urogenital and reproductive ailments
  Irregular menstruation
  Frequent urination
  Nocturnal emission
  Infertility
  Impotence
  Leukorrhea
- Abdominal Pain
- Edema in the face or legs
  ST25 Tensu_: Hinge of Heaven
- Digestive ailments
  Diarrhea
  Indigestion
  Swollen abdomen
  Pain in abdomen
  Nausea
  Constipation
  Tightness around navel
  Water retention (splashing sound in stomach)
- Abdominal pain due to stagnant blood
- Discharge
- Irregular menstruation

LV14 Kimon: Gate of Hope
- Digestive ailments
  Swelling under rib cage (center to side)
  Digestive problems
  Tightness or enlarged liver or gall bladder
  Pain in the intercostal region

  Indigestion
  Nausea and vomiting
- Chest pain due to stagnant blood
- Dryness in mouth due to "liver fire"
- Gynecological ailments (after delivery)
- Constant sweating with alternating fever and chills

LV13 Shomon: Gate of Order
  (One of eight influential points for all yin organs)
- Tightness or enlarged spleen or pancreas
- Loss of weight
- Jaundice
- Indigestion
- Swollen abdomen
- Pain in intercostal (rib) region

GB24 Nichi Getsu: Sun and Moon
- Digestive ailments
  Gastralgia
  Vomiting bile
  Gallstones
- Hysteria (mania/emotional instability), hypochondria

GB25 Keimon: Gate of Capital
- Difficulty in eliminating body fluids
- Lumbago
- Lower abdominal pain
- Gurgling colon
- Swollen abdomen

125

9. OUTSIDE OF ARMS

Large Intestine (LI) Meridian
Vital Points: LI15-LI1

LOCATIONS

LI1
0.1 sun proximal to the radial base
0.2 of the fingernail (index finger)

LI4
On back of hand between the bases of 1st and 2nd metacarpals. (At highest spot of muscle, when a fist is made and thumb is folded inside).

LI5
On radial side on back of wrist. (Clench fist and turn it up; LI 5 is in the middle of cavity at crease on wrist.)

LI10
2 sun (3 fingers) distal to LI11.

LI11
Radial aspect of lateral epicondyle of humerus (corner edge of elbow bone where it curves), beginning of brachioradial muscle (Bend the elbow; LI11 is at tip of crease).

LI15
On the anterior inferior ridge of the acromion (tip of shoulder bone) at the corner of the shoulder. Abduct the forearm; LI15 is the anterior one of the two cavities.

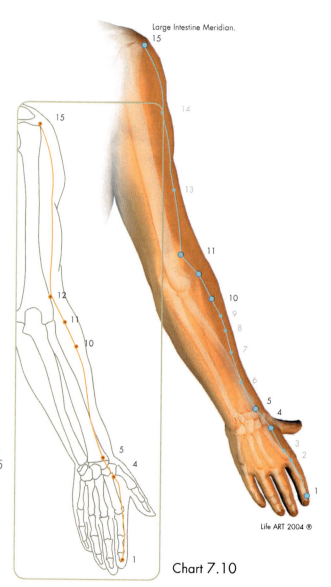

Large Intestine Meridian.

Life ART 2004 ®

Chart 7.10

9. OUTSIDE OF ARMS

Large Intestine (LI) Meridian
Vital Points: LI15-LI1

INDICATIONS

LI15 Kengu: Shoulder's corner
- Pain in shoulders and arms
- Limited R.O.M.
- Skin ailments

LI11 Kyokuchi: Pond at the Corner
- Weakness of upper extremities (Hemiplegia)
- Residual fever after cold
- Skin ailments
- Elbow joint ailments

LI10 Te No Sanri: Three Miles in the Arm
- Toothache
- Pain in shoulders
- Elbow pain
- Mouth distortion (Bell's Palsy)
- Weakness of the upper extremities (Hemiplegia)
- High blood pressure
- Sinus
- Swollen neck and cheeks

LI4 Gokoku: Meeting Valley
(Master point for head, brain and face ailments;
Acupuncture is contraindicated during pregnancy)
- Headache
- Toothache
- Sore throat
- Nose bleed

- Swollen face
- Fever with chills and no perspiration
- Cerebral congestion
- Facial paralysis
- Pain in the face (trigeminal neuralgia -
  inflammation of nerve of the side of the face)
- Speech problems
- Eye ailments
- Skin ailments on the face (including abscess)

LI5 Yokei: Sunny Brook
- Deafness
- Tinnitus (Head noises, ringing in ears)
- Shoulder pains
- Headache
- Wrist joint ailments

LI1 Shoyo: Sho Sound of Yang
- Fever without perspiration
- Congestion in chest
- Coughing
- Toothache
- Back pains
- Shoulder pains
- Tinnitus
- Dizziness
- Sore throat

10. SIDE OF NECK

Small Intestine (SI) & Triple Heater (TH) Meridians
Vital Points: SI17, SI16, TH17, TH16

LOCATIONS

TH17
Beneath the earlobe between mastoid process (round shape bump behind the ear) and angle of mandible (jaw). Open the mouth: TH17 is the middle of the cavity; one feels sharp pain toward the ears.

SI17
Posterior ridge (under corner of jaw) of mandibular angle. On anterior border of sternocleidomastoid muscle (muscle under ear [jaw] which goes to sternum and connects to clavical) at angle of jaw.

SI16
Posterior border of sternocleidomastoid muscle at level of ST9 and LI18 (crossing point from vertical level of SI17 and horizontal line of ST9).

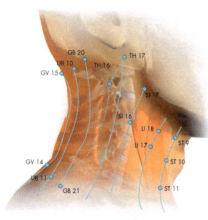

Chart 7.11

Life ART 2004 ®

INDICATIONS

SI17 Tenyo: Face of the Window
- Tinnitus (Head noises, ringing ears)
- Deafness
- Vomiting
- Nausea
- Swelling and pain in the neck
- Jaw joint ailments (TMJ)
- Swollen glands
- Earache

SI16 Tenso: Window of Heaven
- Earache
- Neck pains
- Deafness
- Toothache
- Distorted mouth and eyes (Bell's Palsy)
- Sore throat
- Shoulder pains

TH17 Eifu: Screen of Wind
- Ear problems
- Parotitis (Mumps)
- Tinnitus
- Facial nerve ailments
- Neuralgia
- Paralysis
- Lower toothache

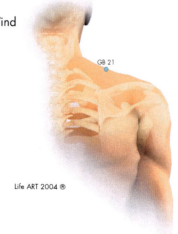

Life ART 2004 ®

11. HEAD

Governing Vessel, Urinary Bladder & Gall Bladder Meridians
Vital Points: INDO - GV20, UB1 - UB7, GB14 - GB17

LOCATIONS

GB14
Directly superior to the pupil, 1/3-way between eye-brow and frontal hairline.

UB1
0.1 sun medial and superior to inner canthus (corner of eye). Put finger on ductus naso lacrimal (tear duct - feels like raised dot); BL1 is superior and posterior to dot, toward bridge of nose, in middle of cavity.

GV20
Highest point on center of head.

GV24
On frontal hairline, crossing point from medial line of head (or, 0.5 sun superior to frontal hairline. Soothe medial line from forehead to hairline; GV24 is in the middle of cavity around hairline).

INDO
Between eyebrows, halfway from medial corners.

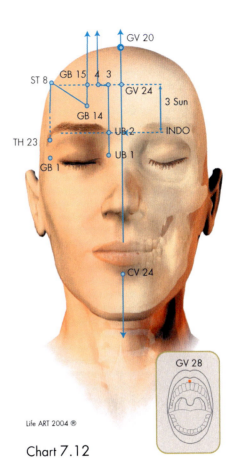

Life ART 2004 ®

Chart 7.12

129

11. HEAD

Governing Vessel, Urinary Bladder & Gall Bladder Meridians
Vital Points: INDO - GV20, UB1 - UB7, GB14 - GB17

 INDICATIONS

INDO: Images of a Palace
- Nose ailments
  Sinus Congestion
- Children's disturbed sleep
- Children's convulsions
- Headache

UB1Seimei: Clear and Bright
- Eye ailments
  Congestion
  Unclear vision
  Mucus
  Red color
  Tired eyes
- Sinus

GB14 Yohaku: Yang White
- Frontal headache
- Facial nerve ailment, pain or weakness
- Eye ailments
  Congestion
  Tired eyes
  Unclear vision
  Distorted shape of eyes

GV20 Hyakue: Hundred Meetings
- Headache
- Hemorrhoid (include Moxibustion)
- Hemiplegia (paralysis on one side of the body
- Dizziness
- Epilepsy
- Speech difficulty
- Forgetfulness
- Excess worry
- Too sensitive emotion
- Fear
- Astonishment, easy to upset

GV24 Shintei: Divine Garden
- Dizziness
- Headache
- Mucus (eyes and nose)

12. BACK OF NECK

Governing Vessel (GV), Urinary Bladder (UB) & Gall Bladder (GB) Meridians
Vital Points: GV15 - GV14, UB10 - UB11, GB20 - GB2

LOCATIONS

UB10
Lateral to GV15 on lateral ridge of trapez-ius muscle (about 1/3 lateral from nape to mastoid process - round bump behind ear).

GB20
Under the skull, about 2/3 lateral from nape to mastoid process.

GV15
At nape, 0.5 sun superior to posterior hair line (where hairline ends in back of middle of the neck). Raise face upward; GV15 is about 1.5 sun (2 fingers) inferior to external occipital bone (bone at the back of the neck), middle of cavity, or between 1st and 2nd cervical vertebrae.

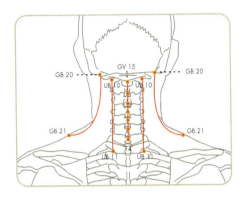

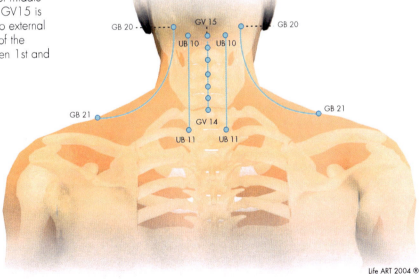

Chart 7.13

Life ART 2004 ®

131

12. BACK OF NECK

Governing Vessel (GV), Urinary Bladder (UB) & Gall Bladder (GB) Meridians
Vital Points: GV15 - GV14, UB10 - UB11, GB20 - GB2

 INDICATIONS

GV15 Amon: Gate of Deaf and Mute
- Speech problems
- Chronic headache
- Nosebleed
- Fever
- Stiffness in spine, neck and shoulder

GV14 Daitsui: Big Vertebra
- Stiff neck and shoulders
- Chronic cold
- Lung congestion
- Intermittent fever
- Upset
- Unable to turn neck
- Stiffness in spine

UB10 Tenchu: Pillar of Heaven
- Headache
- Heaviness in head
- Dizziness
- Stiff neck and shoulders
- Swollen neck and shoulders

GB20 Fuchi: Windy Pool
(Master point in the neck)
- Headache, stiff neck and shoulder
- Eye ailments
- Common cold, sinus
- Dizziness
- Hypertension
- Insomnia

GB21 Kensei: Well at the Shoulder
(Master point for shoulder ailments)
- Shoulder and neck ailments
- Difficult labor, mastitis
- Hemorrhaging after childbirth

13. SHOULDERS

Gall Bladder (GB) and Small Intestine (SI) Meridians
Vital Points: GB21 - LI16, SI13 - SI12 - LI16

LOCATIONS

LI16
At the depression under the acromion (bump at the top of the shoulder), between the lateral end of the clavicle and the lateral end of the scapular spine.

SI13
On the medial extremity of the scapular spine. About midway between SI10 and spinous process (bumps down the back of spine) of the 2nd TV. About 4 fingers next to spine, also 4 fingers behind GB21

SI12
On posterior shoulder, at upper midpoint of scapular spine.

INDICATIONS

LI16 Kokotsu (Huge Bone)
• Pain and disorder in the arm, shoulder and joints
• Limited range of motion in shoulder; difficulty in raising arm

SI13 Kyokuen (Curved Wall)
• Pain and stiffness of the shoulder and scapula (including shoulder blade)

SI12 Eifu (Holding the Wind)
• Numbness and aching of the upper extremity, shoulder and shoulder blade
• Difficulty moving the neck

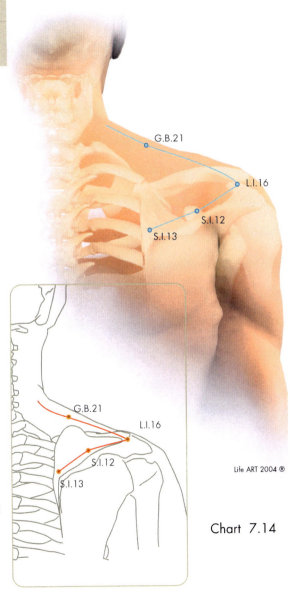

Life ART 2004 ®

Chart 7.14

133

SUMMARY OF 6 MERIDIANS IN THE ARMS

	LARGE INTESTINE	TRIPLE HEATER	SMALLER INTESTINE
SHOULDER	LI15 - Shoulder clavicle	TH14 - Shoulder bone	SI10 - Lower Arm Treatment
RELATED MUSCLES	Brachialis Triceps	Triceps Longus head or triceps muscle (Radial nerve)	Longus head of triceps muscle Medial head of triceps muscle
ELBOW	LI11 - "Curved Pool"	TH10 - "Celestial Wall"	SI8 - "A Small Sea"
ELBOW	LI10 - "Hand Three Miles"	TH5 - "Outer Barrier"	SI7 - "A Straight Branch"
RELATED MUSCLES	Brachioradialis Extensor carpi radialis Radialis longus	Extensor digitorum muscle Extensor carpi ulnaris muscle	Extensor carpi ulnarlis Flexor carpi ulnarlis (Radial nerve)
WRIST	LI5 - "Sunny Brook"	TH4 - "Sunny Pool"	SI5 - "Sunny Valley"
HAND	LI4 - "Meeting Valley"	TH3 - "Central Island"	SI3 - "Curved Wall"
FINGER	LI1 - "Trading Yang"	TH1 - "Barrier for Rush"	SI1 - "Small Marsh

	LUNGS	PERICARDIUM	HEART
SHOULDER	LG1 - "Central Residence"	Heart Constrictor	HT1 - Extremely Important Spring
RELATED MUSCLES	Biceps brachii Brachialis muscle	Middle of biceps Brachii (Medial nerve)	Brachialis m. Medial head of triceps (Ulnar nerve)
ELBOW	LG5 - "Marsh of Foot Depth"	HC3 - "Marshy Corner"	HT3 - "Little Sea"
ELBOW	LG6 - "Opening of the Extreme"	HC6 - "Inner Barrier"	
RELATED MUSCLES	Brachioradialis Flexor carpi Radialis (Radial nerve)	Flexor carpi Radialis muscle Palmaris longus (Medial nerve)	Flexor digitorum Superficialis muscle Flexor carpi ulnaris (Ulnar nerve)
WRIST	LG9 - "Great Abyss"	HC7 - "Big Tomb"	HT7 - "Gate of God"
HAND	LG10 - "Edge of Fish"	HC8 - "The Palace of Labor"	HT8 - "Small Palace"
FINGER	LG11 - "Little Sound of Sho"	HC9 - "Central Rush"	HT9 - "Small Rush"

SUMMARY OF 6 MERIDIANS IN THE LEGS

	STOMACH	GALL BLADDER	URINARY BLADDER
PUBIC BONE	ST30 - "Ki Rushing" (impact)	GB30 - "Bouncing Ring"	UB50 - "To Receive Assistance"
	ST31 - "The Barrier at the Buttocks"	GB31 - "Windy City"	UB51 - "The Gate of Prosperity"
	ST34 - "Hill of Beam"		
CONNECTING MUSCLES	Between rectus femoris and vastus lateralis	Between vastus lateralis and biceps femoris, posterior to tensor fasciae latae	Between semitendinosus and biceps femoris
KNEE	ST35 - "Calf's Nose"	GB33 - "Yang Barrier"	UB54 - "Sending Center"
	ST36 - "Three Miles of the Legs"	GB34 - "Yang Tomb"	UB57 - "Receiving Mountain"
CONNECTING MUSCLES	Between tibialis anterior and ext. digitorum longus, between E.D.L. and peroneus longus	Between peroneus longus and soleus	In the middle of gastrocnemius
ANKLE	ST40 - "Much Abundance"	GB35 - "Yang Intersections" (Outer Hill)	UB58 - "Flying Yang"
	ST41 - "Loosened Current"	GB40 - "Ruin on the Hill"	UB60 - "Elder Brother's Store House" (Mountain in Tibet)
	Between 2nd and 3rd metatarsal bones	Between 4th and 5th tarsal bones	Lateral to 5th metatarsal bones
TOE	ST45 - "Cruel Exchange"	GB44 - "Hole of Yin"	UB67 - "Reaching at Yin"

SUMMARY OF 6 MERIDIANS IN THE LEGS

	SPLEEN/PANCREAS	LIVER	KIDNEY
PUBIC BONE	SP12 - "Gate of Rush" SP11 - "Gate of Dust Basket"	LV12 - "Rapid Pulse"	K11 - "Transverse Bone" "Prosperity"
CONNECTING MUSCLES	Between rectus femoris and vastus lateralis, between vastus medialis and sotorius	Between abductor manus and gracilis	Between semitendinosus and semimembranosus
KNEE	SP10 - "Ocean of Blood" SP9 - "Yin Tomb Spring"	LV9 - "Wrapping Yin" LV8 - "Curved Spring"	K10 - "Shadowy Valley" "Deep Valley" K9 - "Building of Dune" "House of Gulet"
ANKLE	Inferior to tibia bone SP6 - "Yin Intercourse" "3 Yin Crossing"	LV6 - "Central Capital" In the tibia bone LV5 - "Wood Bordered Ditch"	Between soleus & achilles tendon K3 - "Great Brook"
	SP5 - "Hill of Deliberation" (Metal Hill) Sho Sound Medial to 1st metatarsal bone	LV4 - "Central Blockade" LV3 - "Big Rush" Between 1st and 2nd metatarsal bones	K2 - "Light Valley" (Blazing) Sole
TOE	SP1 - "Hidden White"	LV1 - "Great Honesty" "Big Performance"	K1 - "Bubbling Spring"

LOCATING PRESSURE POINTS

ANATOMICAL TERMINOLOGY FOR LOCATING VITAL POINTS

It is important to understand the anatomical term to locate the vital points. These are popular words often used in this text book.

1. Inferior - Lower
2. Superior - Upper
3. Posterior - Back
4. Anterior - Front
5. Distal - Far (or away)
6. Proximal - Near
7. Lateral - Outside
8. Medial - Inside

METHODS OF LOCATING VITAL POINTS

There are a couple ways of locating the vital points. The following are common techniques. Please refer to Figure 7-3A (Pg.100) in Chapter 7.

1. According to finger measurements
   1.5 sun = 2 fingers
   2 sun= 3 fingers
   3 sun= 4 fingers
2. According to proportional segment (based on classic books)
3. According to inspection
4. According to palpation by:
   A. Soothing (skin level)
   B. Kneading (muscle level)
   C. Pressing (main nerves or bones)

FOUR MAJOR POINTS AMONG 365 VITAL POINTS

These are the four most popular points used for common symptoms from the 356 vital points.

1. UB54: Ailments in the POSTERIOR-INFERIOR aspect like lower backache
2. ST36: Ailments in the ANTERIOR-INFERIOR aspect like indigestion
3. LG7: Ailments in the POSTERIOR-SUPERIOR aspect like neck-shoulder pain
4. LI4: Ailments in the ANTERIOR-SUPERIOR aspect like complains in the five sense organs and headache

THE EIGHT INFLUENTIAL POINTS

There are eight additional popular points to apply according to the following group of problems:

1. LV13: Ailments in YIN organs
2. CV12: Ailments in YANG organs
3. CV17: Ailments in KI - breathing/mental
4. UB17: Ailments in BLOOD
5. GB34: Ailments in TENDON/MUSCLE
6. LG9: Ailments in PULSE/VESSELS
7. UB11: Ailments in BONE
8. GB39: Ailments in MARROW

MERIDIANS AND VESSELS

TWELVE MERIDIANS AND TWO VESSELS

Hollow organs[40] are yang in nature; their corresponding meridians are on the outside of the body (sunny side[41]). Since the sun is the source of yang energy, the points of yang meridians start from the face and the tips of fingers (if you hold your hands up, they face toward the sun), and point numbers get larger as you move down the meridians. Yin meridians flow in the opposite direction to the yang meridians.

YANG MERIDIANS

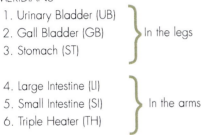

1. Urinary Bladder (UB)
2. Gall Bladder (GB)   } In the legs
3. Stomach (ST)

4. Large Intestine (LI)
5. Small Intestine (SI)   } In the arms
6. Triple Heater (TH)

"Storage" organs (such as the heart and lungs) are yin in nature; their corresponding meridians are on the inside of the body (shadowy side). Since the earth is the source of yin energy, the points of yin meridians start from the feet and end around the chest, and point numbers get larger as you move up the meridians.

YIN MERIDIANS

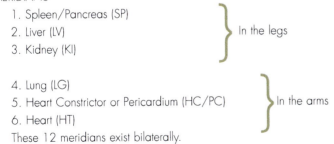

1. Spleen/Pancreas (SP)
2. Liver (LV)   } In the legs
3. Kidney (KI)

4. Lung (LG)
5. Heart Constrictor or Pericardium (HC/PC)   } In the arms
6. Heart (HT)

These 12 meridians exist bilaterally.

VESSELS

1. Governing Vessel (GV): Yang - in the back
2. Conception Vessel (CV): Yin - in the front

These 2 meridians exist in the center of the body

40. All organs are hollow (tubes) except for the gallbladder.
41. "Sunny side" refers to the fact that it faces the sun. That which is inside, or not facing the sun is called "shadowy."

CHAPTER EIGHT
DOANN'S LONG FORM

11 TYPES OF TECHNIQUES IN THE LONG FORM

Soothing (Keisatsu Ho)

Kneading (Jyunetsu Ho)
   A. Cutting (Senjo)
   B. Rotating (Rinjo)

Pressing (Appaku Ho)

   A. Ordinary pressure (Tsujo Appo)
   B. Intermittent pressure (Kanketsu Appo)

RULES OF PRESSURE TECHNIQUE:

1. Sustained (Sasae Atsu)
2. Vertical (Suichoko Atsu)
3. Stable (Antei Atsu)
4. Concentrated (Shuchu Atsu)
5. Coordinated (or Chowa Atsu) breathing
6. Gradual (Kanjo Kangen Atsu)

Exercising (Undo Ho)

Correcting (Kyosei -Streching)

Vibrating (Shindo Ho)

Shaking (Shinsen Ho)

Tapping (Koda Ho)

   A. Side of fist (Shuken Koda Ho)
   B. Fingers together, chopping (Gassho Koda Ho)
   C. Hands apart, chopping (Setsuda Ho)
   D. Cupping hands (Shusho Koda Ho)
   E. Back of fingers (Shuhai Koda Ho)
   F. Back of fists (Shukenhai Koda Ho)

Semi Tapping

   A. "Horse trotting" hand (Tsuki De)
   B. "Rolling" hands (Kuruma De)
   C. "Butterfly" hands (Kujiki De)
   D. "Tail of fish" hand (Yoko De)

1. BACK - PARAVERTEBRAL REGION

Urinary Bladder (UB) Meridians (Bilateral)
Covered Points: UB11 - UB30

Length of time needed to complete this first section: About 10 minutes

Client lies on stomach (prone position)

Back

1. Gassho (greeting)
2. Soothing
3. Kneeling at the head

Top of shoulders to bottom of shoulder blades (diaphragm line)

1. Kneading - Cutting (5 applications)
2. Kneading - Rotating (5 applications)
3. Pressing (1 application, 7 count)
4. Kneeling at the side

Diaphragm line through buttocks

1. Kneading - Cutting (5 applications)
2. Kneading - Rotating (5 applications)
3. Pressing (1 application, 7-count)
4. Correcting-Stretching
   a Stretch shoulder blades to iliac crest
   b. Hands 90 degrees along spine (1 application)
   c. Fingers over the spine with opposite hand above.

Again, for reference, the abbreviations applied in this section include:

PO - practitioner's posture

HA - practitioner's hands

AR - area on client's body to be covered by practitioner

MO - movement of hands

RE - number of times each movement should be repeated

PUR - purpose of method

*** - additional information or notes

ILLUSTRATION 1: WHOLE BACK SOOTHING METHOD

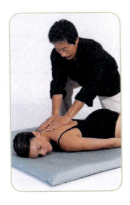
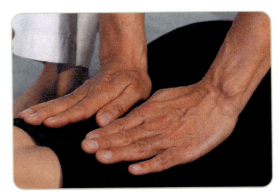
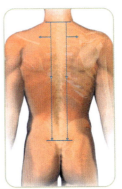

Life ART 2004 ®

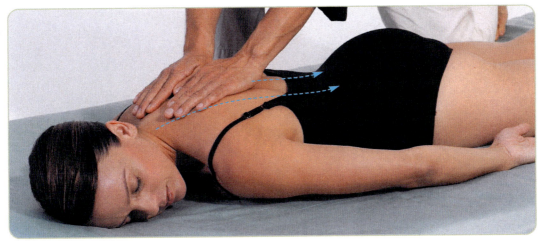

PO: Inside knee on the floor next to the side of client's body, outside knee up.

AR: From top of shoulder to side of hips in one stroke.

MO: Gently soothe with whole palms including fingers, like waves sweeping the seashore.

RE: 3 times.

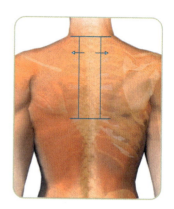

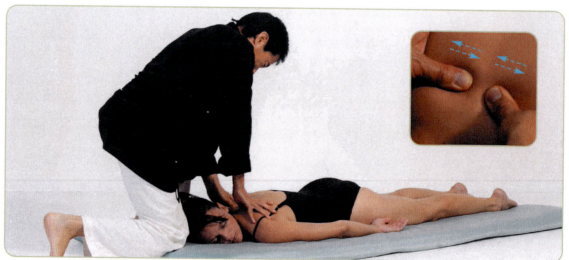

ILLUSTRATION 3: UPPER BACK KNEADING METHOD - ROTATING

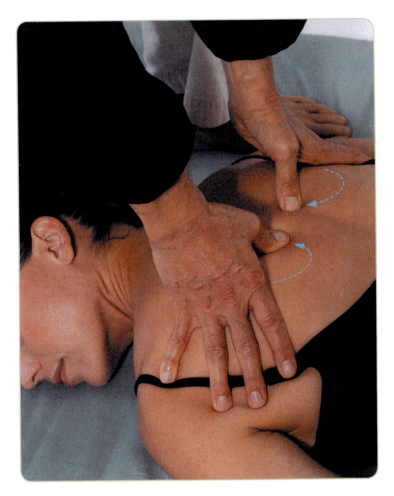

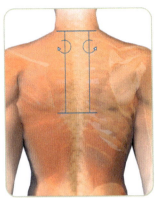

Life ART 2004 ®

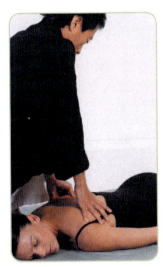

PO: Both knees over client's head, one down and one up.

AR: From top of shoulder to end of scapulas.

MO: Rotate your thumbs over the erector spinae muscles (away from the spine) symmetrically and simultaneously between left and right sides.

RE: 5 times in each spot, but entire sequence only once.

ILLUSTRATION 4: UPPER BACK PRESSING METHOD

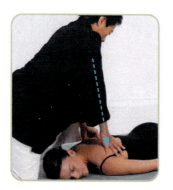

While pressing, Divine force descends from Heaven, the gravity of healing energy penetrating into the body. Heaviness of held emotions leave the mind, filling an empty world with serenity.

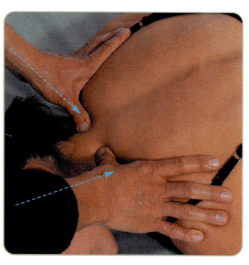
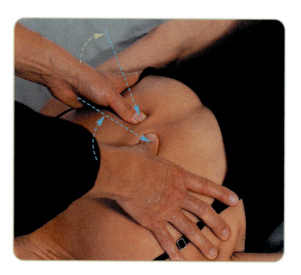

PO: Kneeling with one knee down, one knee up.
AR: From top of shoulder to end of scapulas.
MO: Keep your thumbs and hands relaxed and
     bring your body weight onto your thumbs.
RE: Once in each spot, and entire sequence only once.

ILLUSTRATION 5: MIDDLE AND LOWER BACK - KNEADING, THEN PRESSING

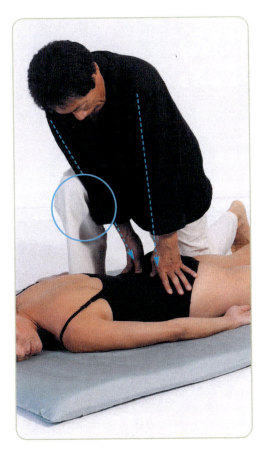

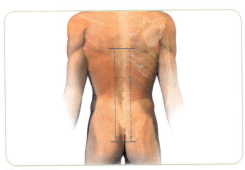

Life ART 2004 ®

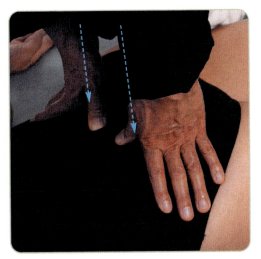

PO: Inside knee on the floor, outside knee up.

AR: Kneading: cutting method from end of scapulas to sacrum, rotating method from end of scapulas to hip. Pressing method from end of scapulas to hip.

MO: Same as Illustration 2.

RE: Kneading method 5 times. Pressing method once for 7 seconds.

149

ILLUSTRATION 6: ADDITIONAL HIP LINES (AHL) FOR KNEADING (ROTATING) &
PRESSING METHODS

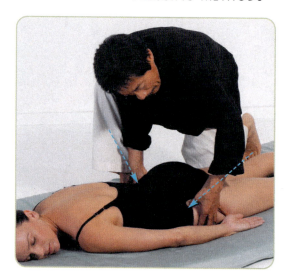

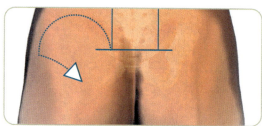

Life ART 2004 ®

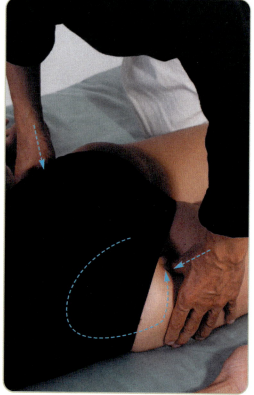

PO: Kneeling with one knee down, one knee up.

AR: From sacrum to hip joints (to GB30).

MO: Rotate your thumbs over the erector spinae muscles (away from the spine) symmetrically and
       simultaneously between left and right sides.

RE: Kneading (rotating) 3 times, pressing once (both continuing from lower back).

***   Additional hip line is not a meridian, but an effective area to include in clinical experience, such
       as for lower backaches, sciatica, piriformis muscle, hip joint and sacro-iliac joint problems.

ILLUSTRATION 7: BACK - SPINE CORRECTING METHOD I

 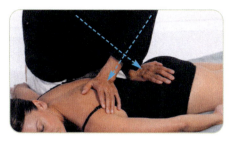 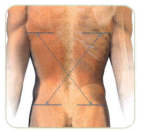

Life ART 2004 ®

PO: Kneeling with one knee down, one knee up.
AR: From top of shoulder to end of scapulas.
MO: Cross arms. Place one on bottom of iliac crest and one on scaupla. Press in opposite directions.
RE: 5 times in each spot, but entire sequence only once.

ILLUSTRATION 8: BACK - SPINE CORRECTING METHOD II

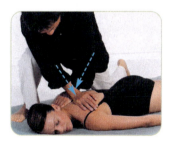 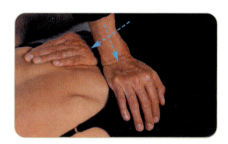 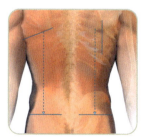

Life ART 2004 ®

PO: Kneeling with one knee down, one knee up.
AR: From shoulder to sacrum
MO: Cross hands and place so that one is on either side of the spine and press along spine
RE: Kneading (rotating) 3 times, pressing once (both continuing from lower back).
*** Additional hip line is not a meridian, but an effective area to include in clinical experience, such as for lower backaches, sciatica, piriformis muscle, hip joint and sacro-iliac joint problems.

ILLUSTRATION 9:   BACK - SPINE CORRECTING METHOD III

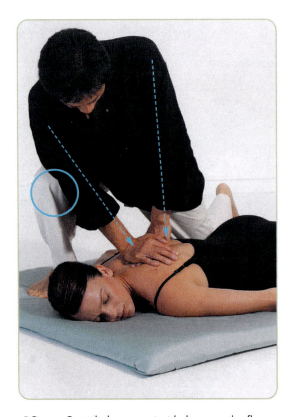 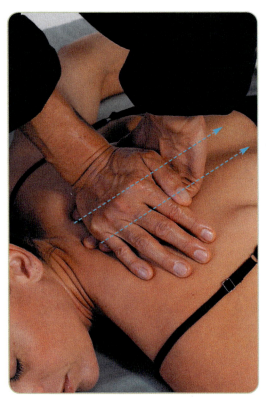

PO: Outside knee up, inside knee on the floor.

HA: Use first and second fingers on either side of spine with the other hand on top. Completely relax your hands.

AR: From end of scapulas to top of iliac bone.

MO: Keep your hands stable and relaxed while bringing your body weight onto your hands.

PUR: Stretching the back. Correcting the pelvis, scapulas and spine.

RE: 1 to 3 times.

***   Although cracking of vertebrae is not intended, often this happens naturally as the body needs correction. This way, the alignment of the spine can be improved softly and indirectly.

2. BACK OF LEGS & FEET

Urinary Bladder Meridians (Bilateral)
Covered Points: UB36 - UB67

Length of time needed to complete this second section of the long form: About 10 minutes

Client lies on stomach (prone position), legs together

Bladder meridian from gluteal fold to baby toe

1. Soothing (3 applications)
2. Kneading - cutting or rotating (3 applications)
3. Pressing (1 application, 3 count)

Bottom of feet (use powder unless socks are left on)

1. Soothe 3 lines (3 applications)
2. Kneading - rotating (3 applications)
3. Intermittent pressing (1 application, 2 - 3 count)
4. Intermittent pressing with fists (1 application, 2 - 3 count)

Legs: correcting Kyosei - stretching

Stretch knee joint (gluteal fold to ankle)

Exercises

1. Open legs and flex legs at knees, press toes toward buttocks (3 applications)
2. In same position, separate legs and press heels to buttocks (3 applications)
3. Shin to shin, press feet down (3 applications)
4. Step along back of thigh as you flex leg forward (3 applications)
5. Step up next to thigh and press back (be cautious for lower backaches)
6. Shake legs up and down, then sideways (do not lift knees off floor)
7. Step on bottom of feet (30 seconds with toes, 30 seconds with heels), do not step on toes
8. Step on calves while standing on feet (3 applications)
9. In same position, vibrate calves with feet

ILLUSTRATION 10: LEGS SOOTHING METHOD - BLADDER MERIDIANS

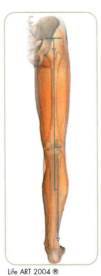

Life ART 2004 ®

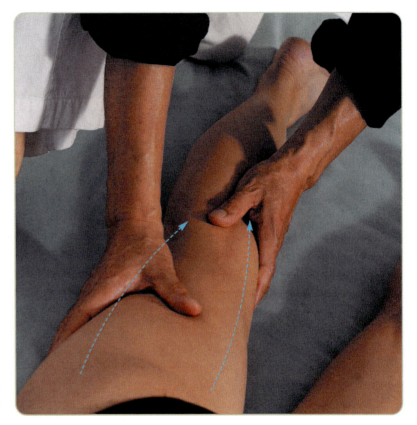

PO: Outside knee up, inside knee on the floor.
HA: Outside palm alongside of hip joint, inside palm further under groin.
AR: From bottom of hip to ankle joints.
MO: Gently soothe with whole palms including fingers, like waves sweeping the seashore (back
       soothing method), but one side at a time.
RE: 1 to 3 times.

ILLUSTRATION 11: LEGS KNEADING (CUTTING) AND PRESSING METHODS - URINARY BLADDER MERIDIANS

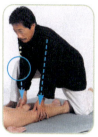

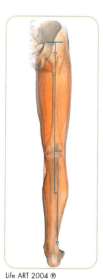

Life ART 2004 ®

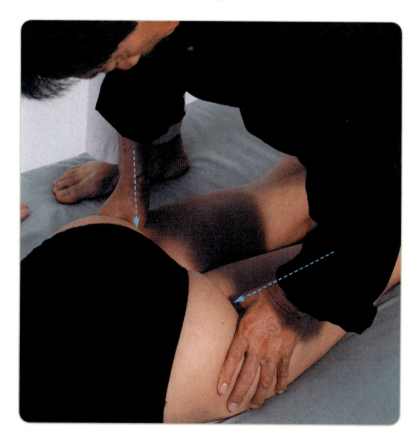

PO: Outside knee up, inside knee on the floor.

HA: Both hands practice at the same level on both legs.

AR: From bottom of hip to ankle joints.

MO: Same as back kneading and pressing methods.

RE: Kneading method 3 times, pressing method once.

*** Treating both legs' bladder meridians together is recommended when client is small and has no specific complaints, thus taking up less time. Behind and just below the knees are sensitive areas DO NOT press hard.

ILLUSTRATION 12: BOTTOM OF FEET SOOTHING METHOD

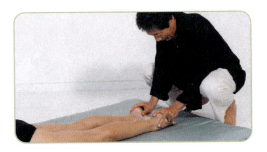  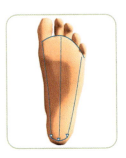

PO: Both knees on the floor or squatting.
HA: Thumb does the work, with index and middle fingers supporting top of foot,
      and ring and little finger on the sole of the foot.
AR: Whole bottom part of the sole in 3 lines (lateral, medial and radial).
MO: Heavy soothing toward heel, pausing halfway up to reposition hands.
RE: 1 to 3 times per line.
***   Powder helps lubrication, keeps sweat away and keeps feet clean.

ILLUSTRATION 13: BOTTOM OF FEET KNEADING AND PRESSING METHODS

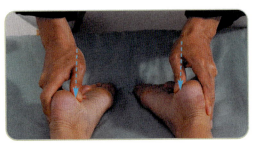  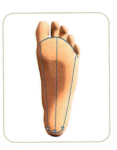

PO: Both knees on the floor or squatting.
HA: Thumb does the work, with index and middle fingers supporting top of foot,
       and ring and little finger on the sole of the foot.
AR: Whole bottom part of the sole in 3 lines (lateral, central and medial).
MO: Kneading (rotating) first, then pressing; same direction and manner as Illustration 12.
PUR: Regulate various organs through nerve reflex effect (zone therapy).
RE: Kneading method once, pressing method once.
***   Most people like stronger pressure on the feet.

ILLUSTRATION 14: BOTTOM OF FEET PRESSING METHOD WITH FISTS

PO: Both knees on the floor or squatting.

HA: Make fists and apply pressure with body weight.

AR: Entire sole.

MO: Pressing; same manner and direction as Illustration 13, but use fists while applying pressure with body weight.

RE: 1 to 3 times.

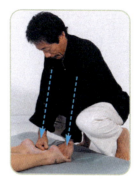 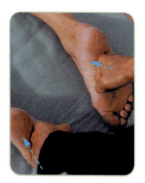

ILLUSTRATION 15: BACK OF LEGS CORRECTING METHOD

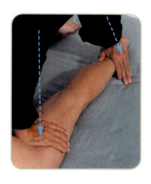 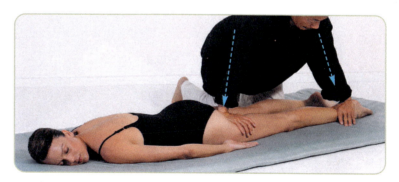

PO: Both knees on the floor.

HA: Separate hands, one inside of ankle, the other inside of sitting bone. Then place hands just above and below the knee, moving outward to original position.

AR: From sitting bone to ankle.

MO: Keep your hands relaxed while applying pressure with your body weight.

PUR: Stretching the legs.

RE: 1 to 3 times.

***   Be careful not to press too hard on the knees and ankles as they can sprain.

ILLUSTRATION 16: LEGS EXERCISING METHOD I

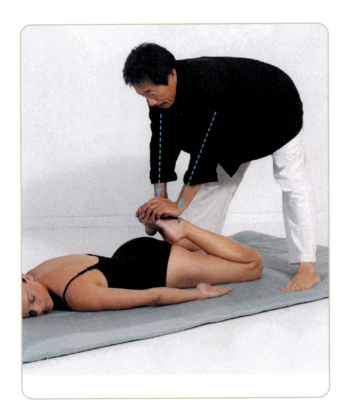
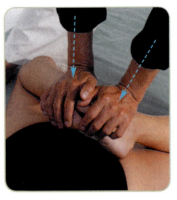

PO: Standing with feet apart and leaning forward.

HA: Open legs wide, overlap feet with the leg with the tighter muscle placed underneath (the more flexible leg should be on top)n then hold toes, press against the hips.

AR: Pelvis, knees, ankles, legs, feet.

MO: Leaning forward, proceed gently as client's flexibility allows.

PUR: Making joints, muscles and tendons flexible; promoting better meridian circulation.

RE: 3 times.

*** More repetitions are recommended for tighter areas; for example, 3 times light pressing, 3 times medium, then 3 times deep, for a total of 9 repetitions. This is especially advisable for very stiff or elderly clients.

ILLUSTRATION 17: LEGS EXERCISING METHOD II

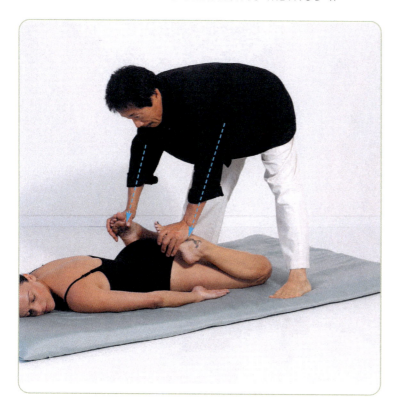
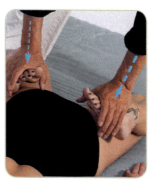
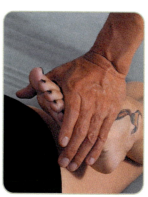

PO: Standing with feet apart and leaning forward.
HA: Holding toes separately.
AR: Pelvis, knees, ankles, legs, feet.
MO: Leaning forward, proceed gently as far as client's flexibility allows.
PUR: Regulate various organs through nerve reflex effect.
RE: 3 times.

ILLUSTRATION 18: LEGS EXERCISING METHOD III

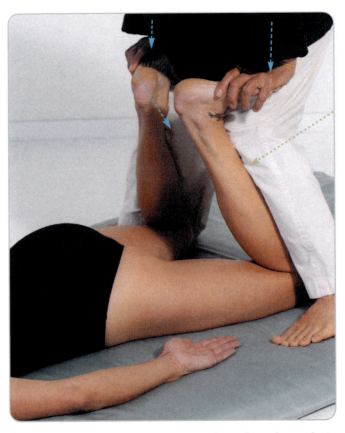

PO: Standing with feet apart and leaning forward, but use legs against client's legs (shin to shin).

HA: Holding bottom of toes and pressing with body weight.

AR: Pelvis, knees, ankles, legs, feet.

MO: Bring your body weight down toward the floor instead of forward.

PUR: Making joints, muscles and tendons flexible; promoting better meridian circulation, especially stretching calves and feet.

RE: 3 times.

ILLUSTRATION 19: LEGS EXERCISING WITH PRESSURE METHOD IV

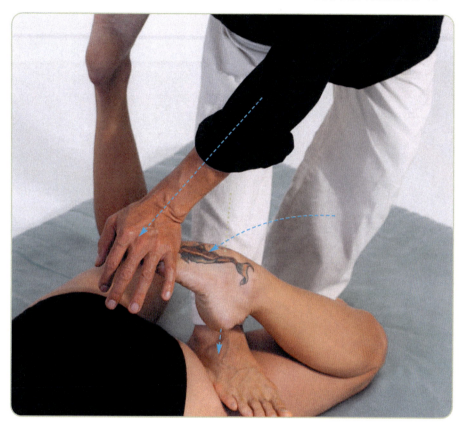

PO: Standing, one foot stepping on the back of client's thigh.
HA: Holding feet. You may bend the client's knee each time you press in.
AR: From sitting bone to the knees.
MO: Relax your foot, bringing body weight down on it.
RE: 1 to 3 times on first leg, then 1 to 3 times on other leg.
***   Do not press too hard while close to the knees.

ILLUSTRATION 20: LEGS EXERCISING/BACK PRESSURE METHOD V

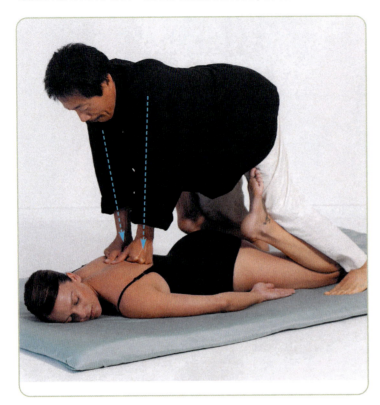

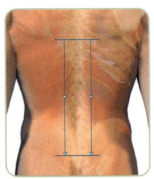

Life ART 2004 ®

PO: Straddle client's body on either side of thighs, with client's ankles locked outside your flexed knees.

HA: Make fists.

AR: Bottom of scapulas to sacrum with fists; back of thigh including knee with feet.

MO: Walk your fists down the client's back along spine.

RE: 1 to 3 times.

*** Avoid this method for serious lower backache clients, as it will aggravate the problem. Also avoid if you, the practitioner, are too awkward.

ILLUSTRATION 21: LEGS SHAKING METHOD (MAINLY CALVES)

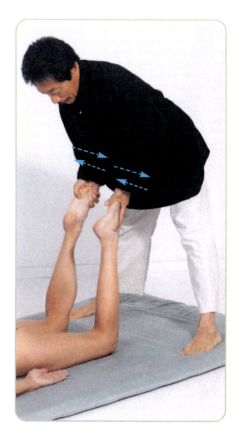 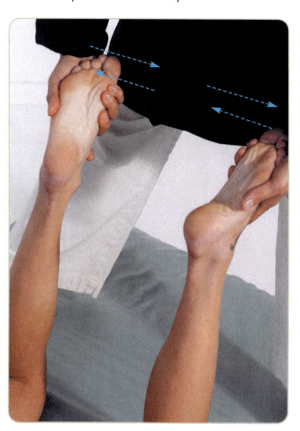

PO: Standing.
HA: Hold client's toes; leave knees on floor.
AR: From knees to ankles.
MO: Shake calves right and left, up and down.
PUR: To relax the calf muscles. To promote energy and blood circulation.
RE: About 5 seconds up and down, 5 seconds right and left, with quick movements.

ILLUSTRATION 22: FEET-ON-FEET PRESSURE METHOD

 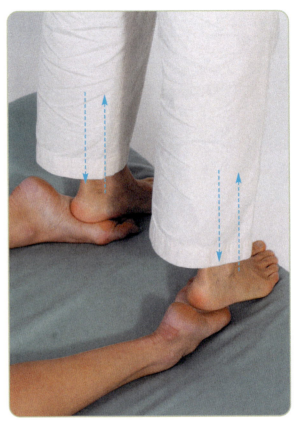

PO: Stand on feet with heels, facing away from client.
HA: Keep interlocked hands above head.
AR: Base of foot.
MO: Walk carefully up and down base of foot, using heel.
PUR: Release tension on feet and create reflexology-like effect on rest of body.
RE: Step on feet gently for 30 seconds with heels and 30 seconds with toes.

3. FRONT OF LEGS & FEET

Stomach (ST) Meridians for Males (Bilateral)
Covered Points: ST31 - ST41
Spleen (SP) Meridians for Females (Bilateral)
Covered Points: SP11 - SP6

Length of time needed to complete this third section of the long form: About 12 minutes

Client lies on back (supine position)

Top of legs

1. Soothing (3 applications)
2. Kneading - rotating (3 applications)
3. Pressing (5 - count)

Top of feet (Powder)

1. Soothe - rub 4 lines between toes including medial aspect of feet (3 applications)
2. Kneading - spiral rotations
3. Intermittent pressing (1 application, 2 - 3 count)

Toes, ankle, knee, hip and leg

1. Snap toes (once per toe), both sides
2. Vibrate toes, grabbing and squeezing sole with other hand (one side)
3. Rotate ankle (3 times each direction)
4. Flex knee and rotate hip joints and sacro-iliac joints (3 times each direction)
5. Hamstrings - straighten leg, pull toes down
6. Hold shoulder, flex knee and rotate hip joints, pressed flexed knee toward floor
7. Open the pelvis and press palm against inside of thigh from top to knee (1 application)
(Then, repeat the same from #2 through #7 on the opposite leg)

1. Flex knees together toward chest and rotate whole pelvis (3 applications)
2. Knees in the same position as #8, press with folded arms back and forth (3 applications)

CHAPTER EIGHT

ILLUSTRATION 23: FRONT OF LEGS SOOTHING METHOD

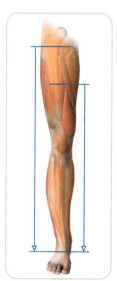

Life ART 2004 ®

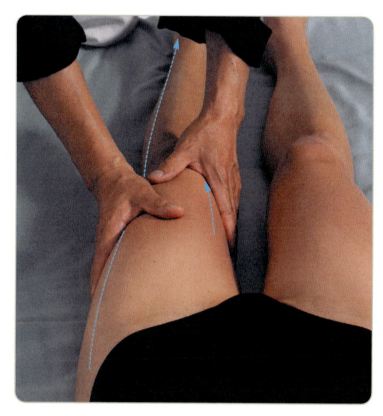

PO: Kneeling with outside knee up and inside knee on the floor.

HA: Outside palm on outside of client's hip, inside palm on inside of client's thigh.

AR: Inside of thigh from below groin area to ankle; outside of thigh from hip joints to ankle, in one stroke.

MO: Soothe down to ankle using both hands, one side at a time.

RE: 3 times.

ILLUSTRATION 24: LEGS KNEADING AND PRESSING METHODS STOMACH MERIDIAN

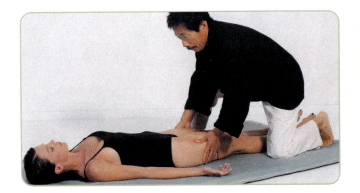

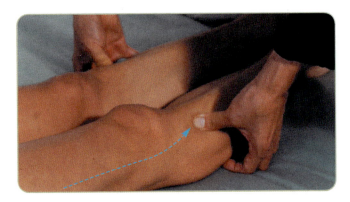

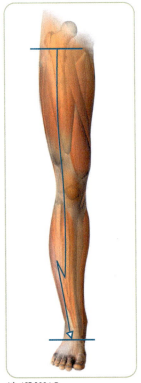

Life ART 2004 ®

PO: Straddle over client's legs with one knee on the floor and other knee up.
HA: Thumbs placed on client's thighs, outside on stomach meridian; 4 fingers holding beneath calves.
AR: From below groin area to ankle.
MO: Perform kneading (rotating) from thighs to ankles symmetrically and simultaneously.

ILLUSTRATION 25: LEGS KNEADING AND PRESSING METHODS - SPLEEN MERIDIAN

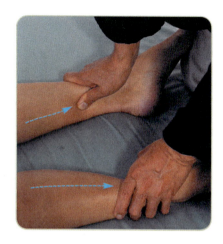
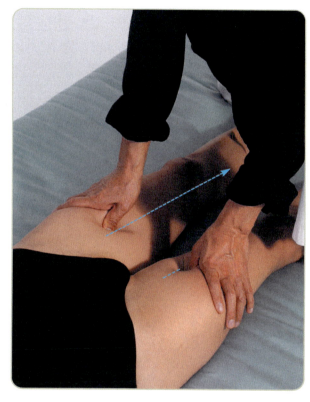

PO: Straddle over client's legs with one knee on the floor and other knee up.

HA: Place thumbs on spleen meridians

AR: Inside of upper thigh, below groin area to ankle.

MO: Perform kneading (rotating) then pressing from thighs to ankles symmetrically and simultaneously.

RE: Kneading method 3 times, pressing method once.

***   For male clients, use outside stomach meridian. For female clients, use the inside (spleen) meridian. You can work stomach and spleen meridians simultaneously using thumb on spleen and knuckle/fingers on stomach meridian.

ILLUSTRATION 26: FRONT OF FEET SOOTHING METHOD -
SPLEEN (SP), LIVER (LV), STOMACH (ST) AND GALL BLADDER (GB) MERIDIANS

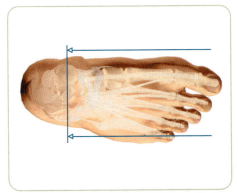

Life ART 2004 ®

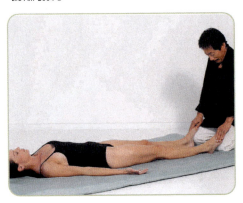

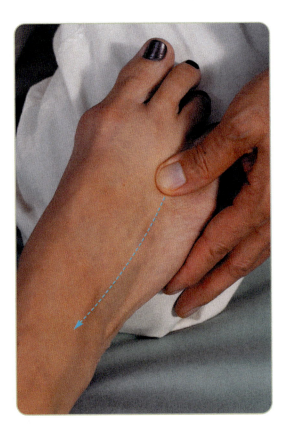

PO: Kneeling, feet flexed, with both knees on the floor.

HA: Secure client's feet by placing them against your knees.

AR: From toes to ankles.

MO: Soothe from client's toes to ankle.

RE: 1 to 3 times.

ILLUSTRATION 27: FRONT OF FEET KNEADING (ROTATING) AND PRESSING METHODS

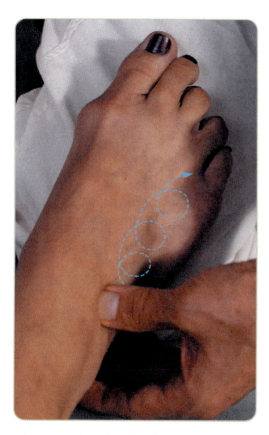 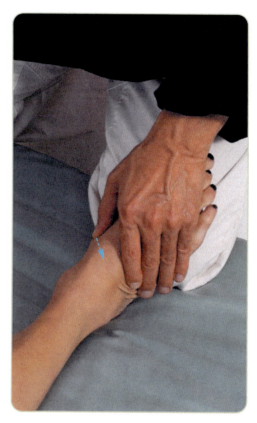

PO: Kneeling, feet flexed, with both knees on the floor.

HA: Secure client's feet by placing them against your knees.

AR: From toes to ankles.

MO: Soothe from client's toes toward the ankles. Use spiral rotation kneading along meridians and intermittent pressure (1 or 2 seconds).

RE: 1 time.

ILLUSTRATION 28: FRONT OF FEET SNAPPING THE TOES METHOD

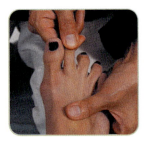 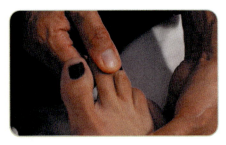

PO: Kneeling, feet flexed, with both knees on the floor.
HA: Simply pinching top and bottom of the toes with index and middle fingers.
AR: Toes.
MO: Squeezing fingers from the bottom of toes to tips, with a quick pull (not crack), snap quickly one toe at a time; left foot first then right foot.
RE: Once.
*** It is a combination of pressing, pulling, sliding then snapping.

ILLUSTRATION 29: TOES SHAKING METHOD

PO: Facing towards the client's feet, with both knees or one knee on the floor. Place client's
foot on your thigh.
HA: One hand vibrating the top of client's toes, the other hand grabbing different parts of the sole of client's foot. (K1, K2)
AR: Toes and the sole of client's foot.
MO: Press the bottom of foot with your bottom hand while vibrating toes with your top hand.
RE: For about 10 seconds.

ILLUSTRATION 30: ANKLE EXERCISING METHOD

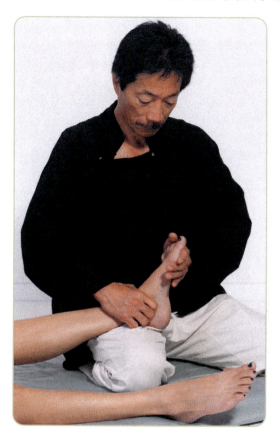 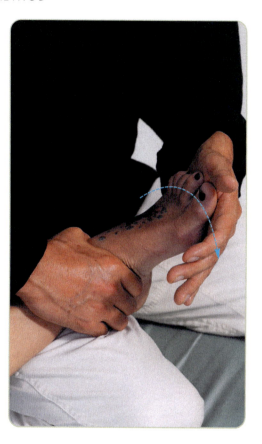

PO: Same as Illustration 29.
HA: One hand holding the ankle, the other hand holding toes.
AR: The foot and ankle.
MO: Rotate the ankle with your top hand while holding it with your bottom hand.
RE: 3 times clockwise, 3 times counterclockwise. If ankle is tight, repeat deeper
       3 times in each direction, then deepest 3 times in each direction.

ILLUSTRATION 31: LEGS EXERCISING METHOD I

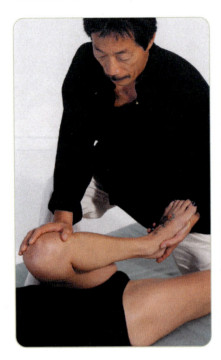
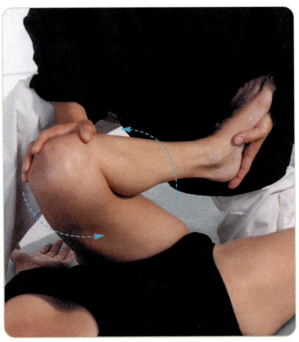

PO: One knee up (outside of client's bent knee), one knee down (kneeling next to client's inside knee).

HA: One hand bends client's knee, while the other hand holds client's heel, and rotates 3 joints
        (hip/knee/ankle) all together.

AR: Hip joint, knee joint, ankle joint.

MO: Rotate hip, knee and ankle in a coordinated manner.

RE: 3x clockwise, 3x counterwise. If tight, repeat deeper 3x in each direction,
        then deepest 3x in each direction.

PUR: To promote general flexibility of hip, knee and ankle joints. Promotes circulation of energy flow
        in the pelvis and legs.

***   Do not overwork your client or yourself by fully using your body weight constantly against hip
        joints. Begin with light pressure and end leg rotation by accentuating body weight.

ILLUSTRATION 32: LEGS EXERCISING METHOD II - BLADDER MERIDIAN

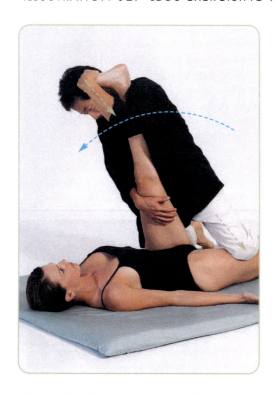 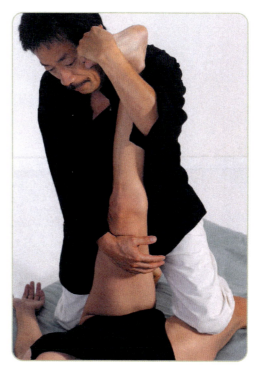

PO: Outside knee on floor, inside knee against client's thigh above knee - holding client's leg down without heavy pressure.

HA: Outside hand holding client's other thigh above knee, inside hand press down bottom of client's foot against your shoulder.

AR: Bladder meridian, sciatic nerve, or hamstring, from sitting bone to ankle and bottom of the foot.

MO: Raise your body and hand up to 90 degrees and press client's foot.

RE: 3 times.

PUR: To promote flexibility and restrict hyperactivity of the nerve and energy flow by stretching ham strings and sciatic nerve.

ILLUSTRATION 33: LEGS EXERCISING METHOD III - GALL BLADDER MERIDIAN

PO: One knee up (in front of client's straight knee), one knee down (kneeling in back of to client's hips). One foot stretches client's resting knee on the floor.

HA: One hand pressing lightly against client's shoulder, the other hand against outside of client's knee, pressing and rotating the knee towards the floor.

AR: Side of the body from chest to hip joint.

MO: Rotate hip twice, then on the third rotation, press client's knee slowly toward the floor gently if no pain.

RE: 3 times.

PUR: To promote flexibility and restrict hyperactivity of the nerve and energy flow by stretching the side of the body along the gall bladder meridian.

***   Great care is needed. Never apply forceful thrust. This is not a chiropractic adjustment.

ILLUSTRATION 34:   PELVIS CORRECTING METHOD

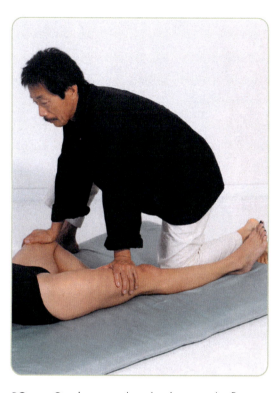 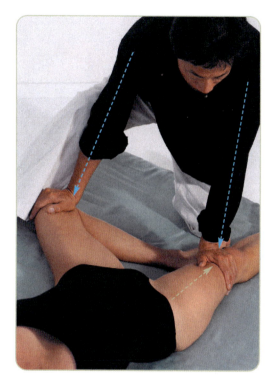

PO: One knee up, the other knee on the floor.

HA: One hand on inside of client's knee, the other hand on outside and top of pelvis.

AR: From pelvis to knee.

MO: Press hand down below the pelvis and shift to knee while other hand remains on inside of client's knee.

RE: 1 to 3 times.

PUR: To promote flexibility of the pelvis and create restriction-free environment to the organs within.

***   Great care is needed. As with all of the exercises, a gentle approach is required. DO NOT FORCE. If area is stiff, then evaluate the condition to see how flexible it is, and work within that range. If there is pain, stop for safety reasons.

ILLUSTRATION 35:   LOWER BACK EXERCISING METHOD I

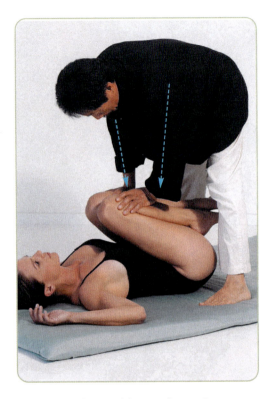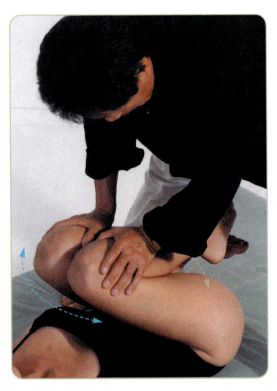

PO: Standing and leaning forward.

HA: Both hands on the kneecaps.

AR: Lower back and knees.

MO: Rotating the knees and pelvis, using body weight against the abdomen. Reverse, then
        rock towards abdomen again.

RE: 3x clockwise, 3x counterclockwise. If tight, repeat deeper 3x in each direction,
        3x deepest in each direction.

PUR: To relax back tension and reduce back pain by curling and stretching the back muscles.

ILLUSTRATION 36: LOWER BACK EXERCISING METHOD II

 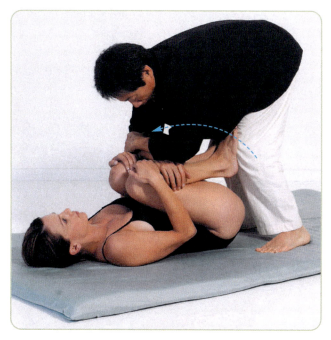

PO: Standing, leaning your knees against client's feet.
HA: Press with hands or crossing arms, hold client's legs to keep them closed.
AR: Middle to lower back and knees.
MO: Press client's knees toward their chest, gently rocking back and forth with your body weight, using your knees. Rotate, reverse, then rock. Client can raise their feet up to therapist's chest (not appropriate for female therapists) at which point the therapist can lean onto the client's knees.
RE: 3 times.
PUR: To relax back tension and reduce back pain by curling and stretching the back muscles.
***   This is an excellent exercise for lower backache, which you may practice on yourself as well.
***   Women practitioners may use chest area above the breasts or abdomen area below the breasts.

4. ABDOMEN

Conception Vessel (CV) Meridian
Covered Points: CV14 - CV3

Length of time needed to complete this fourth section of the long form: About 5 minutes

Client lies on back (supine position)

Abdomen - Powder (optional)

1. Soothing
   a. Side of hands sliding to palms, creating diamond shape (9 applications)
   b. Circular, with fingertips, along large intestine (9 applications)
2. Kneading (cutting and rotating) with middle finger (5 applications); SKIP NAVEL
3. Pressing (1 application - 7 count)
4. Palm kneading (Roto no jyutsu)
   Wave: using heels of palms and balls of fingers (9 applications)
5. Vibrate using heel of palm on and around navel, 5 spots (1 application, 3 - 5 count)
6. Lift waist, shake up and down, slide palms on tanden, press and vibrate and quick release (1 application)

Special Note

A healthy person has a warm lower abdomen. The lower abdomen should be firmer than the upper abdomen.
Pulse beat around the navel usually indicates weakness.

1. Pulse above navel: Weakness in stomach, spleen/pancreas energetic function
2. Pulse below navel: Weakness in kidney energetic function
3. Pulse right of navel: Weakness in lung, large intestine energetic function
4. Pulse left of navel: Weakness in liver energetic function
5. Pulse under the sternum bone: Weakness in heart energetic function

ILLUSTRATION 37: ABDOMEN SOOTHING METHOD I

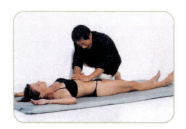

Life ART 2004 ®

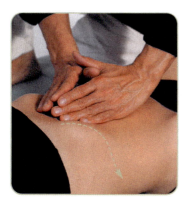
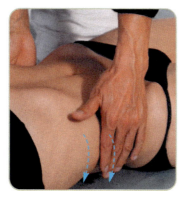
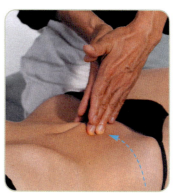

PO: One knee up, one knee on the floor, facing the client's face.

HA- MO: First put your palms together, then slide down and start soothing from just below the sternum bone. Then separate your palms gradually until they reach the lower back, then along the pelvic bone. Reverse directions and come back forward towards the lower abdomen, and then lift hands, palms joining, to finish.

AR: Whole abdomen under the ribs, above the pubic bone, including a small portion of the lower back.

RE: 9 times.

***   If abdomen is sensitive, speed and pressure should be moderate.

***   Fade in at the beginning, fade out at the end, finish soothing with slight pinch of the abdomen (bring hands together with a sweeping motion which brings the tips of the fingers together at the end).

***   Corn starch is good on the abdomen but is optional, you can practice on lightly clothed abdomen.

ILLUSTRATION 38: ABDOMEN SOOTHING METHOD II

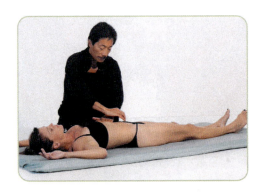

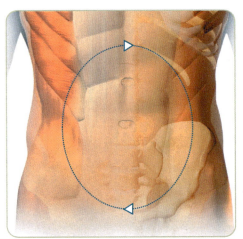

Life ART 2004 ®

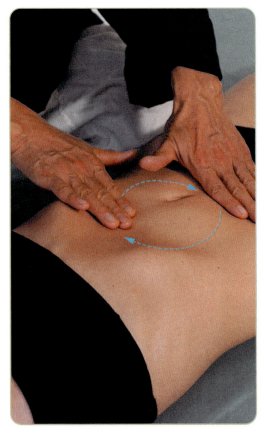

PO: Sitting on the floor[42] to the left of client's body (stomach side).

HA & MO: Rotate your hands and soothe with your fingertips, hands separate, clockwise.

AR: Abdomen.

RE: 9 to 36 times (100 - 108 for constipation).

PUR: To promote digestive movement along the colon.

42.   This is the first time the therapist sits during the Long form.

ILLUSTRATION 39: ABDOMEN KNEADING METHOD (CUTTING AND ROTATING) CONCEPTION VESSEL MERIDIAN

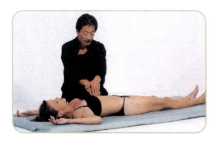 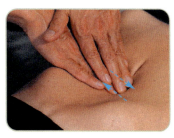 

PO: Sitting on the floor to the left of client's body (stomach side).
HA: Overlap 3 fingers and apply with both hands.
AR: Center line under the sternum bone through the navel to pubic bone.
MO: Cross-fiber movement inwards and outwards (like waves) in cutting kneading, and clockwise circle in rotating kneading.
RE: 5 times at each level, but only once for entire sequence.

ILLUSTRATION 40: ABDOMEN PRESSING METHOD - CONCEPTION VESSEL MERIDIAN

 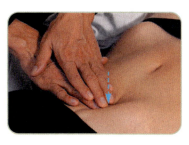 

PO: Sitting on the floor to the left of client's body (stomach side).
HA: Overlap 3 fingers and press with both hands.
AR: Center line under the sternum bone through the navel to pubic bone.
MO: Press overlapped hands, but concentrate pressing balls of middle fingers down at 90 degrees.
RE: 7 seconds in each spot, entire sequence only once.

ILLUSTRATION 41: ABDOMEN PALM KNEADING METHOD (ROTO NO JYUTSU)

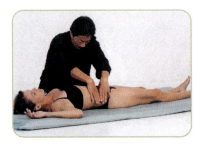 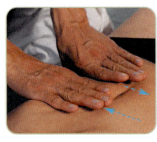 

Life ART 2004 ®

PO: Sitting on the floor to the left of client's body (stomach side).
HA: Palms over client's abdomen.
AR: Around the navel from side to side.
MO: Knead like waves, pressing away with heel of hands and pressing in with the tips of fingers.
RE: 9 times.
***   For a smaller abdomen, knead with palms overlapped.

ILLUSTRATION 42: ABDOMEN VIBRATING METHOD

 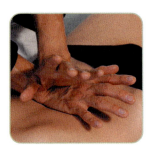 

Life ART 2004 ®

PO: Sitting on the floor to the left of client's body (stomach side).
HA: Overlap your palms over client's abdomen.
AR: 5 spots around the navel (about 3 fingers away from navel in each direction).
MO: Vibrate the heels of your hands.
RE: Once per spot for about 5 seconds.
***   You may perform vibrating method in 2 ways: One, gentle at the surface level with bigger motion. Two, at a deeper level in small, specific motions.

ILLUSTRATION 43: LIFTING BACK AND SHAKING METHOD

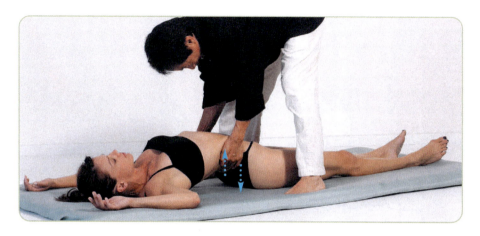

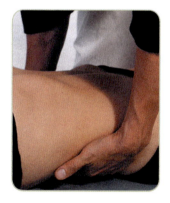 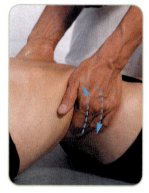 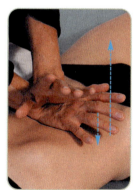

PO: Standing, legs straddling client's abdomen area.

HA: Lift client's back at waist level, slightly elevating the hips.

AR: Both back and abdomen.

MO: Vibrate abdomen up and down. At conclusion, slide hands around and place them on the tanden, then give palm pressure with vibration and a quick release at the end.

RE: Once for about 5 seconds.

PUR: To stimulate bowel movement through possible nerve reflex.

5. ARMS & HANDS

Large Intestine (LI) Meridians (Bilateral)
Associated Points: LI15 - LI5

Length of time needed to complete this fifth section: About 10 minutes

Client lies on back (prone position)

Arms

1. Soothing (3 applications)
2. Kneading - rotating (3 applications)
3. Pressing (5 count)

Hands - Powder

1. Soothe - 4 lines (3 applications)
2. Kneading - rotating (3 applications)
3. Intermittent pressing (1application - 2 count)

Fingers, palm & arm

1. Snapping fingers
2. Squeeze web area[43] between thumb and index finger in the palm with knuckles (3 applications)
3. Turn palms over and squeeze opposite side of palms, base of 5th finger in the palm (3 applications)
4. Hold wrist with one hand, fingers with the other, then rotate wrist (3 applications each direction)
5. Stretch fingers; straighten fingers to tips (3 applications)
6. Drop hand and press fingers down
7. Optional: twist palm at wrist (Kote gaeshi) (3 times each direction)
8. Stand up and bring arm straight up along ear, shake off floor
9. Flex arm and palm - press from armpit to palm
10. Straighten arm and shake off floor, toss arm to side of body

43.   Area of the hand between the thumb and forefinger that resembles a web.

ILLUSTRATION 44: ARMS SOOTHING METHOD

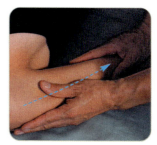

PO: Kneeling with outside knee up, inside knee on the floor or both knees on the floor.
HA: One hand on the outside of client's arm, one hand on the inside.
AR: From shoulder to wrist.
MO: Soothe inside and outside of the arm at the same time.
RE: 3 times.

ILLUSTRATION 45: ARMS KNEADING METHOD - LARGE INTESTINE MERIDIAN

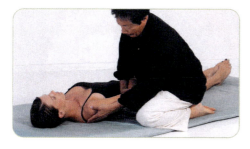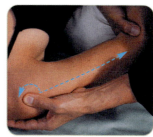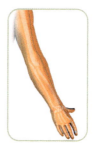

PO: Sitting beside client, between the body and the arm.
HA: The first half (up to elbow): lift, twist inward and pull client's arm with your inside hand.
       The second half (up to wrist): hold client's wrist with your outside hand. Be careful not to
       let client's hand touch your inside thigh.
AR: From shoulder to index finger.
MO: On the first half, perform rotation kneading with your outside hand; on the second
       half use your inside hand.
RE: 3 times each spot, but entire sequence only once.

ILLUSTRATION 46: ARMS PRESSING METHOD - LARGE INTESTINE MERIDIAN

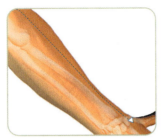

Life ART 2004 ®

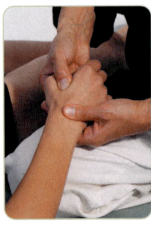

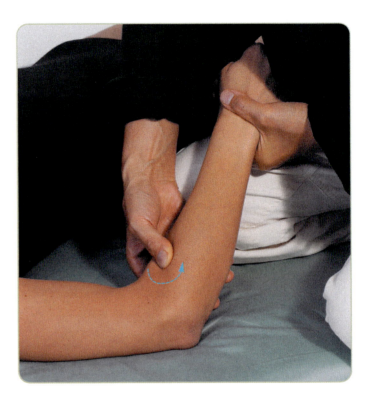

PO: Sitting beside client.
HA: The first half (up to elbow): lift, twist inward and pull client's arm with your inside hand.
The second half (up to wrist):hold client's wrist with your outside hand. Be careful not to let client's hand touch your inside thigh.
AR: Shoulder to index finger.
MO: Press with your thumb; if not creating enough pressure, kneel with one knee down and press with body weight.
RE: Once for about 5 seconds.

ILLUSTRATION 47: HANDS SOOTHING METHOD

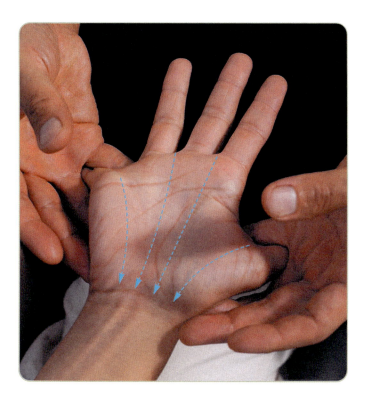

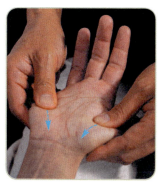

PO: Sitting beside client.

HA: Support hands by hooking your 4th and 5th fingers into client's thumb and 2nd finger and client's 4th and 5th fingers. Then hold underneath. You may brace client's elbow against the floor.

AR: Whole palm in 4 lines.

MO: Soothe 4 lines toward wrists.

RE: 1 to 3 times in 4 lines.

*** Usually people like stronger pressure in the hands.

ILLUSTRATION 48: HANDS KNEADING METHOD

 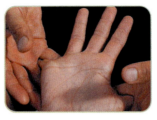 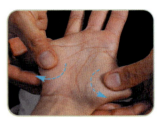

PO: Sitting beside client.
HA: Support hands by hooking your 4th and 5th fingers into client's thumb and 2nd finger and client's 4th and 5th fingers. Then hold underneath. You may brace client's elbow against the floor.
AR: Whole palm in 4 lines.
MO: Perform rotation-kneading along 4 lines toward wrist.
RE: 4 times.

ILLUSTRATION 49: HANDS PRESSING METHOD

 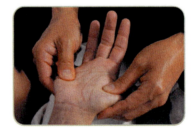

PO: Sitting beside client.
HA: Support hands by hooking your 4th and 5th fingers into client's thumb and 2nd finger and client's 4th and 5th fingers. Then hold underneath. You may brace client's elbow against the floor.
AR: Whole palm in 4 lines.
MO: Perform intermittent pressure along 4 lines toward wrist.
RE: Once (intermittent pressure is recommended).

ILLUSTRATION 50: FINGERS SNAPPING METHOD

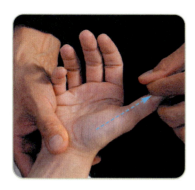
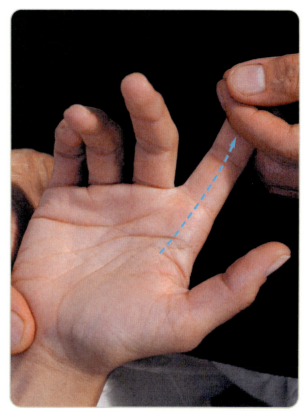

PO: Sitting beside client.

HA: Your thumb and index finger together, holding client's finger with your middle finger, other hand holding client's palm.

AR: Entire finger (including thumb) to the tip.

MO: Squeeze client's fingers, one at a time, from root of finger to the fingertip, quickly snapping at the tip.

RE: Once.

ILLUSTRATION 51: HANDS SQUEEZING METHOD

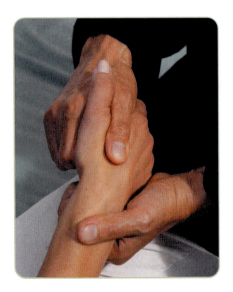
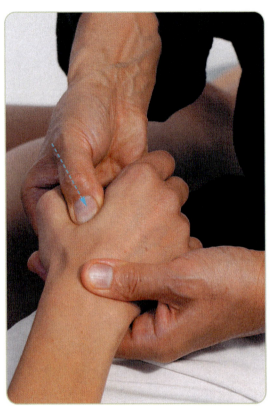

PO: Sitting beside client.
HA: Hold the web between client's thumb and index finger with your thumb and knuckles.
       Other hand holds the other side.
AR: Web between thumb and index finger. Also applies to the pad of the little finger.
MO: Squeeze both sides of client's hand.
RE: Repeat 3 times.

ILLUSTRATION 52: HANDS EXERCISING METHOD I - ROTATING WRISTS

PO: Sitting beside client.
HA: Your right hand (if right-handed) holds client's hand gently but securely.
AR: Wrist joint.
MO: Rotate wrist joint while your left hand holds client's wrist to prevent rest of arm from rotating.
RE: 3 times in each direction (clockwise, then counterclockwise).

ILLUSTRATION 53:   HANDS EXERCISING METHOD II -
WRIST JOINTS AND FINGERS STRETCHING METHOD

PO: Sitting beside client.
HA: Your right hand (if right-handed) holds client's hand gracefully.
AR: Wrist joint.
MO: Press fingers toward elbows while holding client's wrist.
RE: 3 times in each direction (up, down).

ILLUSTRATION 54:   ARMS STRETCHING AND SHAKING METHOD (Kyosei - Stretching)

 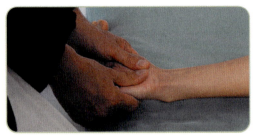

PO: Stand on knee, then squat or kneel on the floor.
HA: Hold client's hand with both hands.
AR: Hand to shoulder joint.
MO: Stretch whole arm above client's head, right next to the ear.
RE: Stretching once, and shaking for about 5 seconds.

ILLUSTRATION 55:   ARMS-SHOULDER JOINT CORRECTING METHOD (Kyosei - Stretching)

 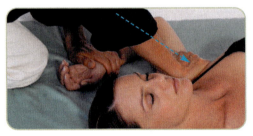

PO: Squatting or kneeling on the floor.
HA: Bend client's elbow and place it on the floor, with the client's hand close to the ear.
AR: From chest (Lung 1-2/pectoralis muscle) to palm.
MO: While your outside hand holds client's wrist, use the palm of your inside hand to press
        against the inside of client's arm.
RE: 1 to 3 times
***   Great care needed for severely stiff and aged shoulder joints.

ILLUSTRATION 56:   ARMS TOSSING METHOD

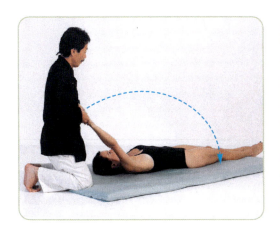
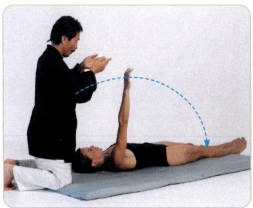
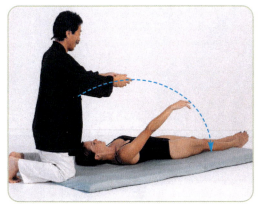
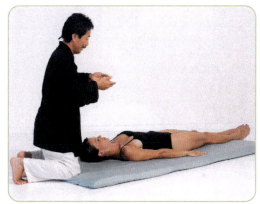

PO: Squatting or kneeling on the floor.
HA: Stretch client's arm and place it on the floor next to the ear.
AR: Whole arm and shoulder joint.
MO: Gently toss the arm forward to floor. This should produce a comfortable sensation for the
        client. You can bring client's arm up to about 45 to 60 degrees, then toss it.

6. NECK, TOP OF HEAD & SHOULDERS

Large Intestine (LI) Meridians (Bilateral)
Covered Points: LI15 - L15

Length of time needed to complete this seventh section of the long form: About 3 minutes

Client lies on back (supine position)

Neck - Powdering is helpful, but avoid in cases of allergy

1. Soothing (3 applications)
2. Kneading - rotating (3 applications)
3. Pressing neck (5 count)

Head

1. Intermittent pressing (1 application - 2 - 3 count)

Neck, shoulder and head

1. Squeezing the shoulder and shaking
2. Traction[44] of the neck and gently shake the head at the end
3. Vibrating the head with both hands
4. Kyosei - Stretching neck and shoulders, into 3 directions (left, right and center)

---

44. Pull upward towards the therapist.

ILLUSTRATION 57: NECK SOOTHING METHOD

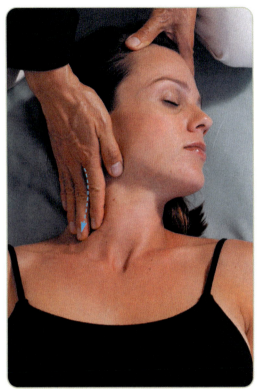

PO: Sitting above client's head.
HA: Turn client's face to one side, keeping the practicing hand's four fingers closed and stretched out.
        Keep the thumb separated.
AR: Under the chin to the supraclavicle fossa.
MO: Soothe from below ear to clavicle bone while placing other hand on client's forehead.
RE: 3 times.
***   Take care not to irritate the front of the throat. Powder may be helpful.

ILLUSTRATION 58: NECK KNEADING AND PRESSING METHODS -
SMALL INTESTINE MERIDIAN - INSIDE NECK

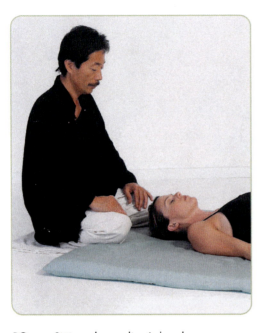
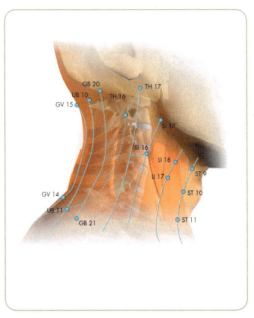

PO: Sitting above client's head.

HA: Turn client's face to the center, keeping the practicing hand's four fingers for the first neck section. Then keep the thumb separated, while using the thumb to front of shoulder.

AR: Under the chin to the supraclavicle fossa.

MO: Perform rotation-kneading from the corner of the jaw toward the shoulder
Then pressing the same area.

RE: 3 times for kneading method, once for pressing method.

*** You may carefully work on both sides of the body at once. SI meridian is almost along the
vein in the neck, not on the carotid artery[45].

45. This is a very important artery which supplies blood to the brain.
It is important NOT to press both sides of this artery at the same time. It can cause choking and fainting.

ILLUSTRATION 59: NECK KNEADING AND PRESSING METHODS - TRIPLE HEATER MERIDIAN - OUTSIDE NECK

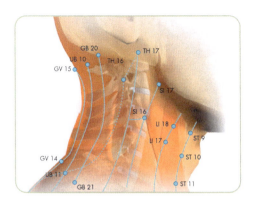
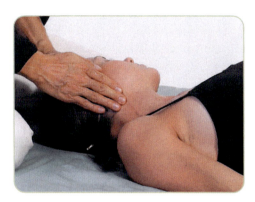

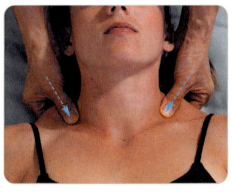
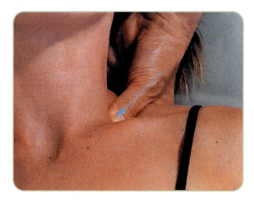

PO: Sitting above client's head.

HA: Keep client's face in the center, keeping the practicioner's four fingers closed behind the neck. Keep the thumb separated, while using the thumb to the supra clavicle fossa.

AR: Under the earlobe to the supraclavicle fossa.

MO: Perform rotation-kneading from below the earlobe to clavicle then pressing in the same area.

RE: 3 times for kneading method, once for pressing method.

ILLUSTRATION 60: FACE AND HEAD PRESSING METHOD - GOVERNING VESSEL MERIDIAN

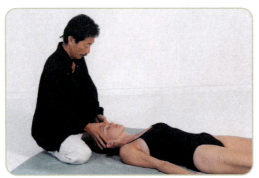

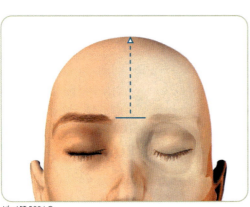

Life ART 2004 ®

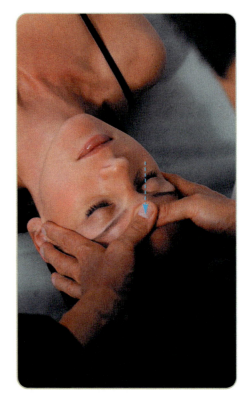

PO: Sitting above client's head.
HA: Overlap thumbs.
AR: From eyebrow line to top of head.
MO: Apply intermittent pressure from "third eye" to top of head.
RE: Once.
***   Avoid pulling the client's hair by lifting fingers and by using proper perpendicular pressure[48].

48. Create a 90 degree angle with the fingers.

ILLUSTRATION 61: FACE AND HEAD PRESSING METHOD - URINARY BLADDER MERIDIAN

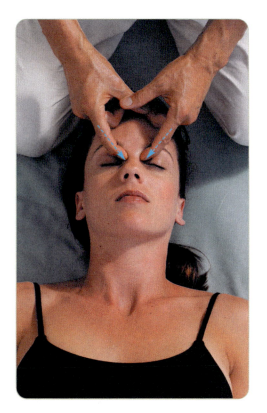
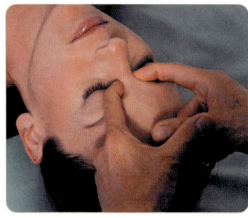
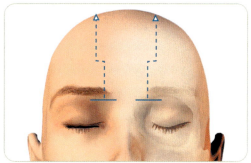

Life ART 2004 ®

PO: Sitting above client's head.
HA: Use index fingers for points UB1 and UB2, then thumbs for the remainder.
AR: From inside corner of eyes to top of head.
MO: Apply intermittent pressure from inside corner of eyes to top of head.
RE: Once.
*** Do not touch the eyes. You can press with index fingers first, then thumbs from forehead. People usually prefer harder pressure on the head as well as on hands and feet.

ILLUSTRATION 62: FACE AND HEAD PRESSING METHOD -
GALL BLADDER MERIDIAN

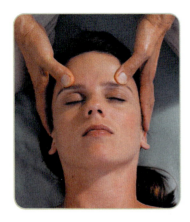

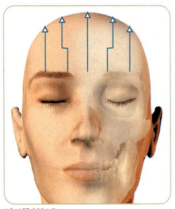

Life ART 2004 ®

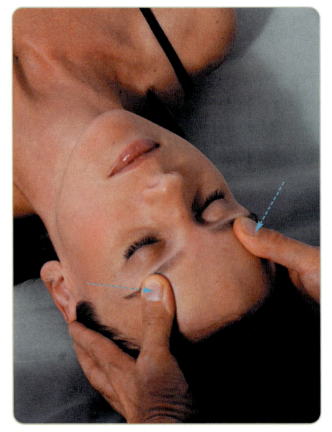

PO: Sitting above client's head.
HA: Practitioner's hands are apart, practicing with thumbs in unison bilaterally.
AR: From the middle of the eyebrow line to top of head.
MO: Apply intermittent pressure from eyebrow line to top of head.
RE: Once.

ILLUSTRATION 63: NECK AND SHOULDERS EXERCISING METHOD (TRACTING)

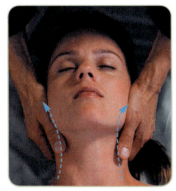

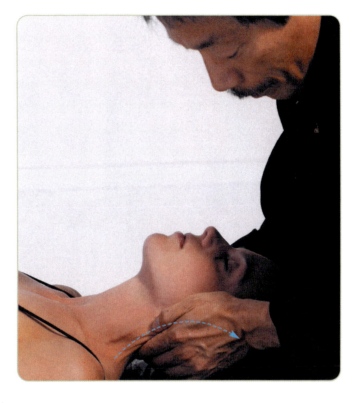

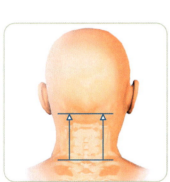

Life ART 2004 ®

PO: Sitting above client's head.
HA: Practitioner's hands overlap behind client's neck.
AR: From the top of shoulders to the base of the skull.
MO: Gradually produce traction of the neck with a rolling or wave-like movement (pull head up toward the therapist, moving it up, then dropping it down in 3 to 4 motions).
RE: 1 to 3 times.
*** This is a wonderful exercise for neck sprain which causes an irregular condition in the arms and fingers like numbness, pain and tingling, after inflammatory periods. Do not pull too vigorously or suddenly when lifting the head. Great care is needed.

ILLUSTRATION 64: HEAD EXERCISING METHOD (VIBRATING)

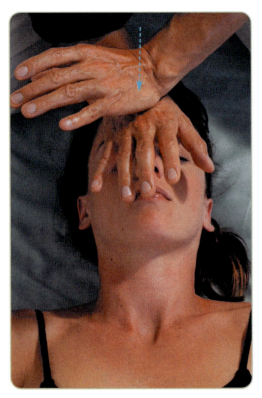 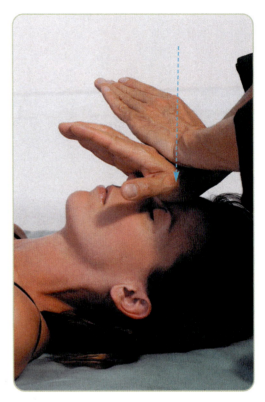

PO: Sitting above client's head.
HA: The heels of the practitioner's hands overlap; if right-handed, the right hand goes under the left which is just resting.
AR: Top of forehead. Also vibrate sides of the head by placing hands around ears.
MO: Increase pressure first then combine vibration with pressure.
RE: About 5 to 10 seconds each for the forehead and sides of the head.
***   Very effective for headaches. The therapist can practice this method in two steps: 1) general and surface vibration, then 2) specific and deep vibration.

ILLUSTRATION 65: NECK AND SHOULDER KYOSEI STRETCHING METHOD

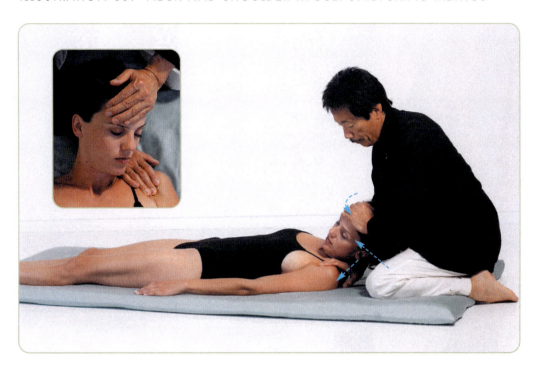

PO: Squatting or kneeling.
HA: One hand on client's forehead, the other on the front of client's shoulder for the left and
        right stretches; both hands on client's shoulders for the middle stretch. In all three stretches,
        client's head rests on your arm.
AR: Trapezius muscle between neck and shoulder and scapulas.
MO: Lean your body forward, thus securing client's head; stretch to the left, then to the right,
        then in the middle.
RE: 3 times.
***   When you get towards the center, you stretch the client's back using both hands against
        client's shoulders. Do not stretch too much; start gradually and proceed gently with great care.

7. BACK OF NECK & SHOULDERS

Neck Governing Vessel (GV) Meridians (GV15 - GV14)
Urinary Bladder (UB) Meridians (UB10 - UB11)
Gall Bladder (GB) Meridians (GB20 - GB21)
Shoulders: Gall Bladder (GB) Meridians (GB21 - LI16)
Small Intestine (SI) Meridians (SI13 - LI16)

Length of time needed to complete this seventh section of the long form: About 10 minutes

Client is in sitting position

Back of neck

1. Soothing (3 applications)
2. Kneading - rotating 3 lines (3 applications)
3. Pressing (1application, 5 count)
Coordinate with hand holding forehead. At the base of head, tilt head back and press inward and upward, pressing horizontally in the middle and downward on the shoulders

Shoulders

1. Kneading - cutting or rotating 2 lines (3 applications)
2. Pressing (1 application, 5 count)

Back of neck and shoulders

1. Rotate neck in small range, holding forehead and base of head (3 times in each direction) - small range
2. Rotate neck in large range, holding forehead and head (3 times in each direction) - large range
3. Holding wrists and lift arms, stretching back while pressing knees into back (3 applications)
4. Sit down and bring arms back, rotate shoulders (3 times in each direction)
5. Same position - shake arms up and down, then sideways (5 seconds each)
6. Same position - place feet on back, press foot and pull arms, moving down the back
7. Place client's hands behind neck, open chest while pressing knees into back (3 applications)
8. Put knees on back and rotate the trunk in both directions (3 application including in the center)
9. Tapping
10. Soothing around the scapulas and back

At conclusion, let client rest for 5 to 10 minutes

ILLUSTRATION 66: SHOULDER-TO-ARMS SOOTHING METHOD

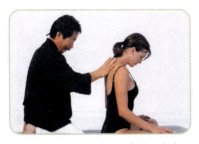 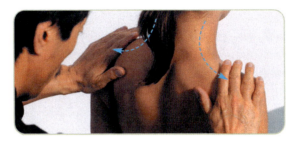

PO: Kneeling down behind client.
HA: Fingers together, separated from thumbs.
AR: From neck through shoulder to upper arms.
MO: Soothe neck, shoulder and upper arm in one movement.
RE: 3 times.

ILLUSTRATION 67: NECK KNEADING AND PRESSING METHOD - GOVERNING VESSEL MERIDIAN

 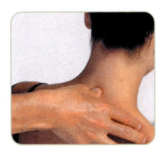 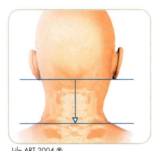

Life ART 2004 ®

PO: One knee on the floor, the other supporting client's back comfortably (be careful not to let your groin touch client's back).
HA: One hand against client's forehead, the other kneading and pressing.
AR: From the bottom of client's skull to the shoulder.
MO: First press up toward "third eye" at the base of skull, gradually moving down toward the chest at the shoulder.
RE: Once.
*** Coordinate your left and right hands to create effective pressure angle.

ILLUSTRATION 68: NECK KNEADING AND PRESSING METHOD -
URINARY BLADDER MERIDIANS

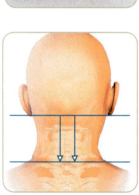

Life ART 2004 ®

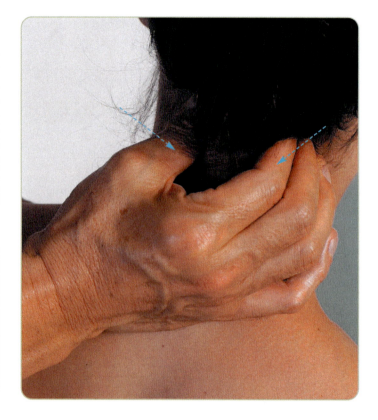

PO: One knee on the floor, the other supporting client's back comfortably (be careful not to let your groin touch client's back).

HA: Separate thumb from index finger, you can practice on both sides simultaneously.

AR: From the bottom of client's skull to the shoulder.

MO: First direct your thumb toward opposite eyes at the base of client's skull, gradually moving toward the chest at the shoulder.

RE: Once.

ILLUSTRATION 69: NECK PRESSING METHOD - GALL BLADDER MERIDIANS

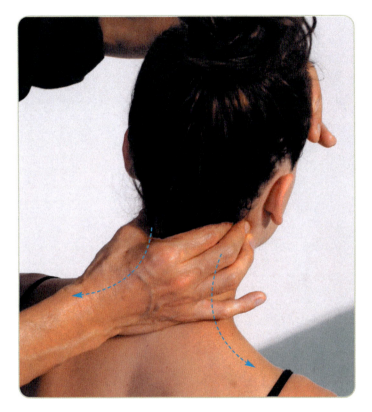

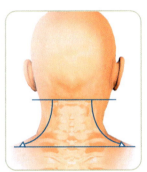

Life ART 2004 ®

PO: One knee on the floor, the other supporting client's back comfortably (be careful not to let your groin touch client's back).

HA: One hand against client's forehead, the other kneading and pressing.

AR: From the bottom of client's skull to the shoulder.

MO: First direct your thumb up toward "third eye" at the base of skull, gradually moving down toward the chest at the shoulder.

RE: Once.

ILLUSTRATION 70: SHOULDER KNEADING AND PRESSING METHODS - GALL BLADDER MERIDIANS

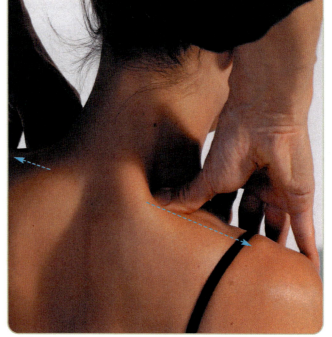

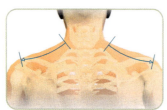

Life ART 2004 ®

PO: Standing with knees against the client's back for comfortable support.

HA: Four fingers on supraclavicle fossa[47].

AR: From corner of neck to shoulder.

MO: Lean forward to increase pressure as you move from corner of neck to shoulders.

RE: Kneading, 3 times; pressing, once.

***   Shaking client's body uncomfortably as you knead is called "earthquake Anma." Which should be avoided. On the last point (LI16[48]), you can perform cutting-kneading sideways.

47. Cavity above the clavical.
48. Refer to Chart on page 133.

ILLUSTRATION 71:   SHOULDER KNEADING AND PRESSING METHODS -
SMALL INTESTINE MERIDIANS

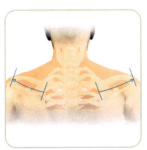

Life ART 2004 ®

PO: Standing with knees against the client's back for comfortable support.

HA: Four fingers on supraclavicle fossa.

AR: From corner of scapula to shoulder.

MO: Lean forward to increase pressure as you move from corner of neck to shoulders.

RE: Kneading, 3 times; pressing, once.

***   The ending point for this practice is same as for previous one (LI16).

ILLUSTRATION 72: NECK ADDITIONAL EXERCISING METHOD I (ROTATING)

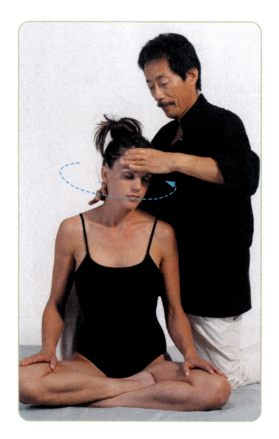 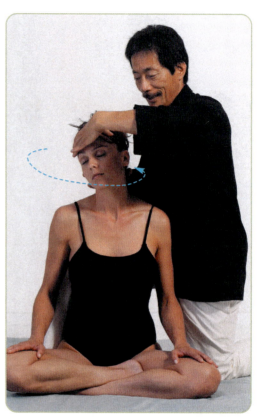

PO: One knee on the floor, the other supporting client's back comfortably.
HA: One hand is on client's forehead, the other against client's skull.
AR: Neck to shoulder.
MO: Rotate neck clockwise, then counterclockwise; first making small circles, then bigger, deeper ones.
RE: 3 times in each direction.
*** Proceed carefully with the deeper rotations.

ILLUSTRATION 73: BACK ADDITIONAL EXERCISING METHOD II
(KYOSEI STRETCHING)

 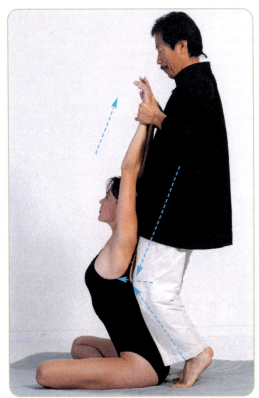

PO: Standing with knees against client's back, palms facing forward and client's arms next to ears.

AR: Practitioner's knees move up each time a stretch is finished.

MO: Stretch client's back, creating a slight arch by pressing your knees against client's back.

RE: 3 times. (Elevate knees from client's middle back to upper back).

*** Avoid pressing your knees against the client's spine. The exercise focuses not only lifting the client's arms but also swinging them back.

ILLUSTRATION 74: BACK-SHOULDER ADDITIONAL EXERCISING
METHOD III (ROTATING SHOULDER JOINTS)

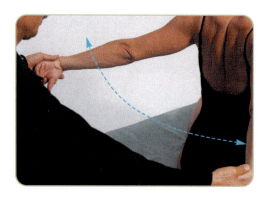

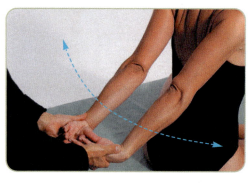

PO: Kneeling behind client.
HA: Practitioner holding both of client's wrists, palms up.
AR: Around the shoulder joints.
MO: Rotate client's shoulder gently and symmetrically, then reverse.
RE: 3 times.
***   Make sure client relaxes shoulder so that it drops. You may lift client's arms higher and higher,
        and also bring client's hands together to open up the chest area. If shoulder is tight, do it at a
        lower angle.

ILLUSTRATION 75: NECK-SHOULDER ADDITIONAL SHAKING METHOD

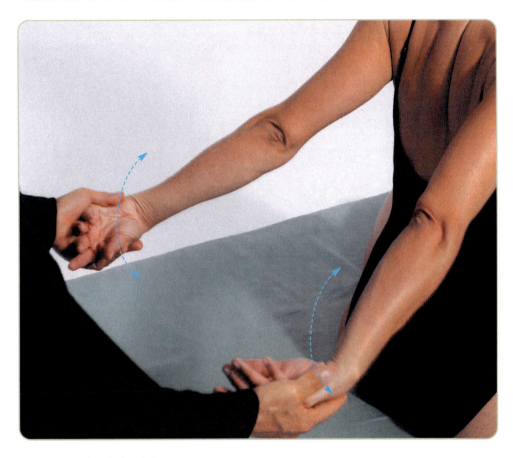

PO: Kneeling behind client.
HA: Holding client's wrists (palms up).
AR: Vibration reaches from hands to arms to shoulders to neck.
MO: Shake client's arm first up and down, then sideways.
RE: About 5 seconds per direction.

ILLUSTRATION 76: NECK-SHOULDER ADDITIONAL EXERCISING METHOD IV
(KYOSEI STRETCHING - FOOT PRESSURE AGAINST BACK)

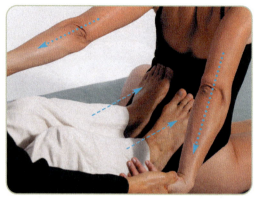
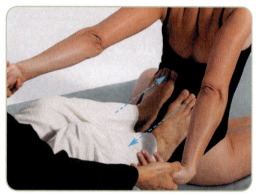

PO: Drop hip on the floor and extend your feet toward client's back.

HA: Same as Illustration 75.

AR: Press on the bladder meridians with feet from end of scapula to buttocks.

MO: Press your foot against the client's back next to the spine on the same side as you are
       pulling his or her hand.

RE: 1 to 2 times.

ILLUSTRATION 77: NECK-SHOULDER ADDITIONAL EXERCISING METHOD V
(KYOSEI STRETCHING - OPENING THE CHEST AND ARMS)

PO: Standing - same as Illustration 73.

HA: Ask client to interlock the fingers against the back of the head.

RE: 1 to 3 times.

MO: Press outward on the inside of the client's elbows (opening the chest), as you press the client's back with your knees.

AR: Practitioner's knees move up after each opening of the client's chest.

***   This exercise opens the client's chest gently, but be careful not to over-twist.

ILLUSTRATION 78:   NECK-SHOULDER TAPPING METHOD I
(SHUKEN KODA HO - FIRST TAPPING)

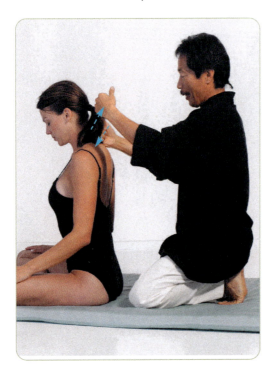
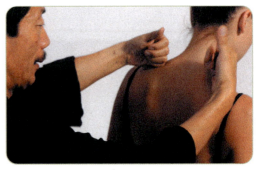
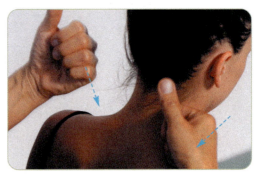

PO: Kneeling behind client, drop shoulders and open armpit slightly so that elbow is nicely bent.
HA: Make a moderate fist, neither too tight nor too loose, and tap alternately.
AR: Top of shoulders.
MO: Tap alternately (not simultaneously) between bottom of neck and shoulders.
RE: About 10 seconds.
***   1. Practitioner should relax and use the soft and gentle part at the bottom of fist.
2. Tap as much as possible, as quickly as possible.
3. Strong tapping should be avoided for whiplash cases.
4. Turn your wrists in and rotate them well.

ILLUSTRATION 79: TAPPING METHOD II
(GASSHO KODA HO - PRAYING HAND TAPPING)

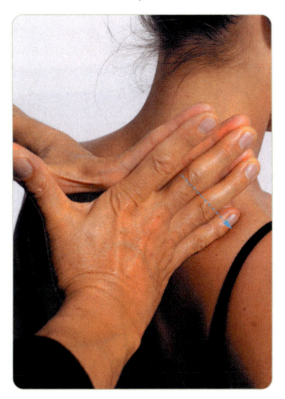
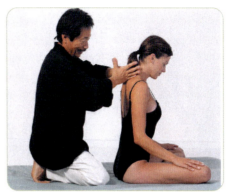
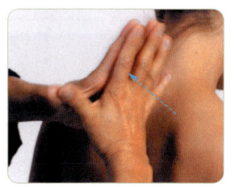

PO: Kneeling down behind client.
HA: Put your palms together, closing fingers momentarily while you tap, then opening them again.
AR: Shoulder blade, along the spine (first bladder meridian), to mid-back;
     also along the second bladder meridian.
MO: Tap with hands together on client's left side of back first, then right, from top to bottom.
RE: About 10 seconds.
*** Rotate wrists well. Bottom of palms being open creates good tapping sounds.

ILLUSTRATION 80: TAPPING METHOD III
(SETSUDA HO -CHOPPING HAND TAPPING)

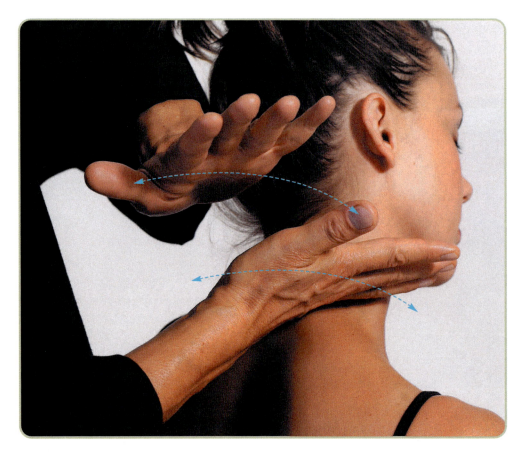

PO: Kneeling down behind client.
HA: Separate palms and open fingers when you tap. Palms or fingers may touch each other.
AR: Side of the neck. (Ask client to turn the neck to the side).
MO: Tap on client's left side between top of neck and shoulder first, then on the right.
RE: About 10 seconds.

ILLUSTRATION 81: TAPPING METHOD IV
(SHUSHO KODA HO - CUPPED HAND TAPPING)

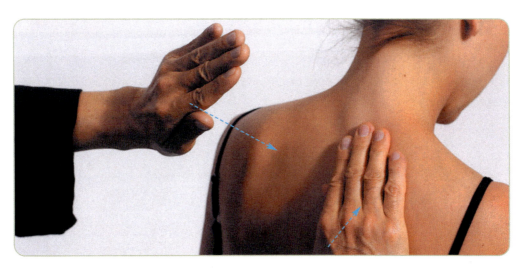

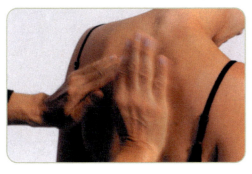 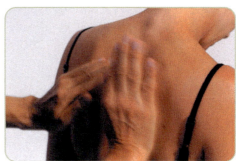

PO: Kneeling down behind client.
HA: Cup your palms and tap.
AR: General area on the upper back and shoulders, as well as over the scapulas.
MO: Tap alternately at random.
RE: About 5 seconds.

ILLUSTRATION 82: TAPPING METHOD V
(SHUHAI KODA HO - BACK OF HAND TAPPING)

 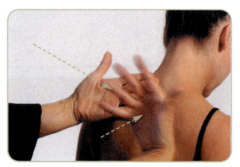

PO: Kneeling behind client.
HA: Use the back of your fingers.
AR: Middle back.
MO: Tap alternately from shoulders to middle back region.
RE: About 5 seconds.

ILLUSTRATION 83: TAPPING METHOD VI
(SHUKENHAI KODA HO - BACK OF FIST TAPPING)

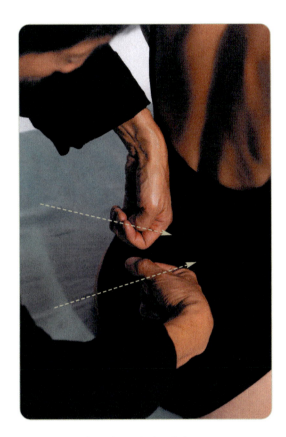
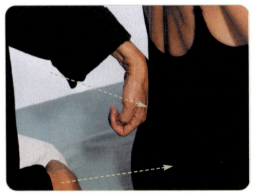
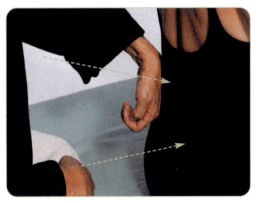

PO: Kneeling down behind client.
HA: Use the back of your fists.
AR: Lower back and buttock regions.
MO: Tap alternately from the lower back to bottom.
RE: About 5 seconds.

ILLUSTRATION 84: KYOKUDE METHOD I
(TSUKI DE - STRIKING OR HORSE'S HAND)

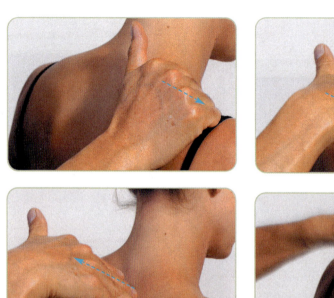

PO: Kneeling down behind client.
HA: Stretch and separate fingers. Tap with the fingertips and heels of hands.
AR: Upper back and shoulder.
MO: Tap with the fingertips and heels of hands on same areas alternately, like horse-trotting.
RE: About 5 seconds.
***   1. Good coordination between right and left hands is required.
      2. An important movement is the immediate collapse of the finger joints and a swift jumping.
      3. A good rhythm should be maintained, like the trotting of a horse.
      4. This is strong yet soft tapping.

ILLUSTRATION 85: KYOKUDE METHOD II (KURUMA DE - ROLLING HAND)

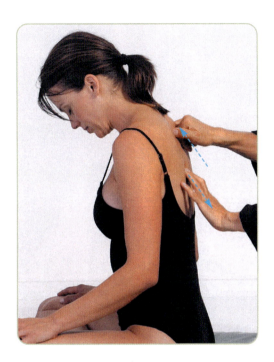

PO: Kneeling down behind client.

HA: First open your hands and flatten palms on the back, then start rolling one hand, using knuckles to apply pressure.

MO: Roll hand up, until a nice fist is formed. Then reverse the movement until the fingers are open. Next the other hand starts rolling upward in the same way. Alternate the two rolling motions.

AR: Upper back to the neck.

RE: Roll up about 3 times.

***   The rolling motion will produce nice pressure. On top of the shoulder, you may roll both fists at the same time.

ILLUSTRATION 86: KYOKU DE METHOD III (KUJIKIDE - BUTTERFLY HAND)

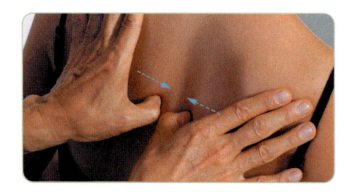

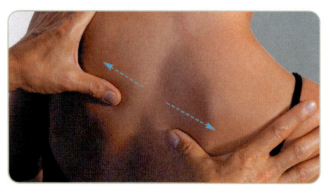

PO: Kneeling down behind client.
HA-MO: Stand with hands raised (not flat) at 90 degrees against client's back, separate thumbs
        from fingers, then flex thumb joint in so that knuckles hit each other; bring thumb knuckles
        in and out as you move your four fingers inward in a quick, light brushing motion,
        constantly moving from the bottom of the scapulas to the top of the shoulders.
AR: Along the spine of the shoulder blade upward only .
RE: 3 times.

ILLUSTRATION 87: KYOKUDE METHOD IV (YOKO DE - FISH HAND)

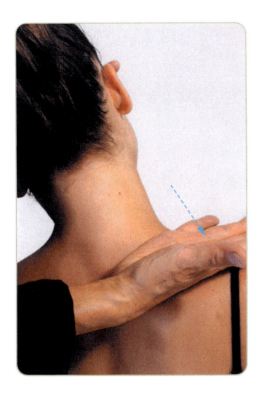 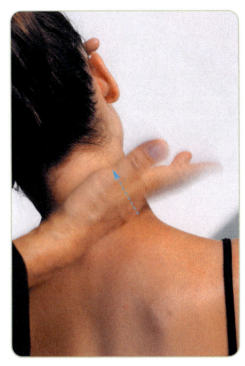

PO: One knee down, the other supporting client's back (same as Illustration 69).

HA-MO: One of your hands holds and presses the side of client's head toward you so that the other hand can practice well. Stand the hand, little finger side down, and apply slight pressure against the surface of the neck with the ball of the small finger and constantly vibrate side ways until you reach the base of the skull.

AR: Side of neck and shoulder, including triple heater, gall bladder and urinary bladder meridians.

RE: 3 times.

ILLUSTRATION 88: SHOULDER-TO BACK SOOTHING METHOD

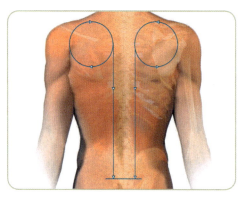

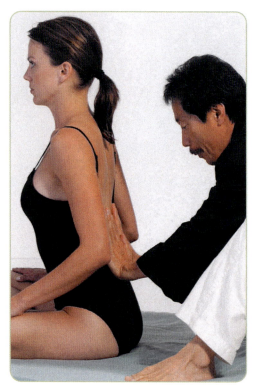

PO: Kneeling down behind client.

HA: Fingers together, separated from thumbs.

AR: Neck to shoulders to lower back.

MO: Soothe outward and symmetrically around the scapulas[17] twice; then on the third rotation, bring hands down on both sides of spine to the lower back.

RE: 3 times.

***   This is the very end of all the sequences. This is the time to reflect and to make prayers and wishes for your client's well-being and peace.

17. Shoulder blade bones.

ILLUSTRATION 89: ENDING / GASSHO

During this concluding blessing, the therapist may inwardly pray the following for well-being and harmony in our universe:

To all gods, saints and guardians of our souls: Thank you for your love. We will try to follow your teaching of love, healing and Tao, the divine order of the universe, so that we can realize peace, harmony and infinity beyond any conflicts between yin and yang. May love and healing prevail among family, friends, clients and all living creatures in the universe.

Shiatsu Anma is a meditation.
It is a prayer for the client's total well-being.

CHAPTER NINE
DOANN'S SHORT FORM

1. Gassho.

2. Soothing.

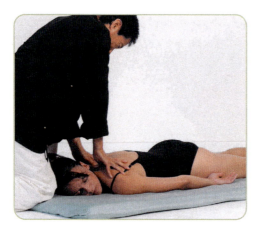

3. Sekisaisen: upper back pressing method.

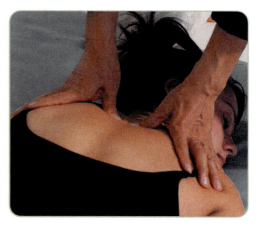

4. 1st Urinary Bladder meridian: upper back pressing method.

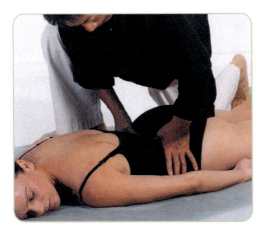

5. Sekisaisen middle and lower back pressing method.

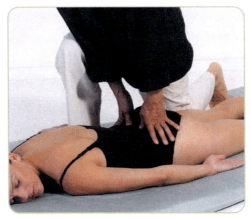

6. 1st Urinary Bladder meridian: middle and lower back pressing method.

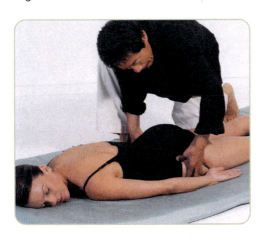

7. Additional hip line pressing method.

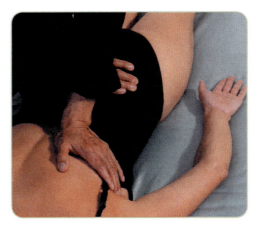

8. Back spine correcting method I.

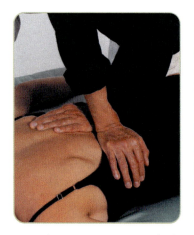 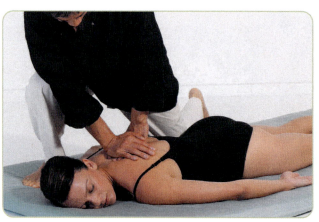

9. Back spine correcting method II. 10. Back spine correcting method III.

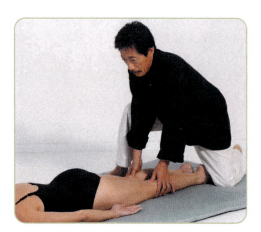 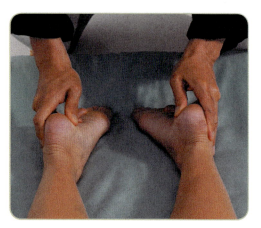

11. Legs - Urinary Bladder meridian: pressing method.

12. Feet - 3 lines: pressing method.

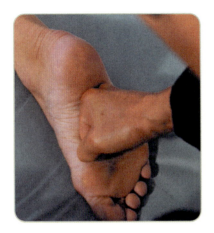

13. Feet: fist pressure method.

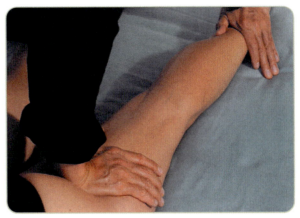

14. Back of the legs correcting method.

15. Legs exercising method I.

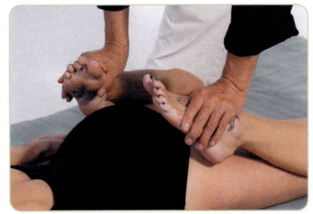

16. Legs exercising method II.

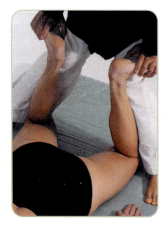

17. Legs exercising method III.

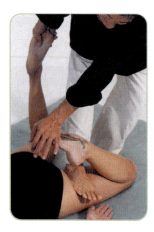

18. Legs foot pressure method.

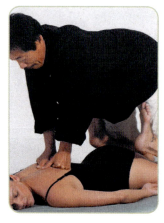

19. Legs exercising and back pressure method.

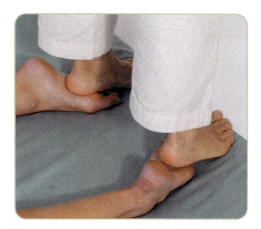

20. Feet-on-feet pressure method.

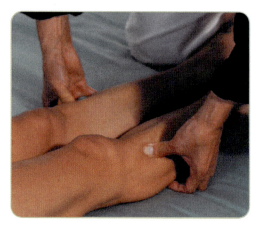

21. Legs - Stomach meridian pressing method.

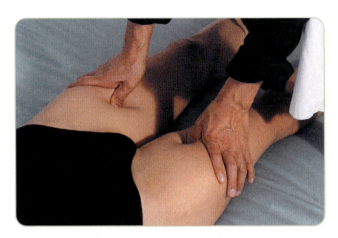

22. Legs - Spleen meridian pressing method.

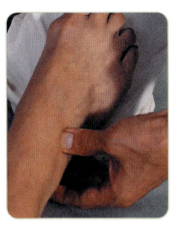

23. Front of feet pressing method.

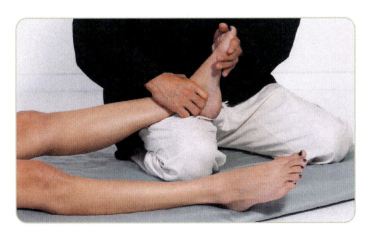

24. Ankle rotating exercise method.

25. Hip joint rotating exercise method.

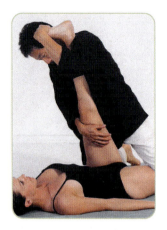

26. Leg - Urinary Bladder meridian stretching method.

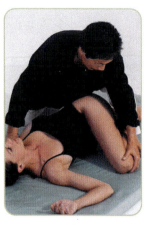

27. Leg - Gall Bladder meridian stretching method.

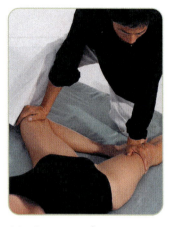

28. Opening pelvis correcting method.

29. Lower back exercising method I.

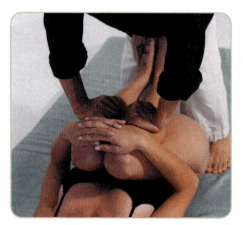

30. Lower back exercising method II.

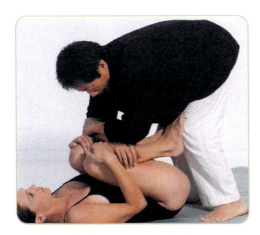

31. Lower back exercising method II. (Deep application)

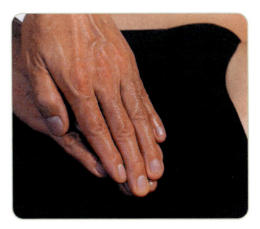

32. Abdomen - Conception Vessel: pressing method.

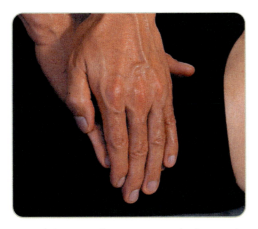

33. Abdomen palm pressing method around the navel (5 spots).

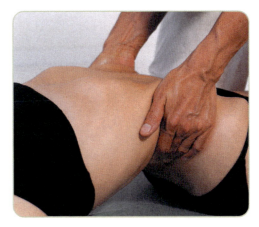

34. Lifting back and quick release method.

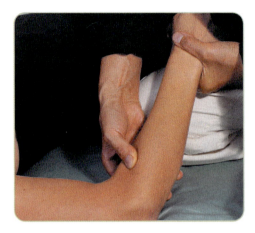

35. Arm - Large Intestine meridian: pressing method.

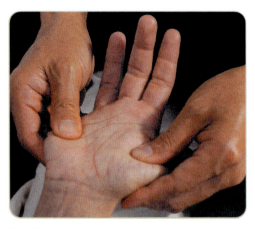

36. Hand pressing method (Seiza).

37. Hand exercising method I - rotating wrists.

38. Hands exercising method II - wrist joints and fingers.

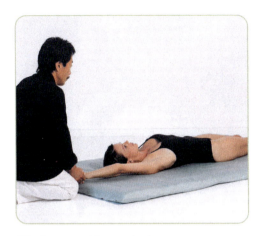

39. Arm stretching method.

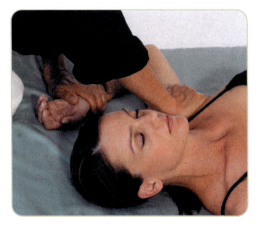

40. Arms: shoulder joint correcting method.

41. Arms tossing method.

42. Neck - Small Intestine meridian: pressing method.

43. Neck - Triple Heater meridian: pressing method.

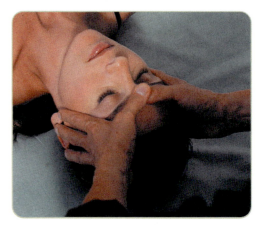

44. Face and head - Governing Vessel pressing methods.

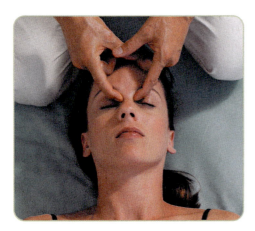

45. Face and head - Urinary Bladder meridian: pressing methods.

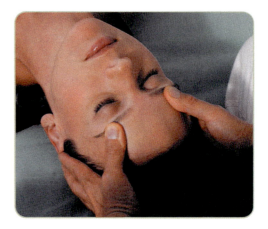

46. Face and head - Gall Bladder meridian: pressing methods.

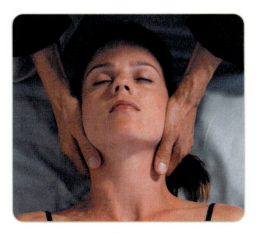

47. Neck and shoulders correcting method: traction the neck method.

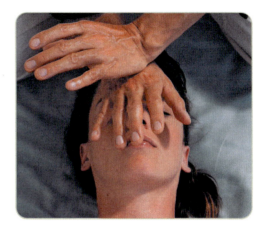

48. Palm pressing on the head method.

49. Stretching the neck and shoulder toward one side.

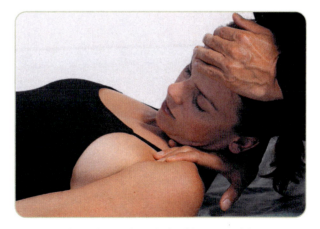

50. Stretching the neck and shoulder toward the center.

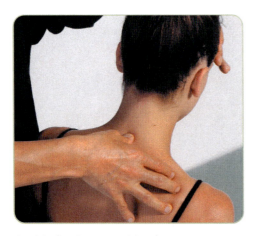

51. Neck - Governing Vessel: pressing method.

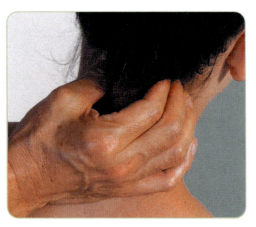

52. Neck - Urinary Bladder meridian: pressing method.

53. Neck - Gall Bladder meridian: pressing method.

54. Shoulder - Gall Bladder meridian: pressing method.

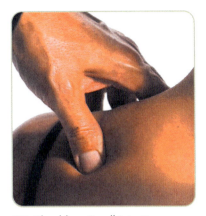

55. Shoulder - Small Intestine meridian: pressing method.

56. Neck additional exercising method I: rotating.

57. Neck additional exercising method II: stretching back and arms.

58. Neck and shoulder additional exercising method III: rotating shoulder joints.

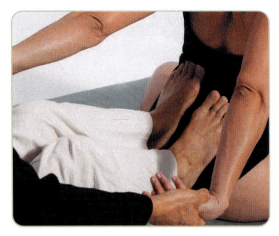

59. Neck and shoulder additional exercising method IV: foot pressure against back.

60. Neck and shoulder additional exercising method V: opening chest and inside of arms.

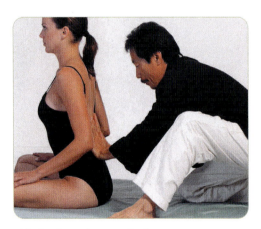

61. Back soothing method.

62. Gassho at completion.

12 Divergent Channels 104
Aches and Pains 66
Acquired Energy 66
Acupuncture 2, 3, 5, 6, 13, 15, 18, 76
Acute Ailments 4, 34, 37, 74, 75, 118
Adult entertainment 81
AIDS 76, 77
Alcohol 73, 75,76
Anma Tebiki 6
Anma (Ankyo Doin) 6
Anma-Shiatsu 17, 6, 62, 63, 37, 80, 74, 45, 18, 75, 66
Anpuku (Abdominal massage) 6, 3, 7
Appaku-ho 34, 62, 142
Appendicitis 75, 98
Arthritis 75, 98, 118
Attsuten 19, 62, 78, 98
Autonomic Nervous System 20, 66
Blood Diseases 75
Bo (alarm) points 19, 20, 67, 99, 123, 125
Breathing 36, 76, 142, 13, 69
Breathing difficulties 76
Cancer 14, 44, 75, 76
Cerebro-spinal meningitis 75
Chi 3, 6, 10, 13, 14
Chi Qong III
Cholera 75
Choma no jyutsu 24
Client education 81
Client feedback 81
Cold 4, 5, 10, 25, 78, 132, 122, 12, 5, 13, 11
Compression 62, 75
Concentrated pressure (Shuchu atsu) 35
Congested energy 66, 107
Constipation 76, 114, 118, 111, 125, 24
Constitutional 74
Contagious diseases 73, 74, 75

Contra-indications 72
Coordinated pressure 36
Correcting technique 44, 45, 46, 142, 62, 151, 152, 157
Cutting kneading 28, 30, 62, 248
Depression 66
Discomfort 34, 110, 54, 124, 14, 75
DoAnn T. Kaneko III
Doin III, 72, 6, 82, 74, 5
Dosage 80
Dry 10, 4, 2, 110
Dysentery 75
Earth 8, 10, 12, 11, 67, 139, 5, 106
Eiki 24
Electromagnetic current 103, 99, 107, 12
Electromagnetic field 124
Embolism 75
Emperor Fu Shi 2
Extreme debility 75
Fatigue 75, 63, 122, 66, 110, 52, 124, 24, 118
Febrile Disease 75
Fever 76, 76, 25, 132, 144, 111, 122, 125, 110, 5
Fire 10, 11, 8, 125, 13
Five Elements 3, 8, 10,11
Fujibayashi Ryohaku 6
Gassho 72, 73, 142, 143, 229
Genki 106
Gonorrhea 75
Gradual pressure 36
Hau Tuo 3
Hau Tuo Jiaji (Sekisaisen) 3
Half-sick, half-healthy condition 66
Hands Kneading 190
Hands Exercising Method 192, 193, 204
Headache 130, 132, 19, 127, 122, 118, 111, 115, 18, 75
Heart failure 75
Hepatitis 77, 75

Herbal treatment 3, 2, 18, 75, 5, 13
Herbs 6, 5, 15, 77, 4, 2
High fever 75
Honji-Ho 19, 20, 5, 10, 12, 20
Huangdi, the Yellow Emperor 2
Huangdi Nei Jing: Yellow Emperor's Classic of Internal Medicine 2
Humidity 111, 10, 11
Hyoji-ho 19, 20
I shoku dogen 14
I wa jinjutsu 14
Ice 75
ICERS 75
I-Ching 2
Infectious 3, 73, 74, 75
Infinite electromagnetic field 12, 10
Inflammation 34, 75
Insomnia 66
Insurance 78, 79
Intermittent pressure 34, 35, 90, 67
Ishi no ue ni mo san nen 86
Jesus Christ 18
Jitsu 10, 34
Jyo ko wa mibyo o iyu 10, 39, 14
Kagawa Genetsu 6
Kagawa Genteki 6
Kagawa Shuan 6
Kaishaku-junetsu-ho 28
Kanketsu appo 21
Kato, Fusajiro 7
Katsusuke Serizawa I
Keiko 86
Keiraku Anma Massage II, 103, 7
Keiraku Shiatsu 7
Keisatsu-ho 142, 24
Ketsu 107, 103, 98
Ki 13, 12, 6, 34, 24, 8, 42, 28

Kneading technique 28, 20, 142, 146 - 149, 150, 156, 168-171, 183
Koda 54, 142
Kujikide (butterfly hand) 58
Kurumade (wheel hand) 58
Kyo 10, 34
Kyokude 58, 224-227
Kyosei-ho 44, 62
Leprosy 44, 75
Liver cirrhosis 75
Local heat 75
Low energy 66
Lower backache 76, 118, 120, 138, 72
Ma 6
Manual of Anma 6
Master Oki III
Master Namikoshi 7
Master Yanagiya I
Master Masunage 7
Medical Advice of Ippondo 6
Meditation 72, 62, 18, 13, 74
Menken/Meigen 74, 80
Meridian 98-139, 62, 21, 29, 7, 244, 219, Chapter 14
Meridian: Urinary Bladder 105, 108-115, 129, 130, 131-132, 136, 139, 153, 154, 175, 201, 206
Meridian: Kidney 105, 115, 137, 139
Meridian: Stomach 105, 117, 118, 122, 136, 139, 168, 170
Meridian: Spleen/Pancreas 105, 119, 120, 121, 122, 137, 139, 165, 169, 170
Meridian: Gallbladder 105, 122, 129 - 132, 136, 139, 176, 202, 206
Meridian: Conceptual Vessel 123, 124, 125, 139, 180, 183
Meridian: Large Intestine 126, 127, 135, 186, 188, 196
Meridian: Small Intestine 105, 128, 135, 198, 206
Meridian: Triple Heater 105, 128, 135, 199
Meridian: Governing Vessel 131, 130, 132, 139, 200
Meridian: Pericardium 135, 139

Meridian: Lungs 135, 139
Meridian: Heart 135, 139
Meridian: Liver 137
Metal 10, 11, 8, 4
Moxibustion 4, 5, 6, 15, 6, 252, 130, 18
Mukyoku 12
Muladhara chakra 13
Negative Restrictive Cycle 10
Occupational Injuries 66
Oketsu 74
Ordinary Pressure 34, 35, 142, 74
Oriental bodywork III
Origins of Chinese Medicine 2
Ota Shinsai 6
Pain 122, 120, 125, 124, 18, 34, 3, 14, 76, 24, 98
Palm kneading (Roto No Jyutsu) 184
Para-vertebral region 67, 11, 108, 110, 112, 201
Payment agreement 79, 78
Peritonitis 75
Pneumonia 75
Polio 75
Positive creative cycle 10
Pregnancy 75
Pregnant clients 75
Pressing technique 34, 142, 149, 150, 157, 164, 168, 188
Pricing 81
Primordial Energy 106, 107
Professional associations 82
Psychosomatic 74
Pyemia 75
Qin Yueren 3
Redness 75
Release forms 78
Rest 75
Rikan-no iyutsu 42
Rinjo junetsu 42

Rotating Kneading 29, 150
Ryusui fubu 14
Scarlet fever 75
Sciatica 14
Seiki 167
Sekisaisen 3, 232, 233
Self-anpuku 6
Self-healing (Doin) 72, 6, 82, 76, 5
Self-massage 72, 13, 15
Semi-tapping technique 52, 142
Senjo Junetso 28
Serizawa Katsusuke I
Shaking technique 142, 185
Shen Nong 2
Shiatsu Massage School of California III
Shindo-ho 50
Shinsen-ho 50
Shoulder techniques 207, 211, 228
Side posture 63, 80, 76
Skeletal system 62, 44, 66, 7
Skin ailments 127, 75
Small pox 75
Snapping technique 60, 172, 191
Soki (ancestral energy) 107
Soothing technique 24, 25, 142, 156, 157, 167, 170, 181, 187, 189, 228
Spinal nerves 20
Spinal nervous system 66, 24
Spirit (seishin) 13
Spirit (shin) 106, 107
Spitting up blood (75)
Spleen 67, 20, 76, 10, 67, 76
Sports injuries 75
Squeezing technique 192
Stable pressure 35
States of altered consciousness 75

Stiffness in shoulders 76
Stomach 168, 165, 10
Stress 18
Stress-related 18, 74
Sugiyama Waichi 6
Sugiyama-rhyu 6
Sujimomi (Keiraku Anma massage) II
Support 75
Sustained pressure (sasae atsu) 35
Su Wen 13
Swelling 75, 110, 111, 120
Swollen glands 75
Synopsis of Prescriptions in the Golden Chest (Jin Kui Yao Lue
Lue Fang Lun) 3
Syphilis 75
Tai Chi Chuan 74
Takagi Rokubai 7
Tanden 20, 76, 36, 185
Tao 2, 9, 10, 14, 82
Taoism 3
Tapping technique 54, 142, 218-223
Techniques 142
Tenohira-ryho-ho 25
The Illustration of Anpuku 6
Three Minute Shiatsu 7
Thrombosis 75
Time 81
Tokugawa Tsunayoshi Shogun 6
Tossing 6, 89, 92
Trachoma 75
Traumatic 74
Treeatise on Febrile Diseases (Shang Han Lun) 3
Trigger point 62
Tsubo 6, 98
Tsujo appo 142
Tsukai 35

Tsukide (horse hands) 58
Tuberculosis (75)
Typhoid 75
Tzu, Lao 8
Ulceration 75
Undo-ho 42, 63
Varicose veins 34, 75, 78
Vertical pressure (Suichoku Atsu) 35, 142
Vibrating Technique 50, 142
Vital force 6
Vital points 98, 100, 138, 107, 78, 3, 80, 6, 68
Vitality (sei) 13
Warau kado niwa fuku kitaru (14)
Water 10, 8, 11, 111, 124, 134, 116
Weakness 114, 118, 124, 34, 116
Weil's Disease 75
Whooping Cough 75
Wind 10
Wood 10
Yamai wa kikara 14
Yanagiya Masako I
Yang 4, 25, 8, 12, 13, 107, 139
Yank ki 107, 13, 12, 34, 72, 8, 106, 25, 10, 6
Yang Meridians 105, 139
Yin ki 107, 13, 12,106, 8, 25
Yin Meridians 105
Yin-Yang Theory 2
Yokode (fish-tail hand) 58
Yoshimasu Todo (6, 20)
Yu (associated points) 19, 67
Zhang Zong Jing 2
Zen Shiatsu 7
Zo fu 20

REFERENCES

Anmatebiki (Manual of Anma Therapy) by Ryohaku Sugibayashi (Idononihonsha)

Aupukuzukai (Illustration of Anpuku Therapy) by Shinsai Ota (Idononihonsha)

A Color Atlas of Human Anatomy by R.H.McMinn & R.T. Hutchings (Nankodo Publication)

A Color Illustration of Acupuncture Points by Santon Science Technology Publication

Chen's History of Chinese Medical Science by Houg-yen Hsu, Ph.D., William, G. Peacher, M.D.
(Oriental Healing Arts Institute USA.)

Chinese Acupuncture & Moxibustion by Cheg Xinnong (Foreign Languages Press, Beijing)

Effective Tsubo therapy by Katsusuke Serizawa (Japan Publication, Inc.)

Illustration of Acupuncture point by Haruto Kinoshita (Idononihonsha Pub.)

Illustration of Anma Massage Therapy by Sorei Yanagiya (Idononihonsha Pub.)

Japanese history nenphyo Kota Kodama (Yoshikawa Kobunkan)

Kampo Oriental Medicine- Vital Points by Zenkokuyoseishisetsu Association (Ishiyaku Publication)

Medical History by Eiichi Nagano (Ishiyaku Publication)

Shiatsu theory and practice by Serizawa Katsusuke (Ishiyaku Publication)

Shiatsu Therapy by Shizuto Masunaga (Sogen Igaku Shinsho)

Summary of Acupuncture & Moxibustion medicine by Sorei Yanagiya (Toyo Acupuncture college)

Tsubo Vital Points for Oriental Therapy by Katsusuke Serizawa (Japan Publication, Inc)

The way to locate Acu-points by Guoji Shudian (China Publication Center)

TP Myofacial Pain Syndromes by Joseph J.Smolders (The motion Palpation Institute)

"Lifeart Images" used with permission of Lippincott William & William

14 MAJOR MERIDIANS & THEIR VITAL POINTS

LUNG CHART

POINT	TRANSLATION	LOCATION	INDICATION
LU1 Chufu **Zhongfu**	Central Residence {Alarm Point for Lung}	1 sun inferior to LG2 at the same level as the 1st intercostal space.	Common cold, cough, panting asthma, pain in the chest and other respiratory disorders, shoulder pain and stiffness.
LU2 Unmon **Yunmen**	Gate of the Cloud	At the center of the infraclavicular fossa.	Cough, asthma, pain in the chest, shoulder, shoulder joint, and arm.
LU3 Tenpu **Tianfu**	Heavenly Residence	3 sun inferior to the tip of the axillary fold.	Asthma, nosebleed, and pain in the radial side of the arm.
LU4 Kyohaku **Xiabai**	Pure White or Guarding White	4 sun inferior to the tip of the axillary fold.	Coughing, short breath, and pain in the radial side of the upper arm.
LU5 Shakutaku **Chize**	Marsh with Foot Depth {Water Element}	On the cubital crease on the radial aspect of the biceps brachii tendon.	Coughing, sore throat, fever followed by chills, elbow problems (radial side), also shoulder and back pains.
LU6 Kosai **Kongzui**	Opening of the Extreme or Collection Hole {Cleft Point}	5 sun inferior to LG5 on the medial border of the radius – stretch the forearm & highest spot where you make a fist.	Coughing, tonsilitis, pain on the radial side of the arm and finger, hoarse voice, and Moxibustion for hemorrhoids.
LU7 Rekketsu **Liegue**	Pile of Cavities or Broken Sequence {Connecting Point}	1.5 sun superior to LG9 at the origin of the styloid process (proximal end).	Headache, neck pain, coughing, nasal congestion, pain and numbness of the radial side of the arm and fingers. One of the four major points for neck and shoulder ailments.
LU8 Keikyo **Jingqu**	Drain of the Meridian {Metal Element}	1 sun superial to LG9 at the radial artery.	Coughing, asthma, sore throat, and pain in the wrist.

1

POINT	TRANSLATION	LOCATION	INDICATION
LU9 Taien Taiyuan	Great Abyss {Earth Element & Source Point}	At the palmar aspect of the wrist on the radial side of the crease.	Coughing, chest pain, tendonitis at the wrist, and pain in the shoulder.
LU10 Gyosai Yuji	Edge of Fish {Fire Element}	Proximal to the metacarpalphalangeal joint of the thumb, – at about the middle of the metacarpal bone on the palmar radial aspect.	Fever, headache, coughing, sore throat, tendonitis, also pain and numbness in the thumb.
LU11 Shosho Shao Shang	Little Sound of Sho (Music Note) or Little Trade {Wood Element}	On the radial side of the thumbs, .1 sun proximal to the base of the nail.	Sore throat, fever, weak breathing numbness of the fingers and hands, bloodletting for emergency cases such as faintness. Effective point for pediatric diseases such as convulsions in children.

LARGE INTESTINE CHART

POINT	TRANSLATION	LOCATION	INDICATION
LI1 Shoyo Shangyang	Sho Sound of Music Note or Trade Yang {Metal Element}	On the radial side of the index fingers, .1 sun proximal to the base of the nail.	Fever, sore throat, skin problems, pediatric complaints such as convulsions, night crying, and colics.
LI2 Jikan Erjian	Second Space or Between Two {Water Element}	On the radial side of the index finger, distal to the metacarpalphalanageal joint.	Flash, nasal bleeding, toothache, sore throat, and bloodletting for childrens' hysteric constitution.
LI3 Sankan Sanjian	Third Space or Between Three {Wood Nature}	On the radial side of the index finger, proximal to the metacarpalphalangeal joint.	Eyeache, lower toothache, sore throat, and trigeminal neuralgia.

POINT	TRANSLATION	LOCATION	INDICATION
LI4 Gokoku **Hegu**	Merging Valley {Source Point}	On the dorsal side of the hand between the junction of the 1st and 2nd metacarpal bones and the margin of the web, – the highest spot when you make a fist.	One of the four major points for any complaints in the face, such as teeth, throat, nose, eye, facial paralysis, neuralgia, and headache, delayed labor, "Lock Jaw" after stroke, and hemiplegia. This point can cause miscarriage.
LI5 Yokei **Yangxi**	Sunny Brook {Fire Element}	On the radial dorsal of the wrist in the depression, (the depression on the wrist when you make a fist).	Headache, tinnitus, difficulty in hearing, and wrist pain on the radial side.
LI6 Henreki **Pianli**	Biased Tract or Partial Order {Connecting Point}	3 sun superior to LI5 in the depression of the lateral radius.	Sore throat, facial paralysis, neuralgia of the forearm, and nasal bleeding.
LI7 Onru **Wenliu**	Warm Dwelling {Cleft Point}	5 sun superior to LI5.	Headache, sore throat, pain in the shoulder and upper back, and stomatitis.
LI8 Geren **Xialian**	Lower Ridge	4 sun inferior to LI11.	Headache, pain and numbness on the radial side of the arm.
LI9 Joren **Shanglian**	Upper Ridge	3 sun inferior to LI11.	Hemiplegia, numbness of the radial side of the arms, and abdominal pain.
LI10 Te No Sanri **Shousanri**	Three Miles in the Arm	2 sun inferior to LI11.	Hemiplegia, pain in the elbow, arm, and shoulder, high blood pressure syndromes, headache eyeache, and indigestion.
LI11 Kyokuchi **Quchi**	Pool at the Corner {Earth Element}	At the radial aspect of the lateral epicondyle of the humerus and at the head of the crease when the elbow is flexed.	Hemiplegia, pain in the elbow, arm, shoulder, high blood pressure sydromes, fever, skin disease, eyeache, and pain and numbness of the radial side of the arm and elbow.

3

POINT	TRANSLATION	LOCATION	INDICATION
LI12 Churyo Zhouliao	Elbow Bone	1 sun superior to LI11, slightly lateral, about $1/2$ way between TH10 and LI11.	Pain and numbness in the elbows and arms.
LI13 Te No Gori Wuli	Five Mile in the Arm	3 sun superior to LI11, slightly lateral, and 3 sun inferior to LI15.	Pain in the elbow and arm.
LI14 Hijyu Binao	Forearm and Upper Arm	On the lower border of the deltoid muscle and on the line between LI10 and LI15.	Pain of the shoulder and upper arms, weakness of the arm.
LI15 Kengu Jianyu	Shoulder Bone	On the anterior inferior ridge of the acromion, – in the middle of the depression when the arm is abducted.	Pain in the shoulder and upper arm, high blood pressure syndromes.
LI16 Kokotsu Jugu	Huge Bone	At the depression between the acromion of the clavicle and the spine of the scapula.	Pain and disorder in the arm, and shoulder joints.
LI17 Tentei Tianding	Celestail Tripod	1 sun directly inferior to LI18.	Sore throat, swollen throat, and hoarseness of the voice.
LI18 Fototsu Futu	Support the Prominence	At the level of Adam's Apple, just between the two heads of the sternocleidomastoid muscle, – lateral to ST9.	Cough, asthma, excessive phlegm, and flushes.
LI19 Karyo Helioa	Grainy Seam	.5 sun lateral to GV26, directly below the lateral margin of the nostril.	Nasal bleeding and congestion, numbness and weakness of the facial muscles.
LI20 Geiko Yingxiang	Welcoming Smell	In the nasolabial sulcus, at the level of the mid point of the lateral border of ala nasi (nose).	Nasal congestion, facial neuralgia, also numbness and weakness of the facial muscles.

4

STOMACH CHART

POINT	TRANSLATION	LOCATION	INDICATION
ST1 Shokyu **Chengqi**	Tear Container	.7 sun inferior to the pupil at the infraorbital ridge.	Eye problems such as, red eyes, twitching eyes, poor eye sight, hypermetropia (farsighted), itchy eyes, night blindness, minor glaucoma, and minor cataract.
ST2 Shihaku **Shibai**	Four White	1 sun inferior to the pupil at the infraorbital foramen.	Facial paralysis, trigeminal neuralgia, conjectivitis, and facial convulsions.
ST3 Korho **Juliao**	Huge Seam	Directly inferior to the pupil at the level of the lower border of ala nasi (the nose).	Numbness and weakness of the face, facial convulsion, trigeminal neuralgia, nasal conjestion, and upper toothache.
ST4 Chiso **Dicang**	Ground Storehouse	Lateral to the corner of the mouth below ST3.	Deviation of the mouth, numbness and weakness of the face.
ST5 Taigei **Daying**	Big Welcome	1.3 sun anterior and inferior to the angle of the mandible, – in the middle of the depression when you bite the teeth, in front of the muscle where you can feel pulsation.	Tregeminal neuralgia, lower toothache, numbness and weakness in the face, swollen glands, and TMJ.
ST6 Kyocha **Jiache**	The Wheel of the Chain	1 sun anterior and superior to the angle of the mandible, at the posterior border of the muscle (masseter).	Pain of the lower teeth, facial paralysis, and TMJ.
ST7 Gekan **Xianguan**	Below the Joint	Opposite side of GB3 at the inferior border of the zygomatic arch, – when you open the mouth the finger on this point is pushed upward.	Toothache, TMJ, tregeminal neuralgia, numbness and weakness in the face.

5

POINT	TRANSLATION	LOCATION	INDICATION
ST8 Zuii Touwei	Head Corner	At the angle of the forehead, 4.5 sun lateral to GV24.	Headache, migraine headache, and eyeache.
ST9 Jingei Renying	Welcoming Human Being	1.5 sun lateral to laryngeal prominence, where pulse is felt, in front of the sternocleidomastoid muscle.	Sore throat, coughing, goiter, swollen lymph, asthma, Basedow's disease (hyperthyroidism).
ST10 Suitotsu Shuitu	Water Prominence	Midway between ST9 and ST11 in front of the sternocleidomastoid muscle.	Coughing, asthma, sore throat, and swollen lymph node.
ST11 Kisha Qishe	Residence of Ki	On the superior ridge of the clavicular fossa, directly below ST9 to the clavicle.	Sore throat, coughing, torticollis, flushes, and hiccup.
ST12 Ketsubon Quepen	Cavity at the Basin Clavicle or Cavity at the Clavicle	In the depression at the middle of the superior border of the clavicle and directly above the nipple, also 4 sun lateral to CV22.	Coughing, common cold, pain in the upper arm.
ST13 Kiko Qihu	Door of Ki	At the lower border of the middle of the clavicle on the mammillary line – 4 sun from CV21, and 2 sun lateral to K27.	Coughing, pain in the chest and intercostals, also hiccup.
ST14 Kobo Kufang	Store House	First intercostal space, 2 sun lateral to K26.	Coughing, pain in the chest and intercostals, also hiccup.
ST15 Okuei Wuyi	Screen in the Room	Second intercostal space, 2 sun lateral to K25.	Pain in the chest, and coughing.

POINT	TRANSLATION	LOCATION	INDICATION
ST16 Yoso **Yingchuang**	Window of the Breast	Third intercostal space, 2 sun lateral to K24, and 4 sun lateral to CV18.	Pain in the chest, coughing, and mammary gland ailment.
ST17 Nyuchu **Ruzhong**	Middle of the Breast	Fourth intercostal space 2 sun lateral to K23, and 4 sun lateral to CV17, in the middle of the breast.	Insufficient lactation, no accupuncture, or .
ST18 Nyukon **Rugen**	Root of the Breast	Fifth intercostal space, 2 sun lateral to K22, and 4 sun lateral to CV16.	Insufficient lactation, and mammary gland ailment.
ST19 Fuyo **Burong**	Uncontainable (Allowed)	6 sun above the umbilicus, 2 sun lateral to CV14, and 1.5 sun lateral to K21.	Abdominal distention, gastric pain, vomiting, anorexia, and liver ailments.
ST20 Shoman **Chengman**	Receiving Fullness	5 sun above the umbilicus, 2 sun lateral to CV13, and1.5 sun lateral to K20.	Abdominal distention, gastric pain, vomiting, anorexia, and liver ailments.
ST21 Ryoman **Liangmen**	Gate of a Beam	4 sun above the umbilicus, 2 sun lateral to CV12, and 1.5 sun lateral to K19.	Gastro intestinal ailments including liver and gall bladder complaints.
ST22 Kanmon **Guanmen**	Gate of Barrier	3 sun above the umbilicus, 2 sun lateral to CV11 – 1.5 sun lateral to KI8.	Pain and distention in the abdomen, diarrhea, and edema.
ST23 Taiitsu **Taiyi**	Great Unity	2 sun above the umbilicus, 2 sun lateral to CV10, and 1.5 lateral to K7 – 1.5 sun lateral to KI7.	Pain and distention in the abdomen, diarrhea, and edema.
ST24 Katsunikumon **Huaroumen**	Gate of Smooth Flesh	1 sun above the umbilicus, 2 sun lateral to CV9.	Pain and distention in the abdomen, diarrhea, and edema.

POINT	TRANSLATION	LOCATION	INDICATION
ST25 Tensu **Tianshu**	Hinge of the Heaven {Alarm Point for Large Intestine}	2 sun lateral to center of the navel, 1.5 sun lateral to K16.	Abdominal pain, diarrhea, constipation, irregular menstruation, lower abdominal distention, hernia, retention of urine, frequent urination, prolapse of uterus, pain and swelling of the external genitalia, stagnant blood, and lower backache.
ST26 Gairyo **Wailing**	Outside of Tomb	1 sun below the umbilicus, 2 sun lateral to CV7, and 1.5 sun lateral to K15.	Abdominal pain, irregular menstruation, and hernia.
ST27 Taiko **Dayu**	Big and Huge	2 sun below the umbilicus, 2 sun lateral to CV5, and 1.5 lateral to K14.	Indigestion, constipation or diarrhea, and gynecological ailments.
ST28 Suido **Shidao**	Water Channel	3 sun below the umbilicus, 2 sun lateral to CV4, and 1.5 sun lateral to K13.	Indigestion, constipation or diarrhea, gynecological ailments.
ST29 Kirai **Guilai**	Returning and Coming	4 sun below the umbilicus, 2 sun lateral to CV3, and 1.5 sun lateral to K12.	Indigestion, constipation or diarrhea, gynecological ailments.
ST30 Kisho **Qichong**	Rushing Ki	5 sun below the umbilicus, 2 sun lateral to CV2, and 1.5 sun lateral to K11.	Indigestion, constipation or diarrhea, gynecological ailments.
ST31 Hikan **Biguan**	The Barrier at the Buttocks	Directly inferior to the anterior, superior iliac spine by the satorius, – bend the knee, ST31 is located in the middle of the crease under the iliac spine. It is also located at just about the inferior border to the pubic symphysis.	Lower backache, hemiplegia (paralysis on one side of the body), paralysis of lower extremities, pain in the anterior thigh, special point for the pain in the lower limb.
ST32 Fukoto or **Futu**	Hidden Rabbit or Crouching Rabbit	6 sun superior to the lateral superior ridge of the patella.	Numbness and weakness of the lower limb, and arthritis of the knee.

POINT	TRANSLATION	LOCATION	INDICATION
ST33 Yinshi **Yinshi**	City of Yin	3 sun superior to the lateral superior ridge of the patella.	Numbness and weakness of the lower limb, and arthritis of the knee.
ST34 Ryokyu **Liangqiu**	Beamed Hill {Cleft Point}	2 sun superior to lateral superior ridge of the patella.	Pain of the knee, special point for acute abdominal pain, gall stones and diarrhea.
ST35 Tokubi **Dubi**	Calf's Nose	Lateral to patellar ligament, in the middle of the cavity just below the patella, – bend the knee, in the middle of the cavity.	Knee joint problems, neuralgia, and rheumatism.
ST36 Ashi No Sanri **Zusanli**	Three Miles in the Leg {Earth Element}	3 sun inferior to the lateral interior ridge of the patella, – sooth top of the tibia bone until finger stops, ST36 is in between this point and the head of the fibula bone. 1 sun lateral to anterior crest of the tibia. (Hold patella with thumb and index finger, ST36 is at the tip of the middle finger).	Gastrointestinal problems, constipation, diarrhea, nausea, vomiting, allergies, seizures, weakness, swollen extremities, breast ailments, anemia, pain in the knee and leg, great fatigue or listlessness, aches and pains, incoherent speech, mental disorder (mania). General wellbeing, (tonic purpose with for longevity). One of the four major points for abdominal ailments.
ST37 Jyokokyo **Shangjuxu**	The Great Emptiness in the Upper Extremity	3 sun inferior to ST36.	Intestinal ailments including chronic appendicitis, fatigue of the leg, and weakness of the lower limbs.
ST38 Jyoko **Tiaokou**	Opening of Line	2 sun inferior to ST37, next to the tibia.	Pain in the knee, legs, weakness of the lower limbs, and gastrointestinal ailments.
ST39 Kakokyo **Xuajuxu**	The Great Emptiness in the Lower Extremity	1 sun inferior to ST38.	Backache referring to testis, gastrointestial ailments, pain and weakness of the lower extremities.

POINT	TRANSLATION	LOCATION	INDICATION
ST40 Horyu Fenglong	Abundant Prosperous {Connecting Point}	1 sun lateral to ST38, – midpoint between middle of the knee and top of the ankle, also 8 sun inferior to ST35.	Swollen lower extremities, gastrointestinal ailments, excessive sputum in the chest and nose.
ST41 Kaikei Jiexi	Separating Brook {Fire Element}	At midpoint of transverse malleolus crease, – stretch foot and bend toes, ST41 is between the two tendons.	Swollen lower eyelids, headache, dizziness, and pain in the ankle.
ST42 Shoyo Chong Yang	Rushing Yang {Source Point}	1.5 sun distal to ST41, at the highest point of the dorsum (top) of the foot, in the cavity between the second and third metatarsal bones, where a pulsation is perceived.	Pain in the foot, abdominal pain, facial or general edema.
ST43 Kankoku Xiangu	The Sunken Valley {Wood Element}	At the corner proximal to the second metatarsal phalangeal joint.	Pain in the foot (dorsum), and facial edema.
ST44 Naitei Neiting	The Inner Garden {Water Element}	At the corner distal to the second metatarsal phalangeal joint.	Gastrointestinal ailments, deviation of the mouth, and nasal bleeding.
ST45 Reida Lidui	Astrict Exchange or Rapid Hole {Metal Element}	On the lateral side of the second toe, about .1 sun proximal to the corner of the nail.	Fever without perspiration, nasal congestion, swollen mouth, face and neck, epilepsy, disturbed dreams and sleep, also mania.

SPLEEN CHART

POINT	TRANSLATION	LOCATION	INDICATION
SP1 Inpaku Yinbai	Hidden White {Wood Element}	Proximal on the medial side of the toe, about .1 sun proximal to the corner of the nail.	Gastrointestinal ailments, gynecological ailments (irregular menstruation), childrens convulsions, mental disorders, and disturbed dreams.

10

POINT	TRANSLATION	LOCATION	INDICATION
SP2 Taito Dadu	Great Capital {Fire Element}	On the medial side of the big toe, distal to the first metatarsal phalangeal joint where white and red skin is separated.	Gastrointestinal ailments, such as pain, distention or diarrhea.
SP3 Taihaku Taibai	Great White {Earth Element and Source Point}	On the medial side of the big toe, proximal to the first metatarsal phalangeal joint where white and red skin is separated.	Gastrointestinal ailments, such as pain, distention or diarrhea.
SP4 Koson Gongsun	Official Grandson or Yellow Emperor's Family Name {Connecting Point}	1 sun posterior to SP3, distal to the base of the first metatarsal bone where white and red skin is separated.	Gastrointestinal ailments, such as pain, distention, diarrhea, or constipation.
SP5 Shokyu Shangqiu	Hill of Merchant or Hill of Sho Sound (Music Note) {Metal Element}	In depression of anterior inferior ridge of medial malleolus.	Gastrointestinal ailments, pain in the toes, ankles and feet.
SP6 Saninko Sanyinjiao or Onna Sanri	Three Yin Channel Crossing or Female Three Miles	3 sun superior to medial malleolus, (ankle at posterior border of tibia bone).	Impotence, gynelogical ailments, such as, irregular menstruation leukorrhea, sterility, difficult labor, failure to discharge placenta. Also gastrointestinal ailments, diarrhea. This point is contraindicated during pregnancy.
SP7 Rokoku Longu	Leaking Valley	3 sun superior to SP6 at posterior border of tibia.	Gastrointestinal ailments, numbness and weakness of the feet.
SP8 Chiki Diji	Mechanism for Earth or Crux of the Earth {Cleft Point}	3 sun inferior to SP9 at the posterior border of the tibia.	Abdominal distention, diarrhea, colic, irregular menstruation, dysmenorrhea, and edema.
SP9 Inryosen Yingling-quan	Spring at Shadowy Tomb {Water Element}	Medial inferior ridge of medial condyle of tibia, – sooth the posterior border tibia, SP9 is where soothing fingers stop at the corner.	Body fluid retention, pain in the knee, abdominal cavity, edema and bladder, incontinence of urine, nocturnal emission, diarrhea, pain in

POINT	TRANSLATION	LOCATION	INDICATION
SP9 con't.			sexual organs, irregualar menstruation, menopause, and impotence.
SP10 Kekkai Xuehai	Ocean of Blood	2 sun superior to superior border of the patella.	Gynecological ailments, irregular menstruation, bleeding, menopause, dysmenorrhea, leukorrhea (discharge), knee pain, body fluid retention, eczema, and urticaria.
SP11 Kimon Jimen	Gate of Basket or Gate of Winnower	Slightly inferior to midpoint between medial superior ridge of patella and superior ridge of symphysis. 6 sun above SP10 – $8/19$ of the way between patella and pubic symphysis.	Hernia, swollen inguinal lymph, and urinary retention. Also, pain and paralysis of the lower extremities.
SP12 Shomon Chongmen	Gate of Pouring or Gate of Rushing	Superior to the lateral end of the inguinal groove, on the lateral side of the femoral artery, at the level of the upper border of the symphysis pubis, 3.5 sun lateral to CV2.	Digestive disorder, hernia, abdominal pain, and swollen lymph.
SP13 Fusha Fushe	Palace of Dwelling	.7 sun above SP12, 4 sun lateral to the point between CV2 and CV3.	Digestive disorder, hernia, abdominal pain, and swollen lymph.
SP14 Fukketsu Fujie	Abdominal Knot	3 sun above ST13, 4 sun lateral to CV7.	Abdominal pain, hernia, diarrhea, constipation, colic pain, hardness in the abdomen, and retention of urine.
SP15 Daio Daheng	Big Horizontal	4 sun lateral to the center of the umbilicus, on the mammary line.	Constipation, indigestion, pain in the epigastric region, intestinal paralysis, worms in the intestine.
SP16 Fukauai Fuai	Abdominal Sorrow	3 sun above SP15.	Intestinal ailments, diarrhea, and constipation.

12

POINT	TRANSLATION	LOCATION	INDICATION
SP17 Shokutoku Shidou	Food Cavity	In the fifth intercostal space, 6 sun lateral to CV16.	Pain and congestion, (intercostal neuralgia) in the chest.
SP18 Tenkei Tianxi	Celestial Brook	In the fourth intercostal space, 2 sun lateral to ST17, 6 sun lateral to CV17.	Gastrointestinal ailments, numbness and weakness of the feet. Also, breast ailments, (deficiency of lactation), coughing.
SP19 Kyokyo Xiongxiang	Village of the Chest	In the third intercostal space, 2 sun lateral to ST16, 6 sun lateral to CV18.	Fullness and pain in the chest.
SP20 Shuei Zhourong	Surrounding Prosperity	In the second intercostal space, 2 sun lateral to ST15, 6 sun lateral to CV19.	Pain in the chest, neuralgia, respiratory ailments, and coughing.
SP21 Taiho Dabao	Big Wrapping {The Great Connecting Channel Point}	In the sixth intercostal space, 6 sun below the middle of the axilla – it is half way between the axilla and the tip of the 11th rib.	Pain in the chest, neuralgia, respiratory ailments, and coughing.

HEART CHART

POINT	TRANSLATION	LOCATION	INDICATION
H1 Kyokusen Juquan	Extreme Spring or Highest Spring	At the center of the axillary artery – extend the arm and at the tip of the crease where the pulse is perceived.	Cardiac pain, stiffness in arms or shoulders, axillary body odor, and hysteria.
H2 Seirei Qingling	Blue Spirit	3 sun superior to HT3.	Pain in the shoulder and arm, also chest pain.
H3 Shokai Shaohai	Little Sea {Water Element}	Medial aspect of the medial epicondyle of the humerus – bend the elbow, H3 is at the tip of the medial cubital crease.	Cardiac pain and ailments, dizziness, tinnitus, vomiting, stiff neck, shoulder numbness, pain in the arms, elbow pain

POINT	TRANSLATION	LOCATION	INDICATION
H3 con't.			(ulnar side), hand tremors, psychosis, neurasthenia and madness.
H4 Reido **Lingdao**	Spiritual Root or Spiritual Channel {Metal Element}	.5 sun superior to H5	Cardiac pain, psychosis, hysteria, pain in the ulnar side of the arms and wrist.
H5 Tsuri **Tongli**	Reaching Miles {Connecting Point}	.5 sun superior to H6.	Psychosis, hysterical aphasia, cardiac pain, palpitations, coughing, dizziness, and pain in the ulnar side of arms and wrist.
H6 Ingeki **Yinxi**	Narrow Space of Yin {Cleft Point}	.5 sun superior to H7.	Neurasthenia, hysteria, palpitations, night sweating, and pain in the ulnar side of the arm and wrist.
H7 Shinmon **Shenmen**	Gate of God {Earth Element & Source Point}	On the ulnar aspect of the wrist at the radial side of the flexor carpi ulnar tendon, on the crease.	Heart murmur, thirst, schizophrenia, insomnia, imbecility, fever, wrist pain, yellow eyes, epilepsy, and amnesia (poor memory).
H8 Shofu **Shaofu**	Little Palace {Fire Element}	Palmar aspect of the hand between fourth and fifth metacarpal bone – clench fist, H8 is at the tip of the fifth finger.	Palpitation, noisiness and chest pains, numbness in elbows, warm palms, and dysuria (difficult urination).
H9 Shosho **Shaochong**	Little Rushing {Wood Element}	On radial side of small finger, .1 sun proximal to the corner of the nail.	Palpitations, acute chest pain, fainting, and apoplectic coma.

SMALL INTESTINE CHART

POINT	TRANSLATION	LOCATION	INDICATION
SI1 Shotaku Shaoze	Little Marsh {Metal Element}	On ulnar side of small finger, about .1 sun proximal to the corner of the nail.	Fever, dryness in mouth, headache, sore throat, cloudiness of cornea.
SI2 Zenkoku Qiangu	Front Valley {Water Element}	On the ulnar side of the finger, distal to the metacarpalphalangeal joint.	Headache, and tinnitus.
SI3 Gokei Houxi	Back Brook {Wood Element}	On the ulnar side of small finger, proximal to the metacarpalphalangeal joint – clench the hand, SI3 is located at the tip of the crease.	Stiff neck, acute sprain of lower back, intercostal neuralgia, seizures, psychosis, hysteria, and hearing diffculties.
SI4 Wankotsu Wangu	The Wrist Bone {Source Point}	On the ulnar side of the wrist, in the cavity between the base of the fifth metacarpal bone and the triquetral bone.	Wrist pain on the ulanr side, headache, neck rigidity, cloudiness of cornea, and ear ailments such as, tinnitus, infections and deafness.
SI5 Yokuku Yanggu	The Sunny Valley {Fire Element}	On ulnar side of the wrist in the depression between the styloid process of the ulnar and triquetral bone.	Dizziness, deafness, swelling in the neck and jaw, and epilepsy.
SI6 Yoro Yanglao	Nourishing Old {Cleft Point}	On the middle of the cavity of the tip of the styloid process of the ulnar – put the palm on the chest, you can find the cavity on the process.	Pain in the ulnar side of wrist and arm, pain in shoulder and back, blurring of eyes, and hearing difficulty.
SI7 Shisei Zhizheng	A Straight Support or Branch to the Correct {Connecting Point}	On ulnar aspect of forearm, 5 sun superior to the wrist.	Pain and weakness of the arms, and posterior shouders, also for feverish conditions.
SI8 Shokai Xiaohai	A Small Ocean {Earth Element}	At the cavity of the cubital joint in between the olecranon of the ulnar and tip of the medial epicondyle of the humerus.	Pain in the elbow joint on ulnar side, shoulders and back, heart problems, epileptic seizure, and swollen cheeks.

15

POINT	TRANSLATION	LOCATION	INDICATION
SI9 Kentei Jianzhen	The Virtue of the Shoulder	1 sun superior to the tip of the posterior tip of the axillary skin fold.	Pain in the scapular and arm, frozen shoulder, tinnitus, deafness, and headache.
SI10 Jyuyu Naoshu	Healing Point of Upper Arm	Directly superior to SI9 under the scapular spine.	Pain, weakness, and immobility of the arms and shoulder.
SI11 Tenso Tianzong	Celestial Ancestor	In the infrascapula fossa about 1/3 of the way from the superior aspect of the scapular spine to the inferior angle of the scapula. SI11 is located in the middle of the depression, when you bring the arm to the back.	Chest pain, high blood pressure, pain in the arms, chest, shoulder, and scapula.
SI12 Heifu Bingfeng	Holding the Wind	In the middle of the superior aspect of the scapular spine, directly above SI11.	Numbness and aching of the upper extremities, neck, shoulder, and shoulder blade, also difficulties in raising the arms.
SI13 Kyokuen Quyuan	Curved Wall	On the medial extremity of the scapular spine, also about midway between SI10, and spinous process of the second TV.	Pain and stiffness of the scapula, shoulder, and shoulder blade.
SI14 Kengaiyu Jianwaishu	The Healing Point for the Outside of the Shoulder	3 sun lateral to the spine, at the level of the first and second TV, 2 sun lateral to UB11.	Rigidity and pain of the neck and shoulder, and headaches.
SI15 Kenchuyu Juanzhongshu	The Healing Point for the Center of the Shoulder	2 sun lateral to the spine at the level between the seventh CV and the first TV, which is GV14.	Headache, cough, asthma, rigidity and pain in the neck and shoulder.
SI16 Tenso Tianchuang	Celstial Window	Lateral to LI18, at the posterior border of the sternocleidomastoid.	Earache, poor hearing, sore throat and rigidity and pain in the neck.
SI17 Tenyo Tianrong	The Face of the Heaven	1 sun superior to SI16 and posterior to ST6 at the anterior border of the sternocleidomastoid.	Tinnitus, poor hearing, swelling and pain in the neck, throat, and jaw problems.

POINT	TRANSLATION	LOCATION	INDICATION
SI18 Kanryo Quanliao	Seam at Cheek or Seam at Bone Hole	Lateral to LI20 and directly inferior to the outer canthus of eye, in the middle of depression of the zygoma.	Toothache, pain, spasm, numbness, weakness of facial muscles, also facial and trigeminal nerve problems.
SI19 Chogu Tinggong	Palace of Listening	Directly anterior to the center of the tragus. Open the mouth, SI19 is in the middle of the triangular cavity.	Ear problems, headache, and facial and trigeminal nerve problems, also TMJ.

URINARY BLADDER CHART

POINT	TRANSLATION	LOCATION	INDICATION
UB1 Seimei Jingming	Clear Light or Bright Pupil	.1 sun medial and superior to the inner canthus (corner of eye), between the bridge of the nose and the tear duct.	Eye ailments, congestion, weak or unclear vision, mucus, and nasal congestion.
UB2 Sanchiku Zanzhu	Gathering Bamboo	In the cavity of supraorbital notch at the medial end of the eyebrow.	Eye ailments, weak eyesight, minor glaucoma, and minor cataract.
UB3 Bisho Meichong	Pouring to the Eyebrow	3.5 sun directly superior to BL2 – .5 sun superior to the frontal hairline, halfway between BL4 and GV24.	Headache, nasal congestion, epileptic seizures, and dizziness.
UB4 Kyokusa Quchai	Discrepancy at the Curve	1.5 sun lateral to GV24.	Headache, nasal congestion, nasal bleeding, and eye ailments.
UB5 Gosho Wuchu	Fifth Spot	.5 sun superior to BL4, 1.5 sun lateral to GV23.	Headache, dizziness, and epileptic seizure.
UB6 Shoko Chengguang	Receiving Light	1.5 sun superior to BL5.	Headache, common cold, nasal congestion, blurring of vision, and dizziness.

POINT	TRANSLATION	LOCATION	INDICATION
UB7 Tsuten Tongtian	Attending Heaven	1.5 sun superior to BL6.	Headache, common cold, nasal congestion, blurring of vision, and dizziness.
UB8 Rakkyaku Luoque	Broken Channel	1.5 sun superior to BL7.	Headache, dizziness, psychosis, and vomiting.
UB9 Gyokuchin Yuzhen	Pillow of Jade or Occipital Bone	1.5 sun lateral to GV17 at the level of TH19 and GB19.	Headache, dizziness, and poor eyesight.
UB10 Tenchu Tianzhu	Pillar of the Heaven	1.5 sun lateral to GV15, approximately 1/3 of the way between GV15 and GB12.	Headache, nasal congestion, heaviness in the head, sore throat, dizziness, rigidity and pain in the neck or shoulders.
UB11 Diajyo Dazhu	A Big Weaver's Shuttle	1.5 sun lateral to GV14, which is between TV1 and TV2.	Common cold, headache, fever, pain and rigidity of the shoulder. One of the eight influential points for bone disease.
UB12 Fumon Fengmen	The Gate of Wind	1.5 sun lateral to the cavity between TV2 and TV3.	Common cold, cough, headache, fever, pain and rigidity of neck and shoulders.
UB13 Haiyu Feishu	Healing Point for the Lung	1.5 sun lateral to GV12, which is between TV3 and TV4.	Common cold, coughing, chills, fever and sinus, allergies, respiratory problems, discomfort and pain in the lung, difficulty in breathing, stiff neck and shoulders. Good for regulating the Metal Element – dryness, skin, and sadness.
UB14 Kecchin Yu Jueyinshu	Healing Point for Pericardium	1.5 sun lateral to the cavity between TV4 and TV5.	Irregular heart beat, palpitations, chest pain, stiffnes and aching between shoulder blades, hysteria, and hypertension.

POINT	TRANSLATION	LOCATION	INDICATION
UB15 Shin Yu Xinshu	Healing Point for the Heart	1.5 sun lateral to GV11, which is between TV5 an TV6.	Circulatory problems, low/high blood pressure, hypertension stroke, palpitation, discomfort and pain in the chest, psychosis, poor memory, and epileptic seizures.
UB16 Tokuyu Dushu	Healing Point for the Governing Vessel	1.5 sun lateral to GV10, which is between TV6 and TV7.	Cardiac pain, hiccup, breast ailments, and abdominal pain.
UB17 Kakuyu Geshu	Healing Point for the Diaphram	1.5 sun lateral to GV9, between TV7 and TV8.	Hiccup, cough, night sweating, anemia, spasm of esophagus, abdominal pain, bleeding. One of the eight influencial points for the blood.
UB18 Kan Yu Ganshu	Healing Point for the Liver	1.5 sun lateral to GV8, between TV9 and TV10.	Distention below ribs, digestive problems, abdominal pain and discomfort, Liver and Gall Bladder ailments, nausea, chest pain on the side (hypochondraic region), enlarged liver, muscle troubles such as cramps, degeneration, eye problems, yellow eyes, turned up eyes, and weak vision.
UB19 Tan Yu Danshu	Healing Point for the Gall Bladder	1.5 sun lateral to GV7, between TV10 and TV11.	Distention below ribs, digestive problems, abdominal pain and discomfort, Liver and Gall Bladder ailments, nausea, chest pain on the side (hypochondraic region), enlarged liver, muscle troubles such as cramps, degeneration, eye problems, yellow eyes, turned up eyes, and weak vision.

POINT	TRANSLATION	LOCATION	INDICATION
UB20 Hi Yu Pi Shu	Healing Point for the Spleen	1.5 sun lateral to GV6, between TV11 and TV12.	Obesity or losing weight, fatigue, aching joints, digestive troubles, discomfort in abdomen, acidity, distention, belching, vomiting, diarrhea, jaundice, diabetes, edema, and a dropped stomach.
UB21 I Yu Weishu	Healing Point for the Stomach	1.5 sun lateral to the depression between TV12 and LV1.	Obesity or losing weight, fatigue, aching joints, digestive troubles, discomfort in abdomen, acidity, distention, belching, vomiting, diarrhea, jaundice, diabetes, edema, and a dropped stomach.
UB22 Shansho Yu Sanjiao Shu	Healing Point for the Triple Heater	1.5 sun lateral to GV5, between LV1 and LV2.	Digestive ailments, vomiting, diarrhea, abdominal pain and gurgling, distention, backache, and urinary retention.
UB23 Jin Yu Shen Shu	Healing Point for the Kidney	1.5 sun lateral to GV4, between LV2 and LV3.	Hot flashes to the head, draining of body fluid, edema, reproductive, gynecological, and uro genital ailments, irregular menstruation, losing sperm without intercourse, impotence, emaciation (becoming thin and feeble), exhaustion, tinnitus, difficulty in hearing, low backache, sciatica, knee pain, coldness, bronchial asthma, and chronic diarrhea.
UB24 Kikaiyu Qihaishu	Healing Point for the Ocean of Ki	1.5 sun lateral to the depression between LV3 and LV4.	Lower back pain, irregular menstruation, diarrhea, constipation, and abdominal pain.
UB25 Daicho Yu Dachagshu	Healing Point for the Large Intestine	1.5 sun lateral to GV3, between LV4 and LV5.	Digestive problems, abdominal pain, diarrhea, constipation, gurgling colon, hemorrhoids, gynecological problems, lower backache, and controls food transformation.

POINT	TRANSLATION	LOCATION	INDICATION
UB26 Kangen Yu **Guanyuanshu**	Healing Point for the Primary Barrier	1.5 sun lateral to the depression, between LV5 and Sac.1.	Low backache (lumbar), sciatica, abdominal pain, diarrhea, and distention of the abdomen.
UB27 Sho Cho Yu **Xiaochangshu**	Healing Point for the Small Intestine	1.5 sun lateral to the first medial sacral crest, .75 sun lateral to UB31.	Lower abdominal pain, distention, diarrhea, constipation, uroreproductive pain, pain in the lumbosacral, sacroilliac region, sciatica.
UB28 Boko Yu **Pang Guang Shu**	Healing Point for the Bladder	1.5 sun lateral to the second medial sacral crest, .75 sun lateral to UB32.	Urogenital, excretory problems, irregular urination, painful and difficult urination, lower digestive problems, controls water metabolism, pain in the lumbo sacral, sacroilliac region, and sciatica.
UB29 Chu Rho Yu **Zhonglu Shu**	Healing Point for Middle Buttocks	1.5 sun lateral to the third medial sacral crest, .75 sun lateral to UB33.	Pain in the lumbosacral region, sciatica, and intestinal ailments.
UB30 Hakukan Yu **Baihuan Shu**	Healing Point for White Ring or Jade Ring	1.5 sun lateral to the fourth medial sacral crest, .75 sun lateral to UB34.	Pain in the lumbosacral region, sciatica, pelvic infection, seminal emission, irregular menstruation, leukorrhea, and hernia.
UB31 Jyo Rho **Shangliao**	The Upper Hole	In the first dorsal sacral, .75 sun lateral to the medial sacral crest.	Sciatica pain in the lumbosacral sacroilliac region, gynecological ailments (irregular menstruation, inducing labor, leukorrhea), reproductive ailments, impotence, and hemorrhoids.
UB32 Jirho **Ciliao**	The Second Hole	In the second dorsal sacral foramen, .75 sun lateral to the second medial sacral crest.	Sciatica pain in the lumbosacral sacroilliac region, gynecological ailments (irregular menstruation, inducing labor, leukorrhea), reproductive ailments, impotence, and hemorrhoids.

21

POINT	TRANSLATION	LOCATION	INDICATION
UB33 Churho Zhongliao	The Center Hole	In the 3rd dorsal sacral foramen, .75 sun lateral to the third medial sacral crest.	Sciatica pain in the lumbo-sacral sacroilliac region, gynecological ailments (irregular menstruation, inducing labor, leukorrhea), reproductive ailments, impotence, and hemorrhoids.
UB34 Gerho Xialiao	The Lower Hole	In the 4th dorsal sacral foramen, .75 sun lateral to the 4th medial sacral crest.	Sciatica pain in the lumbo-sacral sacroilliac region, gynecological ailments (irregular menstruation, reproductive ailments, impotence, and hemorrhoids.
UB35 Eyo Huiyang	The Meeting of Yang	.5 sun lateral to GV1, in the tip of the coccyx.	Sciatica pain in the lumbo-sacral sacroilliac region, gynecological ailments (irregular menstruation, inducing labor, leukorrhea, impotence, and hemorrhoids).
UB36 Shofu Chengfu	Receiving Support	Mid-point of the gluteal fold, directly, inferior to the tip of the ishcial tuberosity (sitting bone).	Constipation, sciatica, backache, hemiplagia, poor urination, and pain in the hamstring.
UB37 Yinmon Yinmen	The Gate of Abundance	6 sun inferior to UB50.	Low backache, difficulty in bending the back, and sciatica.
UB38 Fugeki Fuxi	The Floating in the Narrow Space	1 sun superior to UB39.	Pain or weakness of the knee and hamstring, also sciatica.
UB39 Iyo Weiyang	Bending Yang	1 sun lateral to UB40.	Sciatica, knee pain, lower back and hamstring pain, hemmorhoids, also constipation.
UB40 Ichu Weizhong	Disputing at the Center or Bending Middle {Earth Element}	Mid-point of the patellar fascia – located behind the knee in the middle of the crease when the knee is bent, pulse is perceived and has electrifying sensation.	Fever in the limbs, pain in the low back, sciatica, knee ailments, weakness of lower extemities, spasm of gastrocnemius. One of the four major points for back pain.

POINT	TRANSLATION	LOCATION	INDICATION
UB41 Fubun **Fufen**	Attaching and Dividing	1.5 sun next to UB12, between the second and third TV.	Pain and rigidity of the shoulder, neck and upper back, also numbness of the arms.
UB42 Hakko **Pohu**	The Door of the Inferior Soul or Fighting Spirit	1.5 sun next to UB13, between the third and fourth TV.	Pain and rigidity of the shoulder, neck and upper back, respiratory ailments (coughing, common cold).
UB43 Kokoyu **Gaohuang-shu**	Healing Point for the Fatty Tissue of Invisible Pericardium	1.5 sun lateral to UB14, between the fourth and fifth TV.	Psychosis, neurosis, and degenerative diseases, chronic degenerative disease of respiratory, cardiac, and digestive systems.
UB44 Shindo **Shentang**	The Hall of God	1.5 sun lateral to UB15, between the fifth and sixth TV.	Cardiac ailments, respiratory ailments, and pain on the shoulder blade.
UB45 Iki **Yixi**	Moan of Happiness or Laughing Sound	1.5 sun lateral to UB16, between sixth and seventh TV.	Cardiac ailments, respiratory ailments, and pain in the shoulder blade.
UB46 Kakkan **Geguan**	The Barrier of the Diaphram	1.5 sun lateral to UB17, between the seventh and eigth TV.	Intercostal pain, spasm of the esophagus, and pain in the shoulder blade.
UB47 Konmon **Hunmen**	The Gate of the Soul	1.5 sun lateral to UB18, between the ninth and the tenth TV.	Distention below ribs, digestive problems, abdominal pain and discomfort, Liver and Gall Bladder ailments, nausea, chest pain on the side (hypochondraic region), enlarged liver, muscle problems such as cramps, or degeneration.
UB48 Yoko **Yanggang**	The Principal Yang	1.5 sun lateral to UB19, between the tenth and eleventh TV.	Distention below ribs, digestive problems, abdominal pain and discomfort, Liver and Gall Bladder ailments, nausea,

POINT	TRANSLATION	LOCATION	INDICATION
UB48 con't.			chest pain on the side (hypochondraic region), enlarged liver, and back pain.
UB49 Icha Yishe	The Dwelling of the Idea	1.5 sun lateral to UB20, between the eleventh and the twelfth TV.	Obesity or losing weight, fatigue, aching joints, digestive problems, discomfort in abdomen, acidity, distention, belching, vomiting, diarrhea and back pain.
UB50 Iso Weicang	The Stomach Store House	1.5 sun lateral to UB21, between the twelfth and 1st LV.	Digestive ailments, diarrhea, abdominal pain and gurgling, distention, and backache
UB51 Komon Huangmen	The Gate of an Invisible Organ	1.5 sun lateral to UB22, between first and second LV.	Digestive ailments, constipation, diarrhea, abdominal pain and gurgling, distention, backache, and urinary retention.
UB52 Shishitsu Zhishi	The Room of Will	1.5 sun lateral to UB23, between the second and third LV.	Hot flashes to the head, draining of body fluid, edema, gynecological, and uro genital ailments, irregular menstruation, losing sperm without intercourse, impotence, emaciation (becoming thin and feeble), exhaustion, tinnitus, difficulty in hearing, low backache, sciatica, and knee pain.
UB53 Hoko Baohuang	Uterus of the Invisible Area or Wombs	1.5 sun lateral to UB28, second sacral crest.	Urogenital, excretory problems, irregular urination, painful and difficult urination, lower digestive problems, diarrhea, constipation, gynecological problems, pain in the lumbosacral, sacroilliac region, and sciatica.

POINT	TRANSLATION	LOCATION	INDICATION
UB54 Hippen Zhibian	The Order of Boundary	1.5 sun lateral to UB30, fourth medial sacral crest.	Pain in the lumbosacral region, sacral region, sciatica, pelvic, infection, seminal emission, irregular menstration, leukorrhea, hernia, and difficult urination.
UB55 Goyo Heyang	Merging of Yang	2 sun inferior to UB40.	Low backache, sciatica, cramp of gastrocnemius, and numbness and paralysis of lower extremity.
UB56 Shokin Chengjin	Receiving Muscle or Supporting Muscle	3 sun inferior to BL55.	Low backache, headache, weakness, pain the legs.
UB57 Shozan Chengshan	Receiving Mountains or Supporting Mountains	Halfway between UB40 and UB60, 8 sun inferior to UB40, sooth the skin carefully, UB57 is where the muscle texture changes.	Constipation, hemorrhoids, sciatica, lower backache, and spasm of the gastrocnemius muscle.
UB58 Hiyo Feiyang	Flying Yang {Connecting Point}	1 sun lateral to UB57, also 1 sun inferior to UB57 (2nd opinion).	Hemorrhoids, swollen leg, dizzinesss, eye ache, epilepsy, fatigue, and nasal congestion.
UB59 Fuyo Fuyang	Instepping Yang	3 sun superior to UB60.	Heaviness of the head, headache, low backache, and pain in the ankle.
UB60 Konron Kunlun	Elder Brother's Store House or Name of the Mountains {Fire Element}	Halfway between medial posterior border of external malleolus (ankle bone), and the achilles tendon (use tip of the thumb).	Headache, lower backache, nose bleed, pain the shoulders, pain in the back, swelling and pain in the genital organs. Acupuncture is contraindicated during pregnancy.
UB61 Bokushin Pushen	Serve and Consult	1.5 sun inferior to UB60.	Weakness of lower extremities, pain in the ankle, leg and lower back.
UB62 Shinmyaku Shenmai	Extended Vessels	.5 sun inferior to the inferior border of the external malleolus.	Pain in the ankle, leg and lower back, headache, epilepsy, and dizziness.

POINT	TRANSLATION	LOCATION	INDICATION
UB63 Kinmon Jinmen	Golden Gate {Cleft Point}	Halfway between UB62 and UB64.	Pain in the ankle, legs and lower back, weakness of lower extremities, epileptic seizure, and children's convulsion.
UB64 Keikotsu Jinggu	Capital Bone or Metatarsal Bone {Source Point}	In the depression on the lateral side of the dorsum of the foot, below the tuberosity of the fifth metatarsal bone.	Headache, epileptic seizure, and neck rigidity.
UB65 Sokkoku Shuju	Bundled Bone {Wood Element}	At the corner, proximal and inferior to the fifth metatarsalphalangeal joint.	Psychosis, mental confusion, headache, epileptic seizure, neck rigidity and pain in the lower extremity.
UB66 Tsukoku Tonggu	Going Through Valley {Water Element}	At the corner, anterior and inferior to the fifth metatarsalphalangeal joint.	Psychosis, mental confusion, headache, epileptic seizure, neck rigidity, dizziness, and nasal bleeding.
UB67 Shiin Zhiyin	Reaching Yin {Metal Element}	About .1 sun proximal to the lateral base of the fifth toenail.	Headache, neck rigidity, difficult labor, malposition of the fetus by moxibustion therapy.

KIDNEY CHART

POINT	TRANSLATION	LOCATION	INDICATION
K1 Yusen Yongquan	Bubbling Spring {Wood Element}	On the sole, between the second and third toe – about $1/3$ of the way from the anterior plantar line. K1 is on the line between K2 and the base of the small toe.	Edema, blurring of the eyes, dizziness, cardiac ailment (palpitation, weakness, debility), cold or warm foot, kidney problems, shock, seizure, stroke, psychosis, mental illness, infantile convulsion, and headache.

POINT	TRANSLATION	LOCATION	INDICATION
K2 Nenkoku **Rangu**	A Light Valley or A Blazing Valley {Fire Element}	Anterior and inferior to navicular bone, about the middle of plantar – bend the toes, K2 is located in the middle of the arch, in the depression inferior to the tuberosity of the navicular bone.	Gynecological problems, irregular menstruation, infertility, prolapse of the uterus, sore throat, and bladder problems.
K3 Taikei **Taixi**	Great Brook or Grand Canyon {Earth Element and Source Point}	In the depression, midpoint between the tip of the medial malleolus and the achilles tendon – opposite to UB60.	Sore throat, phlegm, chills, coughing, kidney problems, irregular menstruation, impotence, lower back pain, and weak hearing.
K4 Taisho **Dazhong**	Big Bell {Connecting Point}	.5 sun inferior and posterior to K3.	Sore throat, asthma, pain in the heel, pain in the lumbosacral region, neurasthenia, and hysteria.
K5 Suisen **Shuiquan**	Water Spring {Cleft Point}	1 sun directly inferior to K3.	Gynecological ailments such as irregular menstruation, dysmenorrhea, amenorrhea, and prolapse of the uterus, also for dysuria, and blurring of the vision.
K6 Shokai **Zhaohai**	The Shining Sea	1 sun directly inferior to the tip of the medial malleolus.	Sore throat, irregular menstruation, prolapse of the uterus, epilepsy, and insomnia.
K7 Fukuryu **Fuliu**	Returning Stream {Metal Element}	2 sun superior to K3.	Weak viatality, weak feet, low back pain, night sweats, spontaneous sweating, excretory ailments, (kidney and urinary tract).
K8 Koshin **Jiaoxin**	Exchange of Messages	.5 sun anterior to K7 – 2 sun superior to K3.	Gynecological ailments such as irregular menstruation, uterine bleeding, prolapse of the uterus, and pain and swelling of the testes.

POINT	TRANSLATION	LOCATION	INDICATION
K9 Chikuhin **Zhubin**	House of Guest or Building of Dune	2 sun superior to SP6, and 5 sun superior to K3.	Toxin, (fetus, food, drugs), hernia spasm of the gastrocnemius muscle, excretory and pelvic inflammatory ailemt, psychosis, and seizures.
K10 Yinkoku **Yingu**	Valley of Yin or Deep Valley {Water Element}	Medial corner of the knee in the middle of the depression between tendons – bend the knee, K10 is in between the semimembranosus and semitendinosus.	Impotence, urogenital, reproductive ailments, and knee problems.
K11 Okoku **Henggu**	The Transverse Bone or The Pubic Bone	5 sun below the umbilicus, .5 sun lateral to CV2 on the symphysis pubis.	Lower abdominal pain, hernia, impotence, and urogenital ailments.
K12 Taikaku **Dahe**	The Big Clarity	4 sun below the umbilicus, .5 sun lateral to CV3.	Pain in the external genitalia, seminal emissions, and leukorrhea.
K13 Kiketsu **Qixue**	A Cavity of Ki	3 sun below the umbilicus, .5 sun lateral to CV4.	Irregular menstruation, leukorrhea, infertilty, and diarrhea.
K14 Shiman **Siman**	Full in Four Corners	2 sun below the umbilicus, .5 sun lateral to CV5.	Infertility, irregular menstruation, postpartum, and abdominal pain.
K15 Chuchu **Zhongzhu**	Flowing to the Center	1 sun below the umbilicus. .5 sun lateral to CV7.	Abdominal pain, irregular menstruation, low back pain, and constipation.
K16 Koyu **Huangshu**	Healing Point of the Invisible	Same level as the umbilicus, .5 sun lateral to CV8.	Gastro-intestinal ailments such as, diarrhea, constipation, and colic.
K17 Shokyoku **Shangqu**	The Sound of "Sho" Note in the Music	2 sun above the umbilicus, and .5 sun lateral to CV10.	Gastro-intestinal ailments such as, diarrhea, constipation, and colic.

POINT	TRANSLATION	LOCATION	INDICATION
K18 Sekikan **Shiguan**	The Barrier of the Stone	3 sun above the umbilicus, .5 sun lateral to CV11.	Gastrointestinal ailments, hiccups, and spasms of the esophagus.
K19 Yinto **Yindu**	The Capital of Yin	4 sun above the umbilicus, .5 sun lateral to CV12.	Abdominal pain, distention, and respiratory ailments.
K20 Hara No Tsukoku **Tonggu**	Going Through Valley in the Abdomen	5 sun above the umbilicus, .5 sun lateral to CV13.	Gastro-intestinal ailments, nausea, vomiting, diarrhea, abdominal pain, and distention.
K21 Yumon **Youmen**	The Hidden Gate	6 sun above the umbilicus, and .5 sun lateral to CV14.	Gastro-intestinal ailments, nausea, vomiting, diarrhea, abdominal pain, and distention.
K22 Horo **Bulang**	Corridor for Walking	In the fifth intercostal space, 2 sun lateral to CV16.	Respiratory ailments, and chest pain.
K23 Shinpu **Shenfeng**	Territory of God or Divine Seal	In the fourth intercostal space, 2 sun lateral to CV17.	Respiratory ailments, chest pain, and breast ailment.
K24 Reikyo **Ling Xu**	Ruins of the Spirit	In the third intercostal space, 2 sun lateral to CV18.	Respiratory ailments, chest pain, and breast ailment.
K25 Shinzo **Shencang**	Storing God	In the second intercostal space, 2 sun lateral to CV19.	Respiratory ailments, and chest pain.
K26 Wakuchu **Yuzhong**	Amid Elegance or Lively Center	In the first intercostal space, 2 sun lateral to CV20.	Respiratory ailments, and chest pain.
K27 Yufu **Shufu**	The Palace of Healing Point	In the depression on the lower border of the clavicle, 2 sun lateral to CV21.	Respiratory ailments, and chest pain.

POINT	TRANSLATION	LOCATION	INDICATION
HC1 Tenchi Tianchi	The Pond of the Heaven or Celestial Pool	1 sun lateral to the nipple in the fourth intercostal space.	Heartache, chest ache, pain and swelling below the axilla.
HC2 Tensen Tianquan	The Celestial Spring	2 sun inferior to the tip of the anterior axillary fold, between two heads of the biceps brachii.	Cough, pain in the chest, palpitation, pain in the back and the medial side of the arm.
HC3 Kyokutaku Quze	A Curved Marsh {Water Element}	Middle of the transverse cubit crease – flex the elbow, HC3 is in the middles of the cavity, ulnar side of the biceps brachii.	Pain in the elbow, heartache, feverish body, thirstiness, flash to the head, tremor of the arms and hands.
HC4 Gekimon Ximen	Gate of Narrow Space {Cleft Point}	5 sun superior to the transverse crease of the wrist (HC7).	Special point for stopping bleeding, of the nose, lung, and stomach, palpitations, chest pain, epilepsy, psychosis, hysteria shock (someone easily shocked or astonished), misanthropy (hatred of mankind).
HC5 Kanshi Jianshi	Using the Space or A Messenger in Between {Metal Point}	3 sun superior to HC7, between the radius and ulnar.	Pain in the arm along the median nerve, and chest pain.
HC6 Naikan Neiguan	The Inner Barrier {Connecting Point}	2 sun superior to HC7.	Digestive ailments, nausea, motion sickness, vomiting, palpitations, chest pains, fainting, seizure, red eyes, hysteria, psychosis, and pain the arm and wrist.
HC7 Tairyo Daling	Big Tomb {Earth Element and Source Point}	Midpoint of the transverse crease of the wrist, in the depression between palmaris longus and flexor radialis.	Pain in the wrist, warm palms, chest ache, headache, red eyes, dryness in the mouth, short temper, lunatic speech, numbness or pain in the third and fourth fingers.

POINT	TRANSLATION	LOCATION	INDICATION
HC8 Rokyu Laogong	The Palace of Labor {Fire Element}	In the middle of the palm between the second and third metacarpal bone – on the transverse crease of palm.	Cardiac pain, heat or excessive sweating of the palms, psychosis, mental illness, hysteria, frightfulness, and fainting.
HC9 Chusho Zhongchong	Pouring Through the Center {Wood Element}	On the radial side of the third finger, .1 sun posterior to the corner of the nail – or in the center of the tip of the middle finger.	Special point for acute shock, epyleptic coma, heat exhaustion, chest pain, stiffness of the tongue causing speech trouble, and infantile convulsion.

TRIPLE HEATER CHART

POINT	TRANSLATION	LOCATION	INDICATION
TH1 Kansho Guanchong	Barrier for Rushing {Metal Element}	On the dorsal aspect of the hand, on the ulnar side of the fourth finger, .1 sun posterior to the corner of the nail.	Headache, dizziness, congestion in the eyes, fever, sore throat, and stiff tongue.
TH2 Ekimon Yenmen	Gate for Fluid {Water Element}	On the ulnar side of the fourth finger distal to the metacarpalphalangeal joint.	Numbness and pain in the hand, arms, and fingers, headache, and congestion in the eyes.
TH3 Chusho Zhongzhu	Central Islet {Wood Point}	On the ulnar side of the fourth finger proximal to the metacarpalphalangeal joint.	Headache, ear ailments such as tinnitus, and difficulty in hearing, also sore throat, fever, and congestion in the eyes.
TH4 Yochi Yangchi	Sunny Pond or Pool {Source Point}	On the dorsal aspect of the wrist, in the depression on the transverse crease.	Dryness in mouth, intermittent fever, pain or weakness of the wrist, forearm, shoulder, and ulnar nerve, and tilted uterus. Special point to increase healing power for chronic disease.
TH5 Gaikan Waiguan	Barrier at Outide {Connecting Point}	2 sun superior to TH4, exactly the opposite side from HC6.	Fever, dizziness, eye problems, wrist pain (radial nerve and median nerve), febrile disease, headache, chest pain, weak hearing, and tinnitus.

POINT	TRANSLATION	LOCATION	INDICATION
TH6 Shiko **Zhigou**	A Branch of Ditch Between Radius and Ulna {Fire Element}	1 sun superior to TH5, between radius and ulna.	Pain in the chest, shoulder, arm, rib and axilia, weak hearing, and tinnitus.
TH7 Eso **Huizong**	Gathering of Ancestors' Ki {Cleft Point}	1 sun lateral to TH6, ulnar side.	Numbness and pain of the arm, along median nerve, epileptic seizures, and weak hearing.
TH8 Sanyoraku **Sanyangluo**	Three Yang Channels	1 sun superior to TH6.	Numbness and pain of the arm, shoulder, and back, seizure, difficult speech, and toothache.
TH9 Shitoku **Sidu**	Four Drains or Flow to Four Directions	6 sun inferior to TH10, 5 sun inferior to the olecranon.	Numbness and pain in the forearm, toothache, headache, dizziness, and neurasthenia.
TH10 Tensei **Tianjing**	Celestial Wall {Earth Element}	1 sun superior to the olecranon of ulnar – flex the elbow, TH10 is in the middle of the cavity above the head of the elbow.	Weakness of arms, deafness, sore throat, pain in the corner of eyes, pain behind the ears, coughing, pain in the neck, shoulder, arm, and elbow, and migraine headaches.
TH11 Seireien **Qingleng- yuan**	Clear and Cool Abyss	1 sun superior to TH10.	Pain in the neck, shoulder, elbow, and arms, and migraine headaches.
TH12 Shoreki **Xiaoluo**	Dissolved Lake	2 sun superior to TH11, between TH11 and TH13.	Pain in the neck, shoulder, arms, and radial nerve.
TH13 Jyue **Naohui**	Meeting at Upper Arm	2 sun superior to TH12, or 3 sun inferior to TH14.	Pain in the shoulder, arm, and radial nerve.
TH14 Kenryo **Jianliao**	Shoulder Bone or Shoulder Seam	On posterior inferior ridge of the acromion, 1 sun posterior to LI15.	Pain and weakness in upper arms and shoulder, hypertension, and excessive perspiration.

POINT	TRANSLATION	LOCATION	INDICATION
TH15 Tenryo **Tianliao**	Celestial Bone or A Tip of Scapula	Midway betwen GB21 and SI13, almost 1 sun posterior to GB21.	Stiffness and pain in the neck, shoulder, scapula, and arm, headache, high blood pressure, and palpitation.
TH16 Tenyo **Tianyou**	Celestial Window	Posterior and inferior to the mastoid process, midway between SI17 and UB10.	Neck rigidity, facial swelling, sudden hearing weakness, migraine headaches, blurring of vision, and sinus problems.
TH17 Eifu **Yixfeng**	Screen of Wind	Middle of depression, behind the ear lobe between mastoid process, and angle of mandible.	Ear and hearing ailments, swollen gland, facial nerve problems, neuralgia, paralysis, lower toothache, and painful jaw.
TH18 Keimyaku **Qimai**	Peripheral Blood Vessel	$1/3$ of the way from TH17 to TH20.	Ear and hearing ailments (tinnitus), and headaches.
TH19 Rosoku **Luxi**	Breathing of Skull	$2/3$ of the way from TH17 to TH20, it is about the same level as GB19, UB9, and GV17.	Ear and hearing ailments, headaches, and toothache.
TH20 Kakuson **Jiaosun**	Small Horn	At the tip of ear's apex on the line extended from GV20, GB17, and GB8.	Ear and hearing ailments, headaches, and toothache.
TH21 Jimon **Ermen**	Gate of Ear	Directly anterior to anterior incisure of the ear – open mouth TH21 is in the top of traingular cavity, slightly superior to the condylon process of mandible; pulse is perceived.	Ear and hearing ailments, facial and trigeminal nerve ailments (neuralgia and paralysis), headaches, and T.M.J.
TH22 Waryo **Heliao**	Harmony at Bone (Balance)	Anterior and superior to TH21, level with the roof of the auricle, by the you can palpate the beat of the superficial temporal artery.	Ear and hearing ailments, facial and trigeminal nerve ailments (neuralgia and paralysis), headaches, and T.M.J.
TH23 Shickikuku **Sizhukong**	Silk Bamboo or Hole of Silk Bamboo	On lateral end, outside of the eyebrow.	Eye and vision ailments, headaches, facial paralysis, dizzines, and twitching of the eyelid.

GALL BLADDER CHART

POINT	TRANSLATION	LOCATION	INDICATION
GB1 Doshiryo	Seam at the Pupil	.5 sun lateral to the outer canthus of eyes, on the lateral side of the orbit.	Eye and vision ailments, paralysis and neuralgia of the trigeminal and facial nerve, and headache.
GB2 Choe Tinghui	Collecting of Listening	Directly anterior to the tragal incisure of the ear – open the mouth GB2 is located at the bottom of the triangular cavity.	Ear and hearing ailments, eye and vision problems, lower toothache, paralysis and neuralgia of the trigeminal and facial nerve.
GB3 Jyokan Shangguan also Kyakushujin	Upper Barrier or Main Quest	In front of the ear, superior border of zygomatic arch, in the cavity opposite to ST7.	Ear and hearing ailments, toothache, facial paralysis, and painful jaw (T.M.J.).
GB4 Ganen Hanyan	Satiated Chin	In the hair of the temporal region, about $1/4$ of the way from ST8 to GB7.	Migraine headaches, pain in the eye and face, epileptic seizures, and convulsions.
GB5 Kenro Xuanlu	Suspended Skull	In the hair of the temporal region, about $1/2$ of the way from ST8 to GB7.	Migraine headaches, pain in the eye and face, and convulsions.
GB6 Kenri Xuanli	Suspended Reguation	In the hair of the temporal region, about $3/4$ of the way from ST8 to GB7.	Migraine headaches, pain in the eye and face, and convulsions.
GB7 Kyokuhin Qubin	Corner of the Hair	In the hair of the temporal region cut.	Eye ailments, pain in the cheek, spasms of the temporal region, and jaw, migraine headaches, and childhood convulsions.
GB8 Sokkoku Shuaigu	Leading Valley or Main Valley	About 1.5 sun superior to the apex auricle – it is found on the extended line between TH20 and GV20.	Migraine headaches, dizziness, and eye and vision ailments.

POINT	TRANSLATION	LOCATION	INDICATION
GB9 Tensho **Tianchong**	Celestial Rushing	Superior to the apex auricle, .5 sun posterior to GB8.	Migraine headaches, dizziness, and eye and vision ailments.
GB10 Fuhaku **Fubai**	Floating White	About $1/3$ of the way from GB9 to GB12.	Ear and hearing ailments, insomnia, pain and stiffness of the neck, swelling and pain of the cheek, toothache, and facial paralysis.
GB11 Atama No Kyoin **Qiaoyin**	Shady Hole of Head	About $2/3$ of the way from GB9 to GB12.	Ear and hearing ailments, insomnia, pain and stiffness of the neck, swelling and pain of the cheek, toothache, and facial paralysis.
GB12 Kankotsu **Wangu**	Bone at the End (Mastoid Process)	In the depression posterior and inferior to the mastoid process – drop head forward, GB12 is in the middle of the cavity behind the ears.	Ear and hearing ailments, neckache, headache, swollen glands, insomnia, epilepsy, and facial paralysis.
GB13 Honjin **Benshen**	The Root of God	.5 sun within the hairline, the forehead at $1/3$ of the way from ST8 to GV24.	Headache, epilepsy, facial pain and upper paralysis, eye and vision ailments, and lacrimation on exposure to wind.
GB14 Yohaku **Yangbai**	Yang and White	1 sun superior to the midpoint of the eyebrow, about $1/3$ of the way from the eyebrow to the anterior hairline.	Eyelids, eyes and vision ailments, and headache.
GB15 Atama No Rinkyu **Toulingi**	Opening of Weeping at the Head	Directly above GB14, .5 sun within the hairline, midpoint between GV24 and ST8.	Dizziness, nasal congestion, apoplectic coma, and seizure.
GB16 Mokuso **Muchuang**	Window of the Eye	1.5 sun posterior to GB15.	Headache, eye and vision ailments, dizziness, toothache, and apoplectic coma.
GB17 Shoei **Zhengying**	Proper Management	1.5 sun posterior to GB16, level with midpoint between TH20 and GV20.	Headache, eye and vision ailments, dizziness, toothache, and apoplectic coma.

POINT	TRANSLATION	LOCATION	INDICATION
GB18 Shorei **Chengling**	Receiving Spirit	Halfway between GB17 and GB19.	Dizziness, headache, eye and nose ailments (nasal bleeding).
GB19 Noku **Naokong**	Space of the Brain	Directly above GB20, level with TH19 and GV17.	Pain and stiffnes of the neck, headaches, common cold, and seizure.
GB20 Fuchi **Fenchi**	Pond of Wind or Windy Pool	Under the base fo the skull, about 2/3 lateral from nape (GV15), to mastoid process (GB12) – about 1 sun superior to the hairline.	Headache, stiffness and pain of the neck and shoulder, eyes, common cold, sinus, dizziness, hypertension, and brain ailments.
GB21 Kensei **Jianjing**	Well at the Shoulder	Halfway between GV14 and acromion, at the highest point of he shoulder, it is the extended line from the nipple.	Shoulder pain, stiffness of the neck and upper back, difficult labor, hemorrage after child birth, breast ailments (insufficient lactation), and hemiplegia after a stroke (hand and arm).
GB22 Eneki **Yuanye**	Abyss at the Armpit	In the fourth intercostal space between the fourth and fifth rib, where K23, ST17, and HC1 are located, on the mid axillary line (3 sun below).	Pain in the chest, ribs, shoulder, arm and hypochondriac region.
GB23 Chokin **Zhejin**	Abrupt Muscle (The Inercostal Muscle)	In the fourth intercostal space, 1 sun anterior to GB22 at the nipple level.	Chest pain, and coughing.
GB24 Nichingetsu **Riyue**	Sun and Moon {Alarm Point for the Gall Bladder}	On the mammary line in the seventh intercostal space, between the seventh and eigth rib.	Pain in the chest, ribs, shoulder, liver, and gall bladder, stomach ailments, hiccough, and jaundice.
GB25 Keimon **Jingmen**	Gate of Capital {Alarm Point for Kidney}	On the lateral side of the abdomen, on the lower border of the free end of the twelfth rib.	Kidney ailments, difficulty in eliminating body fluids, lower backache, lower abdominal pain, and a swollen abdomen.
GB26 Taimyaku **Daimai**	Belt Channel	Directly inferior to the end of the eleventh rib, level with the umbilicus.	Lower abdominal pain, gynecological complaints such as irregular menstruation, leukorhhea, and hernia.

POINT	TRANSLATION	LOCATION	INDICATION
GB27 Gosu Wushu	Fifth Axis (Lumbar Vertebra)	On the lateral side of the abdomen, in front of the anterior superior iliac spine, 3 sun inferior to the level of the umbilicus.	Pain in the hip joint and lower back, hernia, gynecological and reproductive ailments.
GB28 Yuido Weidao	Tied Channel	Anterior and inferior to the anterior superior iliac spine, .5 sun anterior and inferior to GB27.	Pain in lower abdomen, lower back, and hip joint, constipation, and prolapse of the uterus.
GB29 Koryo Juliao	Dwelling Bone	Halfway between the superior iliac spine and the greater trochanter of the femur.	Pain in the lower abdomen, lower back, and leg, urogenital ailments, and muscular atrophy of the lower limbs.
GB30 Kancho Huantiao	Bouncing Ring (Head of Femur)	Superior and anterior to the greater trochanter – lie on your side and bend the hip joint, GB30 is on the tip of this crease. Sharp sensation to lower extremities. In Chinese reference it is another $1/3$ medial to the hiatus of the sacrum.	Weakness and paralysis of lower extremities, sciatica, and lower backache.
GB31 Fushi Fengshi	City of Wind	At the midline on the lateral aspect of the thigh, 7 sun superior to the knee cap, stand up and stretch the fingers on the side of the thighs, GB31 is located on the tip of the middle finger.	Weakness and paralysis of lower extremities, sciatica, and lower backache.
GB32 Chutoku Zhongdu	Central Drain	.5 sun superior to GB33.	Knee ailments, weakness and paralysis of lower extremities, and sciatica.
GB33 Hiza No Yokan Xiyangguan	Yang Barrier at the Knee	Directly superior to the lateral epicondyle of the femur, between biceps femoris and femur bone, lateral to ST34.	Pain, swelling, and limited range of motion of the knee, and runners knee.

POINT	TRANSLATION	LOCATION	INDICATION
GB34 Yoryosen **Yanglingquan**	Spring at the Sunny Tomb {Earth Element}	Anterior inferior ridge of the head of the fibula bone, 2 sun inferior to the middle of the knee joint at the lateral aspect.	Acidity in the stomach, migraine headache, pain, swelling, and limited range of movement of the knee, weakness and paralysis of the lower limbs, sciatica, chest pain, and bitter taste in the mouth. One of the eight influential points for the muscles.
GB35 Yoko **Yangjiao**	Yang Intersection	7 sun above the tip of the external malleolus, on the posterior border of the fibula – 1 sun inferior to the midpoint between the middle of the knee and the ankle.	Pain in the side of the chest, stiffness on the side of the neck, knee, pain, and weakness of the legs.
GB36 Gaikyu **Waiqiu**	Outside of Hill {Cleft Point}	1 sun anterior to GB35 and anterior border of the fibula.	Paralysis of the lower extremity, knee pain, pain in the neck, and chest (hypochondriac region).
GB37 Komei **Guangming**	Bright Light {Connecting Point}	5 sun superior to the tip of the external malleolus, on the anterior border of the fibula.	Pain in the leg along the lateral aspect of calf, pain in the lower extremities, pain in the knee, headaches, eye and vision ailments, and night blindness.
GB38 Yoho **Yangfu**	Minister of Yang {Fire Element}	4 sun superior to the tip of the external malleolus, on the anterior border of the fibula.	One sided headache, pain in the outer canthus, hypochondriac region, and lower extremities.
GB39 Zekkotsu **Juegu** or **Kenso**	The Bone Disappearing	3 sun superior to the tip of the external malleolus, in the depression between the posterior border of the fibula, and the tendons of peroneus.	Pain in the knees and ankle joints, sciatica, migraine headache, and atrophic legs.
GB40 Kyu Kyo **Qiuxu**	Ruin on the Hill {Source Point}	In the depression of the anterior inferior ridge of the lateral malleolus.	Distention in the chest and abdomen, pain in the chest, lower back and ankles.

POINT	TRANSLATION	LOCATION	INDICATION
GB41 Ashi No Renkyu Zulinqi	Opening of Weeping at the Leg {Wood Element}	In the depression distal to the junction of the fourth and fifth metatarsal bones.	Dampness and swelling of the foot, pain in the intercostal hypochondriac region, headache, blurring of vision, abscessed breast, menstrual pain, and gallstones.
GB42 Chigoe Diwuhui	Five Meeting at the Ground	At the corner proximal to the metatarsal- phalangeal joint of the fourth metatarsalphalangeal joint.	Pain and swelling of the foot, low back pain, painful breast, also red and painful eyes.
GB43 Kyokei Xiaxi	Narrow Brook {Water Element}	At the corner distal to the fourth metatarsalphalangeal joint.	Fever, dizziness, pain in the neck, pain in the hypochondriac region, tinnitus, blurring of vision, and migraine headaches.
GB44 Ahi No Kyoin Zugiaoyin	Shady Hole in the Leg {Metal Element}	.1 sun proximal to the lateral base of the fourth toenail.	Headache, chest pain, red and painful eyes, and hypertension.

LIVER CHART

POINT	TRANSLATION	LOCATION	INDICATION
LV1 Taiton Dadun	Big Performance or Great Honesty {Wood Element}	.1 sun proximal to the lateral base of the big toenail.	Epilepsy, loss of consciousness, pain in the sexual organs and abdomen, gynecological complaints such as irregular menstruation, and prolapse of the uterus, also bleeding.
LV2 Kokan Xingjian	Space between Lines {Fire Element}	At the corner distal to the first metatarsal phalangeal joint between the first and second toe.	Pain in the hypochondriac region, headaches, blurring of vision, insomnia, and gynecological ailments.

POINT	TRANSLATION	LOCATION	INDICATION
LV3 Taisho Taichong	Great Rush {Earth Element and Source Point}	Between first and second toe, 1.5 sun proximal to the margin of the web – where a pulse is perceived.	Urogenital ailments, abdominal spasms, cramps, hernia, liver ailments, special point for uterine bledding, convulsions in children, headache, epilepsy, dizziness, and insomnia.
LV4 Chuho Zhongfeng	Central Blockade {Metal Element}	1 sun anterior to the medial malleolus – bend the toes up, LV4 is in the depression in front of the medial malleolus, about halfway between ST41 and SP5.	Hernia, pain in the testicles, swollen abdomen. lower backache (side-way movement).
LV5 Reiko Ligou	Woodborder in the Ditch {Connecting Point}	5 sun superior to the top of the medial malleolus, on the middle of the medial surface of the tibia.	Leg pain, gynecological complaints such as irregular menstruation.
LV6 Chuto Zhongdu	Central Capital {Cleft Ppoint}	2 sun superior to LV5 on the middle of the medial surface of the tibia.	Lower abdominal pain, acute liver ailments, hernia, and gynecological ailments.
LV7 Shitsukan Xiguan	Barrier of the Knee	Posterior and inferior to the medial condyle of the tibia – 1 sun posterior to SP9.	Pain in the medial aspect of the knee.
LV8 Kyokusen Ququan	Spring at the Curve {Water Element}	On the medial side of the knee at the tip of the transverse crease of the knee.	Urogenital ailments, colic, hernia swelling of testicle, pain in the external genitalia, knee and the medial side of the thigh.
LV9 Inpo Yinbao	Wrapping Yin or Wrapping Genitals	4 sun superior to the medial epicondyle of the femur.	Gynecological problems, menstruation pains, chills in the lower abdomen, and pain in the lumbosacral region.
LV10 Ashi No Gori Zuwuli	Five Miles in the Leg	3 sun inferior to ST30 on the lateral border of the adductor longus.	Pain or weakness of the lower extremity, and lower abdominal pain.

POINT	TRANSLATION	LOCATION	INDICATION
LV11 Inren Yinren	Space to Yin or Shady Space – Genital and Groin	2 sun inferior to ST30.	Irregular menstruation, hernia, colic, pain in the thigh (top and inside).
LV12 Kyumyaku Jimai	Rapid Pulse	1 sun inferior to ST30, inferior and lateral to the pubic spine – 2.5 sun lateral to the CV channel.	Indigestion, pain in the external genitalia, hernia, prolapse of the uterus, and swelling of the testes, and pain in the groin.
LV13 Shomon Zhangmen	Gate of Order {Alarm Point for Spleen}	On the lateral side of the abdomen, below the free end of the eleventh floating rib.	Tightness or enlarged spleen, pancreas, liver, kidney, distention of the abdomen, indigestion, and vomititng.
LV14 Kimon Qimen	Gate of Hope or Gate of Cycle {Alarm Point for Liver}	On the mammary line in the intercostal space between the sixth and the seventh rib.	Loss of weight, liver ailments, body, pain in the intercostal region, indigestion, nausea, vomiting, hiccups, and depression.

CONCEPTION VESSEL CHART

POINT	TRANSLATION	LOCATION	INDICATION
CV1 Ein Huiyin or Kinmon	Meeting of Yin or Golden Gate	In the center of the perineum, which is between the anus and the scrotum in males, and the posterior labial commissure in females.	Hemorrhoids, gynecological ailments, irregular menstruation, reproductive ailments, seminal emissions, prostate ailments, retention of urine, used to revive from unconciousness, and pain in the genitals.
CV2 Kyokkotsu Qugu	Crooked Bone (Pubic Bone and Symphysis)	On the midline of the bottom of the abdomen on the symphysis pubis.	Reproductive ailments, seminal emission, impotence, swollen prostate, gynelcological ailments, irregular menstruation, leukorrhea, hernia, and retention of urine.

POINT	TRANSLATION	LOCATION	INDICATION
CV3 Chukyoko **Zhongji**	Central Pole {Alarm Point for Urinary Bladder}	4 sun inferior to the navel, $^4/_5$ from the umbilicus to the pubic bone.	Reproductive and urogenital ailments, irregular menstruation, leukorrhea, infertility, enuresis, nocturnal emissions, retention of urine, spermatorrhea, prostate ailments, and impotence.
CV4 Kangen **Guanyuan**	Barrier of Origin {Alarm Point for Small Intestine}	3 sun inferior to the navel, $^3/_5$ from the umbilicus to the pubic bone.	Digestive ailments, reproductive and urogenital ailments, irregular menstruation, nocturnal emission, weak vitality, difficulty urinating, leukorrhea, impotence, enlarged prostate, and pain in the lower abdomen.
CV5 Sekimon **Shimen**	Gate of Stone {Alarm Point for Triple Heater}	2 sun inferior to the navel, $^2/_5$ from umbilicus to the pubic bone.	Urinary ailments such as enuresis and residual urine, gynecological ailments, leukorrhea, irregular menstruation, digestive ailments, and diarrhea.
CV6 Kikai **Qihai**	Ocean of Ki	1.5 sun below the umbilicus and $^1/_2$ between CV7 and CV5.	Gynecological and urinary ailments, irregular menstruation, dysmenorrhea, leukorrhea, impotence, spermatorrhea, digestive ailments such as colic, abdominal pain, and constipation, lower back ache, and degenerative diseases.
CV7 Yinko **Yinjiao**	Intersection of Yin	1 sun below th umbilicus, $^1/_5$ from the umbilicus to the pubic bone.	Gynecological and reproductive ailments, irregular menstruation, leukorrhea, pain in th lower abdomen, postpartum, hemorrhage, uterine bleeding, prolapse of uterus, and hernia.
CV8 Shinketsu **Shenque**	Divine Void or Divine Gate	In the center of the umbilicus.	Digestive ailments, continuous diarrhea, prolapsed anus, constipation, minor food poisoning, loss of concioussnes, and appoplexy. Special point used with salt – moxi-bustion for indigestion (no acupuncture).

POINT	TRANSLATION	LOCATION	INDICATION
CV9 Suibun Shuifen	Dividing Water	$7/8$ of the way from the inferior tip of the body of the sternum to the umbilicus, or 1 sun superior to the umbilicus.	Digestive ailments, abdominal pain, diarrhea, waterish stomach, borborygmus, and edema. Special point for water retention.
CV10 Gekan Xiawan	Lower Stomach	$3/4$ of the way from the inferior tip of the body of the sternum to the umbilicus, or 2 sun superior to the umbilicus.	Digestive ailments, indigestion, stomach ache, prolapsed stomach, and diarrhea.
CV11 Kenri Jianli	Establishing Mile Stone or Interior Strenghtning	$5/8$ between the inferior tip of the body of the sternum and the umbilicus, or 3 sun superior to the umbilicus.	Digestive ailments, stomach pain, vomiting, anorexia, and borborygmus.
CV12 Chukan Zhongwan	Middle Stomach {Alarm Point for Stomach}	About $1/2$ of the way from the inferior tip of the body of the sternum to the umbilicus, or 4 sun superior to the umbilicus.	Digestive ailments, stomach ache, duodenum (small intestine) ache, cramps, nervous stomach, acidity, colic, abdominal pain, gastrectasia, diarhhea, distention, indigestion, gas, vomiting, gallstones, gall bladder disease, and liver disease.
CV13 Jyokan Shangwan	Upper Stomach	$3/8$ of the way from inferior tip of the body of the sternum to the umbilicus, or 5 sun superior to the umbilicus.	Digestive ailment, upset stomach, pain, hiatus hernia, and liver and gall bladder disease.
CV14 Koketsu Juque	Huge Void {Alarm Point for Heart}	$1/4$ of the way from the inferior tip of the body of the sternum to the umbilicus, or 6 sun superior to the umbilicus.	Respiratory ailments such as coughing, chest ache, cardiac ailments such as discomfort or weakness in the heart, digestive ailments, distention under the ribs, vomiting, nausea, psychosis, madness, and mental disorders.
CV15 Kyubi Jiuwei	Tail of Pigeon	$1/8$ of the way from the tip of the body of the sternum and umbilicus – it is at the lower tip of the xiphoid process – 1 sun superior to CV14, or 7 sun superior to the umbilicus.	Cardiac ailments, chest ache, palpitations, psychosis, seizure and hiccough.

POINT	TRANSLATION	LOCATION	INDICATION
CV16 Chutei Zhongting	Middle of Garden	On the midline of the sternum at the level of the fifth intercostal space, about $5/6$ of the way from the jugular notch to the inferior tip of the body of the sternum.	Sensation of the fullness in the chest, difficulty in swallowing food, vomiting, and cough.
CV17 Danchu Shanzhong	Middle of the Chest {Alarm Point for the Heart Constrictor}	On the midline of the sternum at the level of the fourth intercostal space, about $4/6$ or $2/3$ of the way from the jugular notch to the inferior tip of the sternum – midpoint between the nipples.	Respiratory ailments, coughing, weak breathing, congestion in the chest, cardiac ailments, pain in the chest, psychosis, neurosis, and lactation deficiency. One of the eight influential points for ki (mental emotions).
CV18 Gyokudo Yutang	Hall of Jade	On the midline of the sternum at the level of the third intercostal space, about $3/6$ or $1/2$ fo the way from the jugular notch to the inferior tip of the body of the sternum, intercostal space.	Respiratory ailments such as cough, pain in the chest, emphysema, and intercostal neuralgia.
CV19 Shikyu Zigong	Purple Palace	On the midline of the sternum at the level of the second intercostal space, about $2/6$ or $1/3$ of the way from the jugular notch to the inferior tip of the body of the sternum.	Respiratory ailments such as cough, asthma, and pain in the chest.
CV20 Kagai Huagai	Beautiful Covering	On the midline of the sternum at the level of the first intercostal space, about $1/6$ of the way from the jugular notch to the inferior tip of the body of the sternum.	Respiratory ailments such as cough, asthma, and pain in the chest.
CV21 Senki Xuanji	A Spheroid Rotating	On the sternum, $1/2$ way between CV22 and CV20.	Sudden hoarseness of voice, sore throat, cough, pain in the chest, asthma, and bronchia.
CV22 Tentotsu Tiantu	Protrusion to Heaven	In the middle of the supra sternal fossa, jugular notch.	Sudden hoarseness of voice, sore throat, cough, pain in the chest, and asthma.

POINT	TRANSLATION	LOCATION	INDICATION
CV23 Rensen Lianquan	Spring at the Corner	In the depression between Adam's apple and the mandible.	Hoarseness of the voice, sore throat, cough, pain in the chest, difficulty in swallowing, and tongue ailments.
CV24 Shosho Chengjian	Receiving Broth or Source Receptacle	In the depression under the lower lip on the mentolabial groove.	Facial swelling, numbness, pain in the teeth and gums.

GOVERNING VESSEL CHART

POINT	TRANSLATION	LOCATION	INDICATION
GV1 Chokyo Changgiang	Long and Strong	At the bottom of the buttock, midway between the coccyx and the anus.	Hemorrhoids, stiffness, limited range of movement, pain, weakness of lower back, and sacro coccyx region.
GV2 Yo Yu Yaoshu	Healing Waist	In the hiatus of the sacrum.	Uroreproductive ailments, stiffness, limited range of movement, pain, weakness of lower back and lower extremities.
GV3 Koshi No Yokan Yaoyangguan	Barrier of Yang at the Waist	Directly inferior to the spinous process of the fourth lumbar vertebra – medial to UB25.	Uroreproductive ailments, intestinal ailment, impotence, limited range of movement, weakness of the lower back, and lower extremities.
GV4 Meimon Mingmen	Gate of Life	Directly inferior to the spinous process of the second lumbar vertebra – medial to UB23.	Reproductive ailments, impotence, menstrual troubles, stiffness, limited range of movement, weakness of the lower back and lower extremities, digestive ailments, kidney ailments, first aid point for pediactric unconsiousness.

POINT	TRANSLATION	LOCATION	INDICATION
GV5 Kensu Xuanshu	Suspended Hinge	Directly inferior to the spinous process of the first lumbar vertebra – medial to UB21.	Stiffness, limited range of movement pain, weakness of lower back and extremities, and stomach ailments.
GV6 Sekichu Jizhong	Middle of Spinal Cord	Directly inferior to the spinous process of the eleventh thoracic vertebra – medial to UB20.	Stiffness and pain of middle back, spleen/pancreas ailments.
GV7 Chusu Zhongshu	Central Axis	Directly inferior to the spinous process of the tenth thoracic vertebra – medial to UB19.	Stiffness, limited range of movement, and pain, weakness of the middle back, and gall bladder ailments.
GV8 Kinshuku Jinsuo	Muscle Contraction	Directly inferior to the ninth thoracic vertebra – medial to UB18.	Stiffness of the back, intercostal pain, and liver ailments.
GV9 Shiyo Zhiyang	Reaching to Yang	Directly inferior to the seventh thoracic vertebra – medial to UB17.	Stiffness, pain of the spinal column and back, intercostal pain, liver ailments (eyes, muscles).
GV10 Reidai Lingtai	Spiritual Platform	Directly inferior to the sixth thoracic vertebra – medial to UB16.	Stiffness, limited range of movement, pain in the neck and the back, cardiac ailments, and psychological ailments.
GV11 Shindo Shendao	Divine Channel	Directly inferior to the fifth TV – medial to UB15.	Intercostal pain, pain, stiffness, limited range of movement of neck, psychological ailments such as neurosis and hysteria.
GV12 Shinchu Shenzhu	Pillar of the Body	Directly inferior to the third TV – medial to UB13.	Pain, stiffness and limited range of movement of the neck, respiratory ailments, cold, and a tonic point for pediatric care.
GV13 Todo Taodao	Channel of Happiness	Directly inferior to the first TV – medial to UB11.	Pain, stiffness and limited range of movement of neck and shoulder, weakness and pain of the arms, headache, and respiratory ailments.

POINT	TRANSLATION	LOCATION	INDICATION
GV14 Daitsui Dazhui	Big Vertebra (Seventh Cervical)	Directly inferior to the seventh cervical.	Pain, stiffness, limited range of movement of the neck and shoulder, weakness and pain of the arms, headache, respiratory ailments (chronic, psychosomatic).
GV15 Amon Yamen	Gate of Mute and Deaf	At the nape, .5 sun superior to the posterior hairline, (raise face upward, GV15 is about 1.5 sun inferior to the external occipital bone, middle of cavity, between the first and second cervical vertibra.	Headache, deafmutism, stiffness of the tongue, seizures, epilepsy, convulsions, cerebral palsy, post-apoplexy, aphasia, psychosis, sudden hoarseness of the voice, sore throat, speech troubles, and hearing troubles.
GV16 Fufu Fengfu	Windy Palace	1.5 sun posterior to GV17 and .5 sun superior to GV15, directly inferior to the occipital protuberance.	Stiffness, limited range of neck movement, pain, numbness and weakness of the upper extremity, headache, and blurring of vision.
GV17 Noto Naohu	Door to the Brain	1.5 sun posterior to GV18. It is at about the same level as UB9, GB19, and TH19.	Stiffness of the neck, headache, epilepsy, dizziness, and insomnia.
GV18 Gokan Qiangjian	Strong Space	1.5 sun posterior to GV19, $1/3$ of the way between GV17 and GV20.	Stiffness of the neck, and headache.
GV19 Gocho Houding	Posterial Head	1.5 sun posterior to GV20, $2/3$ of the way between GV17 and GV20.	Headache, and dizziness.
GV20 Hyakue Baihui	Hundred Meeting	Higher point on the center of the head and mid point of the line connecting the two apexes of the ears, at the vertex of the head. 5 sun superior to the frontal hairline.	Headache, dizziness, hemorrhoids, prolapsed anus (treated by moxibustion), hemiplagia, hypertension, epilepsy, speech difficulties, psychosis (forgetfulness, excess worry, overly sensitive, fear, and shock).
GV21 Zencho Qianding	Frontal Head	3.5 sun superior to the frontal hairline and 1.5 sun in front of GV20. $2/3$ of the way between GV24 and GV20.	Headache (vertical headache), dizziness, nasal congestion, and seizures.

POINT	TRANSLATION	LOCATION	INDICATION
GV22 Shine Xinhui	Gathering at the Skull	2 sun superior to the frontal hairline, it is $2/5$ from GV20 to frontal hairline. $1/3$ of the way between GV24 and GV20.	Headache (vertical headache), dizziness, nasal congestion, and seizures.
GV23 Josei Shangxing	Upper Star	1 sun superior to the frontal hairline.	Headache (vertical headache), dizziness, nasal congestion, and seizures.
GV24 Shintei Shenting	Divine Garden	On the mid sagittal line of the head, .5 sun superior to the frontal hairline – sooth the medial line from the forehead to the hairline, GV24 is in the middle of the cavity around the hairline.	Frontal headache, dizziness, insomnia, palpitation, seizure, psychosis, and anxiety.
Extra Point Indo Yintang	Impressive Palace Seal Hall	Midpoint between two eyebrows on the forehead.	Sinus problems, children's disturbed sleep and convulsions, also headache.
GV25 Sorho Suliao	Pure Bone	Right on the tip of the nose.	Loss of consciousness, nasal congestion, nose bleed, and swollen nose.
GV26 Suiko Renzhong or Jinchu	Water Groove (Middle of the Human Being)	$1/3$ below the nose in the philtrum.	First aid point for coma and convulsions, epilepsy, facial paralysis, pain in the face, and nasal congestion.
GV27 Datan Duiduan	Exchange at the Edge	Cross section where the philtrum meets the upper lip.	Swelling and pain in the gums.
GV28 Ginko Yinjiao	Intersection of the Gums	Cross section where the gums meets with the upper lip – pull the upper lip back.	Swelling and pain in the gums, and psychosis.

POINT	TRANSLATION	LOCATION	INDICATION
Extra Point Shitsumin	Lost Sleep	Distal to midpoint of calcaneus bone of the heel.	Insomnia.
Extra Point Yogan	Eyes of the Waist	2 sun lateral to UB 25.	Lumbalgia, lumbago, and reproductive ailmetns.